☞ THE DEAF SMITH
COUNTRY COOKBOOK

THE DEAF SMITH COUNTRY COOKBOOK

 *Natural Foods for Family Kitchens*

MARJORIE WINN FORD
SUSAN HILLYARD
MARY FAULK KOOCK

COLLIER BOOKS
A Division of Macmillan Publishing Co., Inc.
New York

COLLIER MACMILLAN PUBLISHERS
London

Photographs by Susan Hillyard

Macmillan Publishing Co., Inc.
866 Third Avenue, New York, N.Y. 10022
Collier Macmillan Canada, Ltd.

Library of Congress Catalog Card Number: 72–12451
First Collier Books Edition 1973

Tenth Printing 1979
Printed in the United States of America

GENESIS 1:29

And God said, "Behold, I have given you every plant yielding seed which is upon the face of all the earth, and every tree with seed in its fruit; you shall have them for food."

PSALM 48:24

and he rained down upon them manna to eat, and gave them the grain of heaven.

Where does the spirit dwell?

It dwells
where the sea
joins earth,
bringing its gift
of renewal—
waves turning green,
then white,
as they caress the shore
with gentle power.

It dwells
where the wind
blows through our hair
as we run,
free and exultant,
under a starry sky.

It dwells
in the heart of a friend.

J.F.F.

SPECIAL THANKS

We would like to thank all of the following for their help and contributions, with a very special thanks to Ruth Warner, who gave unlimited time and energy way beyond the call of duty.

Pilar Abalos
Joanne and Nik
    Amartseff
Barbara Barker
Carol Barney
Beth Barnsley
Ruth Bellomy
Marie Berenger
Carolyn Black
Katherine Black
Charda Bronough
Shirley Bryan
Becca Bush
Marian Calpeno
Carmelite Monastery
Elaine Chapman
Dorothy Clearman

Margie Coates
Irene Coneway
Vicki Crowder
Frances Davenport
Beth Davis
Mama Davis
Alice Feinberg
Sarah Fishburn
Ann Fleming
Davis, Cindy, Dan, and
    Susan Ford
Gwen Ford
Lucile Ford
Boyd and Delores
    Foster
Lynn Foster
Shelley Goldbloom

Lynn Grant
Jim Guiness
Joanne Hairgrove
Susan Hartung
Paul and Dora Hawken
Cyrena and Christopher
    Hillyard
Della Hutchins
Priscilla Jacobsen
Marie Kershen
Phyllis Kincaid
Richard Lee Korst
Michele Lebar
Louise Lieber
Kathy Lindstrom
Maureen Macdonald
John Matheson

Fif McCormick
Micky McDonald
Jean and Mac McGee
Joanne Munro
Brooks Nielsen
Sunny Parks
Sylvia Parsley
Kay Perrin
Catherine Petty
Renee
Martin and Ronny
    Russell
Mary Schooner
Lois Shaw
Thelma Sorrells
Albert Starr
Ginger Swenson
Rod Swenson

Mrs. J. C. Terrill
Tim Tizzano
Peggy Utne
Marie Vanderbeck
Ann Vermont
Warren Vincent
Norma Walden
Waltenspiel Timber-
    crest Farms
Kay White
Lyman White
Susan Wiltshire
Betty and Dan Winn
Margie Winn
Marjorie Daniel Winn
Dr. Ted Winn
Eleanor and Frank
    Wright

Debbie and Will
    Wroth
Joyce Wartes
Elizabeth Wills
Vocational Office of
    Education
        Coop & Lab
            Classes
        Hereford High
            School
Corning Glass Com-
    pany
Home Demonstration
    Agent—Argen Draper
Ekco Stainless Steel
The Hobart Company
Famous Restaurant,
    Lake Worth, Fla.

PREFACE

A phenomenon that might best be described as a revolution of renewal is happening in this land, and it is causing amazing things to happen. A new pioneering spirit is developing, and this time, the frontier is within ourselves. Our technology has conquered mountains, oceans, and space, but many of us are empty and unsatisfied. We have mined our soil, polluted our water and air, often taken unfair advantage of our fellow beings, and now we have begun to pause and ask ourselves a simple question—"Why?" Having defined the question in our minds, we have begun to seek out the answers. It is a very hopeful beginning.

In these days, the Holy Spirit is truly being poured out upon all those who seek, and the right relationship with God, which begins with faith, can logically be extended to the methods used in farming and food preparation as well as our relationships with each other. It may become an exciting adventure for you and your family, and you will be in good company.

As you venture into the world of natural foods cookery, you will be in partnership with the farm families who have labored long and hard to improve the quality of their foods while at the same time improving the quality of their soil. You will feel close to the talented people who are starting bakeries and natural food stores all over America in an effort to secure for themselves and their posterity what should have been our natural birthright—the opportunity to eat pure foods, drink pure water, and breathe pure air in a world in which we work in harmony with nature.

Most important, it will be an adventure for you and your family to gain more self-reliance, individual responsibility, and happier relationships with your immediate surroundings. As you discover the joys of good basic cooking, you will probably become interested in starting an organic garden in a corner of your yard; sprouting beans and seeds that can be "raised" right in your kitchen and turned into delicious, nutritious salads; and, perhaps, growing an herb garden right on your own window sill. These are family projects, and they draw the family of humankind closer together. That is what this book is all about.

Frank Ford

CONTENTS

GATHER 'ROUND

TENGO HAMBRE

THE BREAD BOARD,   189

LOVE 'EM OR LEAVE 'EM

THE THIRST QUENCHERS

HEY DIDDLE DIDDLE

TRAIL FOODS,   311

NATURAL FOODS FROM DEAF SMITH COUNTY,   319

☞ THE DEAF SMITH
COUNTRY COOKBOOK

Introduction

WHO IN THE WORLD IS DEAF SMITH?

Erastus "Deaf" Smith was a frontiersman who was a significant figure in Texas history. Born in New York in 1787, he traveled to Mississippi with his parents when he was 11 years old. The family accumulated an estate there, but Erastus left the security of his inheritance and began his wanderings in the Mexican territory of Texas when he was in his thirties. He had been a frail youth and partially deaf since childhood, but in Texas his health improved greatly, and he became a leading settler in the San Antonio area, where he married Guadalupe Ruiz Duran.

When the Texas Revolution began in 1835, Smith remained aloof from the hostilities because he had friends on both sides. But when he returned from an expedition to see his wife and children in San Antonio and was refused entry into the city by the Mexican authorities, he volunteered his services to Stephen F. Austin and General Sam Houston. His thorough knowledge of the terrain, his exceptional ability to follow a trail, and his courage quickly made him a key figure in the revolution. Information garnered by Deaf Smith enabled General Houston to gain

1

the advantage despite much larger Mexican forces at the decisive battle of San Jacinto. The Texans surprised the Mexican army on April 21, 1836, and routed it in less than an hour. Later, when General Santa Anna was captured, Deaf Smith carried his message, "retreat westward and quit the soil of Texas," to the commander of Santa Anna's Second Army.

Deaf Smith never set foot in the county that bears his name, but he would probably have felt at home there. It's a tough land and requires a sturdy breed of men to farm and ranch on it. Deaf Smith County has also been important in Texas history. Parts of the county were included in the three million acres deeded to the XIT Corporation, builders of the beautiful State Capitol in Austin. Barbed wire fencing from the XIT ranch can still be found, and some of the original windmill holes are still yielding water on farms producing Deaf Smith County wheat.

The present-day fame of this county is due first to its heavily mineralized soil and to the crops that are raised on it. The county, consisting of 1,500 square miles, sits atop a plateau broken by the Canadian River on the north and lower, broken country below a "cap-rock" to the south, east, and west. The 4,000-foot elevation and dry climate cause the wheat roots to go deep into the mineral-rich soil in search of moisture. The resulting nutritive qualities of grains grown in this area have caused many believers in natural foods to turn to the "Deaf Smith Country" for the best in whole grains.

The whole grains, as they pour out of the combines at harvest time, are full and beautiful, so God designed, and it seems a travesty to strip them of their many health-giving attributes and then feed the "leftovers" to mankind. This book is dedicated to the use of whole foods containing all the balanced nutrients that were placed in them by our Creator.

WHY NATURAL FOODS?

First of all, they taste better and they're more satisfying than refined, overprocessed foods! But it is most important to remember that the entire range of vitamins and minerals possessed by whole, natural foods is necessary for good nutrition. Disease can result from a lack or deficiency of a nutrient needed in the most minute amount. Nature requires nutrients to properly assimilate other nutrients. Refining destroys the balance of nutrients, leaving the body poorly armed to cope with refined starches and sugars, hydrogenated fats, improperly assimilated cholesterol, and an onslaught of chemical and external pollutants that requires further nutrients for the body to detoxify them.

Refining is dangerous not only because of the known nutrients that are never replaced but also because of the heretofore unknown vitamins and interrelationships of nutritional factors still being discovered. No pill or system of enrichment can ever equal nature's intricate balance.

Have you read the labels on packaged foods lately? The number of nonfood chemical additives is staggering—in the thousands. The amount of each is supposedly below its harmful level, constituting "no imminent danger." That comforting thought might be soothing if only one or two additives were involved, but most of us consume as many as several hundred every day. It is well known that chemicals reacting with one another may create a danger greatly in excess of one acting alone. And what about the cumulative effect over many years? It is illogical to assume that this internal pollution could be harmless. And the list of additives does not include the chemicals and poisonous sprays used during the growth and processing of the foods.

The demand for natural foods encourages food processors to consider the quality of life desired by the consumer—not just the shelf life of the package. The demand for natural foods also encourages farmers to consider the total health of the crop and the land—not just the size and yield. Yields generally remain constant when scientific organic methods are applied. In instances where the yields drop slightly, the drop is offset by the increase in quality. When crops are pushed chemically for high yields, the quality of the crop frequently degenerates; to take wheat as an example, the result is lower percentages of protein and lower test weights per bushel, as well as higher percentages of cellulose and starch. Soil is a living, creative force—not a mine to be stripped. Its living elements must be nourished by whole foods such as compost. These elements are often weakened or killed by chemical applications. The cycle of health begins with healthy soil that in turn grows healthy crops; these crops, if unrefined and properly prepared as food, build health in the individual.

BEGINNING TO COOK WITH
NATURAL FOODS

In these days, when society is increasingly fragmented, the family unit is more important than ever in providing a center for our lives, physically as well as mentally and spiritually.

As overprocessed, empty foods proliferate in the "outside" world, it is vital that meals eaten at home with the family be as nutritious as only whole, natural foods can make them. Cooking with these foods can be the highest form of creativity, for you not only produce something of beauty and taste but also increase the possibilities for vibrant good health in your family.

While introducing your family to natural and more nutritious foods you will probably want your meals to taste and look like they always have. Start by substituting whole, unrefined foods for refined ones and by eliminating harmful foods and substances from some of your favorite recipes. You may be surprised after a time to find your tastes changing. As you begin to distinguish the many subtle flavors of whole foods, you will find that it is no longer necessary to sweeten and spice foods heavily to give them flavor. Cooking becomes a matter of combining natural flavors rather than of seasoning foods to some preconceived taste. Simplicity is the key to developing a knowledge of the basics of natural foods cooking. Once that is done, go to it. The lid is off!

You and your family also become part of a larger effort. By using organically grown foods you encourage more farmers to join with nature in her own recycling plan by returning organic matter to the soil and by practicing methods of agriculture that increase the humus, beneficial bacterial life, and earthworm population of the soil. The benefits to soil, to crops, and ultimately to man are incalculable, for they will continue for generations.

Cooking with whole foods can enable you to become a positive force in the delicate and beautifully intricate ecological balance that God designed.

USING YOUR OWN TREASURED RECIPES

Everyone has his favorite recipes—perhaps handed down for generations or passed from friend to friend. These familiar recipes can often be made into the best natural food dishes by simply replacing refined foods with the richer flavors of whole, unrefined foods. The resulting improved nutrition may be incidental to the rest of the family, but the cook gets double satisfaction from her efforts.

Learn these simple tricks, then try them in your own special recipes. It you're just beginning to use natural foods, don't try to make all the improvements at once. Introduce new foods gradually.

Omit	Use	Other Changes Required
Cake flour	Whole wheat pastry flour	Requires more liquid
All purpose flour	Whole wheat flour or other whole grain flours	Requires more liquid
Boxed cereals	Granola or whole, flaked, or cracked grains	
Cracker or bread crumbs	Whole wheat bread crumbs, whole grain flakes, or wheat germ	
White rice or other refined grains	Brown rice or whole grains	
Sugars	Raw unfiltered honey (½ honey instead of 1 sugar) Pure maple syrup Unsulphured molasses Fruit juices and purees	Requires more dry ingredients or less liquid
Chocolate	Carob powder (3 tablespoons carob plus 2 tablespoons milk = 1 square chocolate)	

Cocoa	Carob powder (equal amounts)	
Baking soda	Low-sodium baking powder (2 parts instead of 1 part soda)	Add protein, such as milk powder
Baking powder	Low-sodium baking powder (equal amounts) Active dry yeast (amount depends on desired rising time)	Use warm liquids
Cornstarch	Whole wheat flour Brown rice flour Arrowroot powder	
Salt	Sea salt (equal amounts) Kelp powder (equal amounts) Sesame salt Tamari soy sauce	Adjust to taste Adjust to taste
Distilled vinegar	Cider vinegar	
Hydrogenated fats and shortenings	Unrefined oils (safflower, corn germ, olive, sesame) Unrefined safflower oil for deep frying	Requires more dry ingredients or less liquid
Refined oils	Unrefined oils	

Increasing Nutritional Values:
   ADDITIONS: non-instant dry milk powder
               fresh wheat germ
               nutritional yeast

   LIQUIDS: Use liquid that is more nutritious than water whenever possible, such as fruit juice, vegetable stock, milk, or yogurt.
             Milk, yogurt, and buttermilk are usually interchangeable. Use yogurt instead of sour cream.

Top of the Morning
B R E A K F A S T S

A good breakfast sets the pace for your day and puts you right with the world. Whole grain foods give you the protein boost you need so that you don't crave coffee and doughnuts by mid-morning.

A bowl of hot cereal is a wonderful way to start a winter morning. If you like, you can make porridges from whole grains such as rice, barley, and millet, using 4 or 5 times as much water as grain. If you prefer a finer textured cereal, cook cracked grains, flakes, or ground meal. Sprinkle the cooked cereal with roasted nuts or seeds for added protein. Raisins and fresh fruits add natural sweetness to cereals and are particularly enticing to children. For a quick breakfast, summer or winter, try maple-nut granola with milk or yogurt and fresh fruit.

Whole grain muffins, pancakes, and waffles are delicious and provide plenty of opportunity for including other high-quality proteins —fresh yard eggs, milk, non-instant milk powder, fresh toasted wheat germ, and nutritional yeast.

All these breakfasts are easy to prepare and give you energy throughout the day. If you skimp or miss breakfast, your energy level will never be what it should be no matter how well you eat at lunch or supper.

CEREALS

Almost any grain, whether whole, cracked, flaked, or ground, makes a delicious cooked cereal. Cracked, flaked, or ground grains cook very quickly, within minutes. Even whole grains cook in a relatively short time. For precise cooking times, refer to the grain cooking chart on pp. 130–133.

Combine different grains—whole or ground—for interesting flavors. Such combinations give the amino acid (protein) content better balance.

Season the cooked grains any way you like. Try sea salt, tamari soy sauce, or sesame salt for a nut-flavored cereal. Add honey, maple syrup, molasses, or fruits for a sweet cereal. Or you may prefer to leave out all seasonings to let the natural flavor of the grain come through.

Invent your own cold cereal. Granola is fun to make. Try different combinations of flakes, seeds, nuts, and fruits until you come up with a family favorite.

COOKING WHOLE GRAINS FOR BREAKFAST

1 part whole grain or grain mix
(see below)
3 parts boiling water

☞ Add the grain to the boiling water. Bring to a boil again. Remove from heat. Cover and let sit overnight or cover and place in a barely warm oven overnight. In the morning the grain may be reheated or not.

Serve as is or with milk or cream, honey, maple syrup, or molasses if desired. Sea salt may also be added but it really isn't needed because the grains have a delicious nutty taste.

Use a single whole grain, such as wheat, or, to add interest, prepare a combination of grains. The following is an excellent combination.

WHOLE GRAIN MIX

> 4 *cups whole grain wheat or triticale*
> 4 *cups whole grain buckwheat*
> 4 *cups whole grain rye*
> 4 *cups whole grain oats*
> 2 *cups whole grain hulled barley*

☞ Mix and store in a tightly covered container.

KRUSKA

SERVES 6

> 6 *cups boiling water*
> 2 *cups whole grain mix*
> 1 *cup raisins*

☞ Add the grain mix and raisins to the boiling water. Bring to a boil again. Remove from heat. Cover and let sit overnight. The next morning it is ready to eat.

For a nuttier flavor, dry roast the whole grain a few minutes and then grind it in a blender or a hand grinder. (Grind only a small amount at a time in a blender in order not to strain the motor.) Then continue as directed.

BREAKFAST FLAKES

SERVES 4–6

> 2 *tablespoons unrefined oil*
> 2 *cups flaked wheat, rye, oats, or rice,*
>   *triticale, or cracked grains or grits*
> ¼ *teaspoon sea salt*
> 6 *cups boiling water*

☞ Heat a large saucepan. Add the oil and sauté the flakes until they are fragrant, about 5 minutes. Add the water and salt. Cover and cook for 20 to 30 minutes over low flame. Stir occasionally.

Serve with a sprinkling of roasted sesame seeds, sunflower seeds, or nuts and raisins. Flakes are equally good for breakfast or as a grain dish with vegetables.

BULGUR OR CRACKED WHEAT CEREAL

SERVES 4
    1 tablespoon unrefined oil
    1 cup bulgur or cracked wheat
    ¼ cup sesame seeds
    ¼ cup wheat germ
    ¼ cup unsweetened coconut
    3 cups water

    Optional: ¼ teaspoon sea salt
                dried fruits, chopped
                nuts

☞ Heat a heavy pan. Add the oil and the bulgur, sesame seeds, wheat germ, and coconut. Sauté until light brown.
Add the water (and salt and dried fruits if desired). Cover and steam about 25 minutes, until the bulgur is fluffy.
Add nuts to taste. Serve with milk and honey.

THREE BEAR MUSH

SERVES 4
    ⅔ cup buckwheat groats
    ⅔ cup oat flakes
    ½ cup non-instant dry milk powder
    ½ cup raisins

    4 cups boiling water

☞ Combine the buckwheat groats and oats. Add the dry milk and raisins.

Pour boiling water over all and bring mixture to a very low simmer. Cover and simmer 10 to 15 minutes or until the grains are softened. Add honey to taste and serve.

TOASTED OATMEAL
(For Those Who Don't Like Oatmeal)

SERVES 4–6
> 1 tablespoon unrefined oil
> 2 cups oat flakes
>
> 4 cups boiling water
> ¼ teaspoon sea salt
> 2 tablespoons tamari soy sauce

☞ Heat a large skillet. Add the oil and sauté the oats 5 to 10 minutes on medium heat, until they are lightly browned. It is important to roast them well.
Add the boiling water slowly. Add the salt and simmer for 30 minutes.
Add the tamari and simmer 5 minutes more.
Serve with raisins and roasted sesame and sunflower seeds.

This cereal is really delicious and is barely recognizable as oatmeal. The trick is in roasting the oats and adding the tamari before the cereal is completely cooked.

GRANOLA

Vary the following basic recipes any way you like. Make granola for snacks, cookies, and pie toppings as well as for cereals. Place in tightly covered containers and store in a cool, dry place.

ALMOND CRUNCH GRANOLA

YIELD: 3 CUPS
> 2 cups oat flakes and wheat flakes, mixed
> 1 cup almonds, coarsely chopped
> ¼ cup pure maple syrup
> ⅓ cup unrefined corn germ oil
> ¼ teaspoon sea salt
> ½ teaspoon vanilla

☞ Mix all the ingredients together. Spread thinly on a cookie sheet. Bake 20 to 25 minutes at 325° to 350°, or until lightly browned.

VARIATION:
Add other nuts and seeds, such as sesame seeds, chestnuts, cashews, pecans, walnuts. Use honey in place of maple syrup.

If you like almonds, you'll love this one.

CHARISMOLA

YIELD: 3 QUARTS
> 5 cups oat flakes or rye flakes
> 1 cup hulled sunflower seeds
> ½ cup unhulled sesame seeds
> ½ cup unrefined corn germ oil or
>   safflower oil
> ¼ to ½ cup raw honey
>
> 5 cups wheat flakes
> 2 cups raisins

☞ Mix the oat or rye flakes, seeds, oil, and honey. Spread the mixture thinly on a cookie sheet. Roast 2 to 5 minutes in a 400° oven until light brown. Watch very closely; the flakes brown quickly. Remove the roasted flakes from the oven and mix quickly with the untoasted wheat flakes and raisins to prevent the hot mixture from sticking together in lumps. Cool completely. Store in covered containers.

Serve as a cereal with milk. This granola is an excellent snack food when eaten dry.

PANCAKES AND WAFFLES

Homemade pancakes and waffles are so easy and good. It's a shame mixes were ever invented. Once you learn a basic recipe, you can whip out a delicious batter in less than 5 minutes. Make pancakes or waffles a weekly tradition, perhaps on Saturday or Sunday nights— or another night when you don't want to spend time in the kitchen. Let this be a meal the older children prepare and serve.

APPLE PANCAKES

SERVES 4

> 1 cup whole wheat pastry flour
> ½ teaspoon sea salt
> ½ cup wheat germ
>
> 2 tablespoons unrefined corn germ oil
>
> 1 teaspoon dry yeast
> ½ cup warm water
>
> 1 egg, beaten
> 1 cup apple juice
> 1 apple, grated

☞ Mix the flour, salt, and wheat germ together.
Add the oil to the flour mixture and mix well.
Add yeast to the warm water and stir until dissolved. Add the yeast mixture to the flour mixture.
Add the egg, apple juice, and grated apple.
Let the batter sit for 15 minutes. Cook on medium-hot griddle.

Serve with applesauce or pure maple syrup.

BUCKWHEAT CAKES

SERVES 4
(approx. 12 4-inch cakes)
>   1 teaspoon dry yeast
>   ½ cup lukewarm water
>   1 tablespoon unsulphured molasses
>   or raw honey
>
>   1 tablespoon unrefined corn germ oil
>   ½ teaspoon sea salt
>   1½ cups water
>   1½ cups buckwheat flour
>   ½ cup whole wheat flour

☞ Soften the yeast in ½ cup water. Add the molasses to the yeast mixture and let sit until bubbly (about 5 minutes).
Add the oil, salt, 1½ cups water, and the flours. Beat. Cover the batter and let rise at least 2 hours, or overnight for sourdough pancakes. Cook on a hot griddle.

MOUNTAIN FLAPJACKS
(Sourdough)

SERVES 4
>   Feed your starter an extra amount the night before.
>   2 cups sourdough starter, the
>   consistency of a heavy pancake batter
>
>   ½ cup warm water
>   2 tablespoons raw honey
>   2 teaspoons sea salt
>   2 teaspoons low-sodium baking powder
>
>   2 eggs
>   4 tablespoons unrefined oil

Dissolve the honey and salt in the warm water.
Add the baking powder, then stir this mixture into the starter.
Beat in the eggs and oil with a spoon, until the mixture is smooth.
Bake on a medium-hot, oiled griddle.
To make the sourdough go further, add more warm water and whole wheat flour to the batter. Just keep the consistency about the same.

OVERNIGHT SOY PANCAKES OR WAFFLES

SERVES 4
> ¾ *cup soy flour*
> ¼ *cup stone-ground corn meal*
> 1 *cup whole wheat flour*
> 3 *teaspoons low-sodium baking powder*
> ⅛ *teaspoon sea salt*
>
> 1 *cup milk*
> 2 *eggs*
>
> *Optional:* 4 *tablespoons raw honey*

 Mix the dry ingredients.
Beat the liquid ingredients together. Stir the flour mixture into the liquids.
Refrigerate overnight. Add 1 cup warm water in the morning.
Bake on a moderately hot griddle.

QUICK MIX WHOLE WHEAT PANCAKES

SERVES 4
> 2 *cups whole wheat flour*
> 1 *teaspoon sea salt*
> 2 *teaspoons low-sodium baking powder*
>
> 2 *cups milk*
> 2 *eggs, beaten well*
> 2 *tablespoons unrefined corn germ*
>   *or safflower oil*

Mix the dry ingredients together.

Mix the liquid ingredients together and add to the dry ingredients. Stir until just mixed.

Bake on a moderately hot, lightly greased griddle or in a heavy skillet.

This is a thick batter. If a thinner batter is desired, add a few tablespoons of water or milk. The pancakes will rise better if the liquids are warmed slightly before mixing.

VARIATIONS:

1. Substitute some other whole grain flour or stone-ground corn meal for ½ cup of the whole wheat flour.
2. Add ⅓ cup non-instant dry milk powder to the dry ingredients.
3. Use yogurt, juice, or water in place of the milk.
4. Add ½ cup diced, drained fruit to the batter.
5. Omit baking powder. Separate the eggs and beat the whites until stiff. Stir the yolks into the batter, then fold in the beaten egg whites.
6. Add ½ cup soaked or cooked whole grains to the batter.
7. Add ½ cup wheat sprouts or rye sprouts to the batter.
8. Experiment with your own combination of flours. Try whole wheat flour, rye flour, soy flour, and stone-ground corn meal in varying proportions to your taste.

QUICK YEAST PANCAKES OR WAFFLES

SERVES 4

2 cups milk
2 eggs, beaten
2 tablespoons unrefined oil

Optional: 2 tablespoons raw honey

3 tablespoons active dry yeast
2 cups whole wheat flour or a mixture
   of flours
1 teaspoon sea salt

☞ Mix and warm the liquids to lukewarm in a saucepan.
Mix the dry ingredients together. Add the liquid mixture to the
flour mixture and beat 1 minute.
Let the batter sit 5 minutes.
Bake slowly on a medium-hot griddle.

The quantity of yeast in this recipe seems large, but it works
quickly and gives a good yeasty flavor to the pancakes.

WHOLE WHEAT WAFFLES

SERVES 4

4 *eggs*

2 *cups whole wheat flour*
2 *cups water*
¼ *teaspoon sea salt*
1 *cup raisins and/or sunflower seeds,*
   sesame seeds, or granola.

☞ Separate the eggs. Beat the whites until they are stiff.
In a large mixing bowl, mix the egg yolks, flour, water, salt, and
the raisins or seeds. Fold in the beaten egg whites.
Cook on a hot waffle iron until done.

This recipe is easily increased. Double to serve 8.
Waffles are delicious with honey and butter. They make an easy,
quick breakfast.

VERMONT TOAST

☞ Dip slices of whole wheat bread in maple syrup. Bake at medium-
low heat on a buttered grill until golden. Do not let the butter
brown.

Luscious!
This recipe is easy and good and the kids will love it.

OVEN-BAKED FRENCH TOAST

SERVES 4–6
  ¼ cup butter
  2 tablespoons raw honey

  ½ teaspoon cinnamon

  3 eggs, beaten
  ½ cup fresh orange juice
  ⅛ teaspoon sea salt

  6 slices whole wheat bread

☞ Melt the butter and honey in a 9 x 13 inch pan. Mix well, sprinkle
with cinnamon.
Beat the eggs, juice, and salt together.
Soak the bread slices in the egg mixture, but do not let the bread
become so wet that it falls apart.
Arrange the slices close together on top of the honey mixture.
Bake about 20 minutes at 400° until set. Invert the toast when
serving.
Serve with more honey.

EGGS

CORDOBA OMELET

SERVES 2
  An 8 or 9 inch skillet or omelet pan
  2 teaspoons butter or unrefined oil

  4 eggs, beaten
  4 tablespoons milk
  1 tablespoon chopped chives
  1 tablespoon chopped parsley
  ½ teaspoon sea salt
  pinch of pepper

1 tablespoon unrefined oil
1 small onion, chopped
½ bell pepper, chopped
1 small tomato, chopped
¼ cup sliced mushrooms
¼ to ½ cup fresh bean sprouts

½ cup grated cheese

Optional: hot sauce or tamari soy sauce

☞ Heat the omelet pan. Coat the pan with butter or oil.
Mix the eggs, milk, chives, parsley, salt, and pepper and pour into the skillet. Cook over medium-low heat until set.
Heat another skillet. Add the oil and vegetables. Sauté 5 minutes. Pour the vegetables over half the pan of eggs. Add the grated cheese. Fold the other half of the eggs over the vegetables. Heat until cheese melts.
May be served with hot sauce or tamari.

HERBED MUSHROOM OMELET

SERVES 6
½ pound mushrooms
5 tablespoons butter
1 teaspoon tarragon leaves, crumbled

8 eggs
½ teaspoon tamari soy sauce
½ teaspoon sea salt
dash ground black pepper

☞ Rinse, pat dry, and slice mushrooms (makes about 2½ cups).
In a large skillet heat butter. Add mushrooms and tarragon. Sauté 4 to 5 minutes, stirring occasionally.
Beat eggs with tamari, sea salt, and black pepper. Pour over mushrooms in skillet.
Cook over medium heat. Loosen set portion with a spatula; tilt

pan to let uncooked portion run underneath. Continue cooking until omelet is set but not dry. To turn out, loosen edge with spatula.

SCRAMBLED EGGS WITH SPROUTS

SERVES 4–6
   8 to 10 eggs
   ½ cup milk
   4 green onions, including tops,
      finely chopped
   1 teaspoon sea salt or 1 tablespoon
      tamari soy sauce or adjust to taste
   1 cup mung bean sprouts or alfalfa
      sprouts

   1 tablespoon unrefined oil

Beat the eggs with the milk and seasonings. Stir in the sprouts. Heat a large skillet on medium heat. Add the oil. Then add the beaten egg mixture. Cook, stirring often, until the eggs are barely set.

BREAKFAST MENUS

Half Broiled Grapefruit
Scrambled Eggs with Sprouts
Flaky Baking Powder Biscuits
Honey Peach Jam
Herb Tea, grain coffee (available in natural food stores), or milk

Apple juice
Vermont Toast
Omelet
Herb tea, grain coffee, or milk

''CONTINENTAL'' BREAKFAST
Warm Whole Grain Muffins
Lemon Butter
Dried Fruit Preserves
Mu, herb, or breakfast tea

CHILDREN'S BREAKFAST
Apple juice or milk
Toasted Oatmeal
with fresh fruit slices or berries

Whet Your Appetite

HORS D'OEUVRES

The old, jaded cocktail circuit is now passé. Exciting parties with only natural foods and nonalcoholic drinks are much more avant-garde. It is an exciting challenge for you, the host or hostess, to provide an all-natural food menu along with a combination of juices that will please even the most sophisticated palate. With a little imagination you will find your juice bar more popular than the bars of gold rush days.

Offer one or more kinds of drink to your guests, such as a well-seasoned, icy cold tomato juice on-the-rocks with a stick of cucumber or celery in the glass, or fresh apple and lime juice garnished with a thin slice of lime.

Fresh pineapple juice with coconut milk, sweetened with a bit of honey and placed in a blender with ice, is a sure winner. When you find out just how delicious the fresh, natural fruit juices are—and what a lift they give at party time—you may want to add a juicer to your kitchen equipment.

A kabob consisting of a pineapple cube, thin slice of lime, canta-loupe ball, or any other combination of fresh fruit, makes a pretty garnish for a tall drink. Drop a fresh strawberry, fresh cherry, or watermelon ball into juices served in champagne glasses. An orange slice or lemon wedge, a sprig of fresh mint, or a stick of fresh pineapple adds flavor and beauty to a plain glass of juice.

Serve these delicious drinks with a variety of natural food snacks.

EGG AND OLIVE CANAPÉS

YIELD: 3 TO 4 DOZEN CANAPÉS
   ½ cup tree-ripened, pitted olives
   6 hard-boiled eggs
   3 tablespoons homemade mayonnaise
   1 teaspoon fresh lime or lemon juice
   freshly grated black pepper and
   sea salt to taste

   Thin slices of whole wheat bread

   Garnish: thin slices of pimento

Mash all ingredients except bread together, until mixture is smooth.

Trim crust from thin slices of whole wheat bread. (Save crusts for croutons.) Cut each slice of bread into four small squares and toast in a slow oven.

Spread squares with egg and olive mixture; garnish with criss-cross of very thin slices of pimento.

OLIVES ROMANO

YIELD: 20–24
   ¼ pound cheddar cheese, grated fine
   ½ pound butter

1 *cup whole wheat pastry flour*
¼ *teaspoon red pepper*
20 *to* 24 *small stuffed green olives*

☞ Blend cheese and butter in a blender.
Add the flour and pepper and continue blending until smooth.
Chill.
Drain olives on absorbent paper. Pinch off small amounts of cheese
dough and press around each olive. Place on cookie sheet and bake
for 12 minutes at 400°, or until brown.
Make these ahead of time and keep in the freezer to bake when
needed.

STUFFED CELERY

YIELD: APPROX. 1½ CUPS OF STUFFING
Celery stalks

1 *cup homemade cottage cheese or*
  grated cheddar cheese
⅓ *cup homemade yogurt or*
  homemade mayonnaise
¼ *teaspoon sea salt or seasoned sea*
  salt or vegetable salt

Optional: 1 *tablespoon chopped parsley*

¼ *cup chopped pecans*

☞ Wash, string, and dry celery stalks.
Whip the remaining ingredients together.
Fill the celery stalks. Cover them and chill in refrigerator. At serv-
ing time, cut in approximately 2-inch pieces.

PINEAPPLE WITH CHEESE CUBES

☞ Wash, trim, and dry a fresh, pretty pineapple. Make the bottom
steady by smoothing it with a sharp knife. Place the pineapple in

the center of a plate. Cut cubes of a natural white cheese—swiss or jack—and a natural cheddar. Alternating the kinds of cheese, use toothpicks to stick cubes to the pineapple "eyes" (the regularly spaced brown indentations on the pineapple).

VEGETABLE BOUQUET WITH ZIPPY DIP

Carrot sticks
Slices of fresh zucchini
Sweet red pepper ring
Green bell pepper ring
Cherry tomatoes
Cauliflower separated into small pieces

Optional: Any other raw vegetables
          may be added.

☞ Prepare and let stand in crushed ice. At serving time arrange around center of large plate or tray. In center of plate or tray place a bowl filled with:

ZIPPY DIP

YIELD: 1⅓ CUPS
    1 cup homemade cottage cheese
    ⅓ cup homemade yogurt
    2 scallions, chopped fine
    ½ teaspoon sea salt
    ¼ teaspoon tamari soy sauce
    ¼ teaspoon red cayenne pepper

☞ Blend all ingredients for 30 seconds at medium speed. Correct seasoning.

"BREAD 'N BUTTER" CANAPÉS

YIELD: ABOUT 3 DOZEN
Slices of rye bread

¼ pound butter
3 tablespoons green onion tops or chives,
*   cut very fine*
1 tablespoon lime juice

☞ Cut small rounds of bread with a cookie cutter. Save small pieces for croutons.

Stir remaining ingredients together until smooth. Spread this mixture on rye rounds. Make plenty—the very simplest food often gets the biggest rush at a party.

CHEDDAR ROUNDS

YIELD: 2 DOZEN
1 cup finely grated cheddar cheese
¼ cup homemade safflower butter
¼ teaspoon sea salt or 1 teaspoon
*   tamari soy sauce*
¼ teaspoon seasoned pepper or a pinch of
*   cayenne pepper*

⅓ to ½ cup whole wheat flour

☞ Mix cheese, butter, salt, and pepper.
Work enough flour in by hand to form a stiff dough. If it gets too dry, add a few drops of cold water.
Shape the dough into small balls. Place on oiled cookie sheet. Flatten balls.
Bake about 5 to 8 minutes at 400°. Do not overcook.

PARMESAN CROWNS

YIELD: 12 1½-INCH ROUNDS
    ½ *cup homemade mayonnaise*
    ¼ *cup grated Parmesan cheese*
    ¼ *cup finely chopped green onion tops*
    dash of tamari soy sauce

    12 *1½-inch rounds of thinly sliced*
      whole wheat bread

☞ Combine mayonnaise, cheese, green onions, and tamari. Spread on bread rounds. Place on baking pan and sprinkle with additional Parmesan cheese.
Bake about 8 minutes at 450°. The crowns will puff and brown slightly. Serve hot.

WHEAT RUSKS

YIELD: 3 TO 4 DOZEN
    2 *cups whole wheat flour*
    1¼ *cups milk*
    ½ *cup unrefined safflower oil*
    2 *cups fresh wheat germ*
    1 *tablespoon raw honey*
    1 *teaspoon sea salt*

    Caraway seeds
    Sesame seeds

☞ Mix and knead all the ingredients together except the seeds. Roll the dough ¼-inch thick. Cut into sticks about five inches long. Place on an oiled cookie sheet.
Sprinkle some of the sticks with caraway seeds and others with sesame seeds. Bake until golden brown at 350°.

MARINATED CUCUMBERS

YIELD: ABOUT 2 CUPS

    2 cucumbers, sliced very thin
    3 cups water
    1 tablespoon sea salt

    ½ cup unrefined oil
    4 tablespoons cider vinegar

☞ Place the cucumbers, water, and sea salt in bowl. Toss together lightly and allow to soak for 1 hour.
Drain the cucumbers and dry on paper toweling.
Combine the oil and vinegar and pour over the cucumbers. Marinate in refrigerator for 2 hours or longer.
Toss and serve.

MARINATED MUSHROOMS

YIELD: 3 CUPS

    ½ pound mushrooms, with stems

    ¼ teaspoon sea salt or 1 teaspoon
      tamari soy sauce
    ½ teaspoon oregano
    3 tablespoons lemon juice
    ½ cup unrefined olive oil

☞ Rinse and wipe the mushrooms and slice them evenly.
Mix the salt or tamari, oregano, lemon juice, and olive oil. Add to the mushrooms.
Allow to stand at room temperature 2 to 3 hours or overnight.

FRESH DILL PICKLES

YIELD: 3 QUARTS
> *3 quarts water*
> *½ cup sea salt*
>
> *Any or all of the following vegetables*
> *may be pickled. Prepare enough*
> *vegetables to fill a gallon crock*
> *¾ full.*
> > *cucumbers, sliced*
> > *onions, quartered*
> > *green tomatoes, quartered*
> > *carrots, sliced*
> > *celery, sliced*
> > *green pepper, sliced*
>
> *2 heads dill*
> *1 to 2 cloves garlic, chopped*
> *2 bay leaves*

☞ Add the salt to the water. Boil until the salt dissolves. Cool. If you use the water when it is still hot, the pickles will be soft.
Wash the vegetables and drain them on paper towels. In a gallon crock, alternate vegetables and dill. Continue layering until all the vegetables are used up. Add the garlic and the bay leaves. Pour the salt water over the vegetables. Place a plate on top of the vegetables and a quart jar full of water on the plate. This will hold the vegetables under the brine. As the ferment rises to the top, skim it off. Pickling will take 3 to 5 days. Refrigerate when vegetables suit your taste. The longer they are allowed to pickle, the stronger the taste will be.

DIPS

Many dips lead a double life—as salad dressings or sauces as well as dips. Serve natural food dips with homemade crackers or crisp vegetables instead of the same tired old chips.

BEAN DIP

YIELD: 4 CUPS

>4 cups cooked pinto bean flakes or
>   mashed, cooked pinto beans
>1 cup water
>1 cup chopped onion
>1 clove garlic, minced
>1 teaspoon cumin seed
>2 jalapenos peppers, chopped
>1 tablespoon unsulphured molasses
>4 large tomatoes
>
>juice of 1 lemon
>3 tablespoons chili powder
>1½ teaspoons sea salt
>
>½ cup unrefined corn germ oil
>½ pound sharp cheese, grated

In a 2-quart saucepan, place the beans, water, onion, garlic, cumin seed, peppers, molasses, and tomatoes and simmer for 1 hour.
Add the lemon juice, chili powder, and salt.
While the beans are still hot, add the oil and grated cheese. Mash or blend until smooth.

Serve hot or cold with corn munchies or homemade crackers.

CHILI CON QUESO

YIELD: 5 CUPS

1 tablespoon butter or unrefined
    safflower oil
1 medium onion, chopped fine

1 pound cheddar cheese, grated
1 cup whole milk, heated
2 cups cooked tomatoes, chopped
1 tablespoon chili powder, dissolved in
    2 tablespoons of the milk
2 or 3, according to taste, cooked jalepenos
    peppers, seeded and chopped

☞ In top of double boiler melt butter, add onions, and stir until onion begin to soften. Stir in cheese. When cheese begins to melt, add milk slowly, stirring occasionally. Add tomatoes, chili powder, and jalepenos. Pour into top of heated chafing dish and serve with tostados (crisp, deep-fried tortillas).

This is a good main dish for a light supper. Pour chili over toast like a Mexican Welsh rarebit.

HOMOS

YIELD: 1½ CUPS

2 cups cooked chick peas
1 to 2 cloves garlic, minced
2 tablespoons tahini
juice of ½ lemon, or to taste
½ teaspoon unrefined olive oil
sea salt to taste
tamari soy sauce to taste

Garnish: parsley or mint leaves

☞ Purée the peas and mix all the ingredients together—in a blender, if you wish. The consistency should be creamy. Serve in a bowl garnished with parsley or mint leaves, along with crackers or flat bread.

This Middle-Eastern purée is used as a spread which is usually scooped up on pieces of pita or other flat bread, or crackers. A popular Syrian or Turkish appetizer, it is most often served at parties or restaurants rather than with everyday home meals.

OLIVE-NUT DIP

YIELD: 3 CUPS
> 1 cup homemade yogurt
> 1 cup homemade mayonnaise
> ½ cup chopped ripe olives
> ½ cup finely chopped blanched almonds,
>   pecans, or other nuts
> 2 tablespoons chopped pimentos
> 2 tablespoons chopped chives
> ⅛ teaspoon sea salt, or to taste

☞ Mix all ingredients well.
Salt to taste.

A delicious party dip. Serve with homemade whole wheat or sesame crackers, or crisp raw vegetables, for dipping.

SUNFLOWER-YOGURT DIP OR SALAD DRESSING

YIELD: 1½ CUPS
> 1 cup homemade yogurt
> ½ cup sunflower seeds, roasted and
>   ground
> ¼ cup chopped scallion tops or chives
> ½ teaspoon sea salt or kelp or
>   2 tablespoons tamari soy sauce
>   If you use tamari, use less yogurt—
>   ¾ cup.

☞ Blend all the ingredients together.

Serve with corn munchies or whole wheat crackers, or use as a salad dressing.

UMEBOSHI HOT SAUCE

YIELD: ½ CUP
    1 onion, diced
      (for milder flavor, sauté lightly)
    *7 umeboshi plums, pitted
    3 tablespoons unrefined corn germ oil
    1 tablespoon water

☞ Blend all the ingredients together.

Great for tacos or as a dip for raw vegetables such as cucumbers, carrots, or celery.

*Pickled, salted plums. Available in natural food stores and Oriental groceries and markets.

SNACKS AND SANDWICHES

Preparing delicious snacks is one of the easiest ways to introduce your family to natural foods. Now you have some help. Natural food companies are coming up with some great snack foods. Tamari roasted nuts are almost too good to believe. There are even corn chips made from stone-ground yellow corn without preservatives or additives. Occasionally you'll find jellies and some jams with no sweetening other than their own natural sugars. Natural food bakeries are baking delectable cakes and cookies. Really good (nutritionally speaking) candy bars are still few and far between, however.

Of course, the best snacks are still fruits, natural cheeses, home-made breads, old-fashioned nut butters, and raw and roasted nuts.

The recipes that follow are mostly easy, delicious, and nutritious sandwich spreads. Try the beverage and dessert sections for a sweeter selection.

ALFALFA SPROUT SPREAD

YIELD: 1 CUP
   1 cup butter, softened
   ⅓ cup fresh alfalfa sprouts
   juice of 1 lemon
   ¼ teaspoon sea salt
   dash of cayenne pepper

   Optional: chopped fresh parsley

☞ Mix all ingredients together thoroughly.

Spread on homemade dilly bread.

BLUE CHEESE SPREAD

YIELD: ENOUGH FOR 4 SANDWICHES
   2 tablespoons crumbled blue cheese
   2 tablespoons butter or homemade
      mayonnaise
   ¼ teaspoon dry mustard
   ½ teaspoon sea salt, or salt to taste
   1 teaspoon tamari soy sauce
   1 teaspoon toasted sesame seeds

☞ Mash the ingredients together until they form a paste.

This spread is particularly good on all herb or dilly bread but it may be served on any bread.

CHEESE SPREAD

YIELD: ENOUGH FOR 4 SANDWICHES
   ½ pound swiss or muenster cheese,
      grated
   ½ cup chopped chives
   ½ cup green olives, chopped
   ⅓ cup homemade mayonnaise or yogurt
   1 tablespoon milk

☞ Mix well. Spread on dilly bread.

VARIATION:
Add ½ to 1 cup fresh alfalfa sprouts. Roll in a lettuce leaf. Chill and cut in 1-inch pieces.

GARLIC CHEESE SPREAD

YIELD: ENOUGH FOR 2 OR 3 LOAVES OF BREAD
    2 or 3 cloves garlic, finely minced
    4 tablespoons chopped chives
    2 tablespoons chopped parsley
    1 tablespoon tamari soy sauce or
      1 teaspoon sea salt
    4 tablespoons unrefined olive oil
    1 cup butter, softened
    1 cup grated Parmesan cheese

    Optional: 1 teaspoon pepper

☞ Have all ingredients at room temperature. Combine all ingredients and mix well. Chill for several hours.
Slice 2 loaves of bread. Spread the mixture on each slice. Re-assemble the loaves and wrap each whole loaf in foil. Heat through and open when it is time to serve.

HONEY PEACH JAM

YIELD: 3 PINTS
    ¼ teaspoon mace
    ½ teaspoon ground nutmeg
    3 teaspoons cinnamon
    1½ teaspoons whole cloves

    3 pounds fresh peaches, blanched,
      peeled, and puréed

2½ *cups raw honey*
¼ *cup lemon juice*
¾ *cup fresh orange juice*

☞ Tie the spices in a cheesecloth bag. Combine ingredients and simmer together until the mixture thickens.
Remove the spices. Pour jam into hot, sterilized jars. Seal.

VARIATIONS:
Try using fresh apricots or plums.

DRIED FRUIT PRESERVES

YIELD: VARIES WITH FRUITS USED—FROM ONE TO TWO CUPS.
8 *ounces dried fruits*
2 *tablespoons lemon juice*
raw honey

☞ Chop the dried fruits finely.
Add the lemon juice and stir. Cover fruit with raw honey. Cover the bowl and let fruit sit for about 4 to 5 days, until very soft.

VARIATION FOR IMMEDIATE USE:
Use soaked, dried fruit, drained. Place in a blender. Add enough raw honey to make a thick purée when blended.

CRANBERRY RELISH

YIELD: 1 QUART
2 *cups water*
1 *cup raw honey*

1 *pound cranberries*
¼ *teaspoon sea salt*

2 *tablespoons chutney*
1 *teaspoon curry powder*
1 *cup chopped walnuts*

Combine water and honey in saucepan; stir until well mixed.
Add cranberries and salt and bring to boil. Cook 10 to 15 minutes,
or until skins pop. Remove from heat.
Add chutney, curry, and nuts. Mix well and chill.

BASIC NUT BUTTER

YIELD: 1 CUP
   1½ cups roasted nuts, whole or broken
   unrefined oil
   sea salt

 Place 1½ cups whole or broken nuts in a blender. Cover and whirl
until nuts are finely ground. Add the oil (amount varies for each
kind of nut), a small amount at a time, whirling after each addition.
Add salt to taste and blend 30 seconds, or until very smooth.
Note: Start and stop blender as necessary and use a spatula to
keep all the butter in motion. The nut mixture is thick, so make
nut butters in small batches to avoid overtaxing the blender motor.

VARIATIONS:

1. *Almond butter:* Blanch nuts by covering with boiling water,
   let stand about 5 minutes, then drain and slip off skins. Dry in
   a single layer on towels. To roast, place blanched or unblanched
   nuts on a cookie sheet. Bake 10 to 20 minutes at 350°. Blend
   with 2 to 3 tablespoons oil.

2. *Cashew butter:* Buy blanched nuts. To roast, bake nuts 10 to
   15 minutes at 350°. Blend with 4 to 6 teaspoons oil.

3. *Peanut butter:* Roast the peanuts until golden, about 20 minutes at 350°. There is no need to remove the skins. Blend with
   2 or 3 tablespoons of unrefined safflower oil. Add salt to taste.

SAFFLOWER BUTTER

YIELD: 3½ CUPS
   1 pound butter, softened
   1¼ cups unrefined safflower oil

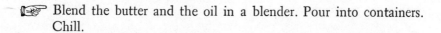 Blend the butter and the oil in a blender. Pour into containers. Chill.

This butter has the rich flavor of natural butter combined with the light flavor of the safflower oil. It is high in unsaturated fats and is free of the preservatives and additives present in commercial spreads.

HONEY LEMON BUTTER

YIELD: 1 CUP

½ cup safflower butter
¼ cup mild raw honey
2 tablespoons fresh lemon juice
1 teaspoon grated lemon peel

In a small mixer bowl cream the butter until fluffy. Continue creaming while adding honey in a fine stream. Add lemon juice and lemon peel. Stir all ingredients until evenly blended. Chill.

LEMON BUTTER

YIELD: ½ CUP

½ cup safflower butter
2 teaspoons lemon juice
1 teaspoon grated lemon rind

Optional: 1 to 2 tablespoons raw honey

Mix all ingredients well.

LIME BUTTER

YIELD: ½ CUP

½ cup safflower butter
1 tablespoon chopped parsley
2 tablespoons lime juice

Mix all ingredients well.

SESAME BUTTER

YIELD: ½ CUP
> *2 tablespoons pan-roasted sesame seeds*
> *⅓ cup butter, softened*
> *1 tablespoon lemon juice*
> *1 teaspoon tamari soy sauce*

 Roast the sesame seeds lightly in a small dry skillet.
Stir all the ingredients together until well mixed.
Chill until mixture can be spread.

Sesame butter is excellent in party sandwiches.

DRY ROASTED NUTS OR SEEDS

 Heat dry skillet over medium heat.
Add nuts or seeds, to cover bottom of skillet.
Stir constantly with wooden spoon until lightly browned. Once hot, seeds will burn very quickly, so watch carefully. Seeds may start popping like popcorn. Remove seeds from pan as soon as they are roasted or they will continue to roast in the hot pan.

VARIATIONS:
1. Nuts and seeds may also be dry roasted in the oven. Spread them on ungreased cookie sheets. Bake 15 to 20 minutes at 300° or until lightly browned. Stir occasionally.

2. Nuts or seeds may be soaked in tamari soy sauce or sprinkled with tamari before roasting.

Do not mix different nuts and seeds, as they cook at different rates.

ROASTED SOYBEANS

YIELD: ½ CUP
> *½ cup dry soybeans*
> *2 cups cold water*

☞ Refrigerate the soybeans in the water overnight. The next day, drain off excess water and dry the beans.

Spread the beans in a shallow pan, and bake 2 hours at 200°. When done, brown lightly in the broiler, stirring frequently.

Use as is, or toss with 1 tablespoon oil and salt lightly. Leave whole for snacks, or grind in a blender or food grinder and use as a nut-like topping.

PARTY MENUS

BUFFET

Vegetable Bouquet with Zippy Dip
Fresh Pineapple with Cheese Cubes with pineapple spears
arranged spoke-wise around base
A board with Brie and Camembert cheeses and white grapes
Whole Wheat Crackers
A bowl of cold, tree-ripened olives
Marinated Mushrooms
Stuffed Celery
Cashew nuts (untoasted)
Tray of stuffed eggs
Egg and Olive Canapés
"Bread 'n Butter" Canapés
Nik's Guacamole with tostados
(crisp, deep-fried tortillas)
A pot of herb tea, a silver compote of Apricot-nut Balls and
a plate of Carob Brownies complete an elegant party buffet.

PREDINNER HORS D'OEUVRES

Cheddar Rounds
Stuffed Celery
Marinated Cucumbers

The Kitchen Kettle
SOUPS

Some like 'em hot, some like 'em cold—and there is nothing more delicious than a hearty soup on a cold winter day or a chilled, light soup for a summer meal. Serving a lunch or supper of soup, green salad, cheese, a crusty loaf of bread, and fruit is a delightful practice adopted from French cooks. Give the soup a special touch by adding your favorite garnish—seeds or nuts, bread crumbs, croutons, chopped parsley, watercress or other greens, grated cheese, a pinch of herb, or sliced hard-boiled eggs.

A good stock is the basis of any fine soup. Soup stock is a great way to use your leftovers and conserve nutrients. It is tempting to use a blender, pressure cooker, or other short cut, but really good soup stock should simmer slowly. Either strain the stock immediately or let it sit overnight and strain in the morning. Freeze or refrigerate any stock over and above your immediate needs. You may even freeze scraps for making stock later. Always keep a jar of stock on hand in the refrigerator to use in soups, breads, casseroles, or sauces.

45

SOUP STOCK

YIELD: 3 QUARTS
>1 quart (approximately) vegetable scraps,
>	cooking liquids, and leftovers
>	from dinner
>2 quarts water
>1 to 2 teaspoons sea salt

☞ Mix all ingredients in a large pot. Cover and simmer 30 minutes or longer.

BARLEY SOUP
(or any whole grain)

YIELD: 4 CUPS
>1 tablespoon unrefined oil
>2 onions, chopped
>1 stalk celery, sliced thinly
>
>1 cup barley, brown rice, oats, millet, or
>	any flaked grain
>
>4 cups water
>
>1 tablespoon unrefined oil
>¼ pound mushrooms, sliced
>2 tablespoons tamari soy sauce
>
>Garnish: Sprigs of parsley

☞ Heat a 2 or 3 quart saucepan. Add the oil, onions, and celery, and sauté. Add the barley or other grain and sauté together with the vegetables for 5 minutes.
Add the water and bring to a boil. Simmer 1 hour or more. (Soups are better the longer they cook.)
Sauté the mushrooms in oil; add 1 teaspoon tamari, and add to the soup.

Add the remaining tamari and simmer 5 minutes longer.

Garnish each bowl with parsley when serving.

Barley soup is an oldtime favorite, something grandmothers always liked to make.

BEAN SOUP

YIELD: 6 CUPS

  4 *cups cooked black beans, pinto beans,*
    or soybeans (or cooked bean flakes)
    and thick juice from cooking.
  2 *cups water or stock*
  2 *tablespoons lime juice*
  4 *teaspoons unrefined oil*
  2 *small onions, finely chopped*
  2 *teaspoons chili powder*
  1 *to 2 teaspoons sea salt*

  Garnish: 6 tablespoons yogurt
    mixed with ½ teaspoon
    chili powder

☞ Simmer all ingredients until thick. Garnish just before serving.

VARIATION:

Simmer the beans, water, juice, and oil with 1 large chopped onion, 1 chopped green pepper, 2 finely chopped cloves of garlic, and 1 bay leaf. Remove the bay leaf before serving.

Serve this thick, hearty soup on a cold evening.

BLACK BEAN SOUP

YIELD: 3 CUPS

    4 *cups water*
    1 *cup black beans*

    2 *tablespoons unrefined oil*
    2 *onions, sliced*
    1 *stalk celery, sliced*

    ½ *teaspoon sea salt*
    1 *bay leaf*
    1 *teaspoon celery seed*
    ¼ *teaspoon basil*

    juice of ½ *lemon*
    1 *tablespoon tamari soy sauce or to taste*

    Garnish: sprigs of parsley or sliced
                  hard-boiled egg

☞ Soak beans overnight in the water.

Next day: Heat a large saucepan. Add the oil and the onions and celery and sauté. Add the black beans and soaking water. Pressure cook beans 1½ hours or simmer 2 to 3 hours until beans are very soft.

Purée the beans in a blender or a food mill and return to the stove. Add the salt and the herbs. Simmer 15 minutes. If the soup is too thin, add 2 tablespoons whole wheat flour mixed with 2 tablespoons water to thicken. Simmer 15 more minutes.

Add the lemon juice and the tamari and heat through.

Garnish each bowl before serving.

Black bean soup is a beautiful and delicate soup to serve company. It is a traditional soup of the Orient and the Southwest. Bean soups are always favorites.

EASY BORSCHT

YIELD: 6 CUPS

    4 *or* 5 *beets, grated*
    4 *cups water*
    4 *tablespoons tamari soy sauce*

1 cup beet greens, chopped
1 teaspoon dill weed
2 teaspoons chopped fresh chives or
   1 green onion sliced

Garnish: homemade yogurt or sour cream

☞ In a soup pot, bring beets, water, and tamari to a boil. Cover and simmer 10 minutes.
Add the beet greens, dill, and chives. Simmer over low heat for 10 minutes.
Serve hot, cold, or at room temperature with a spoonful of yogurt or sour cream in each bowl.

The yogurt makes this soup!

SPIKY CHEESE SOUP

YIELD: 8 CUPS
   4 tablespoons unrefined oil
   4 carrots, chopped
   2 onions, chopped
   4 stalks celery, chopped
   1 or 2 green peppers, chopped

   ½ cup whole wheat flour

   4 cups tamari bouillon or vegetable
      stock seasoned with 2 tablespoons
      tamari soy sauce

   4 cups milk
   ¾ pound cheddar and/or swiss cheese,
      cubed

   sea salt and pepper to taste

☞ Heat a 4 quart saucepan or dutch oven. Add the oil and carrots. Sauté 5 minutes. Add the remaining vegetables. Sauté 5 minutes longer.

Add the flour. Heat gently 3 to 5 minutes, stirring constantly.
Slowly add the broth. Cook until thickened, stirring often.
Add the milk and cheese. Reduce heat to low. Just heat until the
cheese is partially melted. This soup is best when some of the
cheese is still in soft cubes.
Season with salt and pepper to taste.

GAZPACHO

YIELD: 3 CUPS

2 ripe tomatoes
1 cucumber (peel if skin is bitter or
    waxed)
1 green pepper
1 clove garlic, minced
½ cup mixed herbs:
    parsley, basil, thyme, tarragon

1 tablespoon unrefined olive oil
3 tablespoons lemon juice
2 cups chilled water or vegetable stock

1 onion, sliced thinly
1 teaspoon sea salt or 3 tablespoons
    tamari soy sauce

Garnish: dry bread crumbs or yogurt

☞ Place the vegetables in a chopping bowl and chop fine.
Slowly add the oil, lemon juice, and water or stock.
Add the onion and salt or tamari.
Chill 4 hours before serving.
Garnish with dry bread crumbs or yogurt.

Serve gazpacho for the first course when you're having tacos for
dinner. Or, for a special luncheon, scoop out large, firm, red
tomatoes, fill them with gazpacho, and top with sour cream or
yogurt seasoned with curry. Set each tomato on a big romaine leaf
and pass croutons.

COLD GUACAMOLE SOUP

YIELD: 4 CUPS
   ½ cup milk
   2 avocados
   1 green pepper, cut in chunks
   1 small onion, cut in chunks
   2 tablespoons lemon juice
   1 teaspoon sea salt

   3 cups homemade yogurt

   Garnish: fresh mint or parsley, paprika

☞ Blend all the vegetables with the milk in a blender. When smooth,
   add the yogurt.
   Garnish with fresh mint or parsley and paprika.

   Guacamole fans will love this soup.

MALAYSIAN LEMON RICE SOUP

YIELD: 5 CUPS
   1½ quarts vegetable broth
   ½ cup brown rice
   1 bay leaf
   sea salt to taste if broth isn't salted

   ¼ teaspoon summer savory
   4 eggs, beaten
   juice and grated peel of 2 lemons
      (or to taste)

   Garnish: minced green onion or chives

☞ Heat stock to boiling, add rice, bay leaf, and salt if needed. Simmer 30 to 40 minutes or until rice is tender. Remove bay leaf.
   Mix summer savory with beaten eggs. Add lemon juice and grated

peel and mix again. Slowly add one cup of stock to egg mixture, stirring constantly. Add egg mixture to soup. Garnish each bowl before serving.

Serve Malaysian lemon rice soup in demitasse cups in the living room before dinner. You will find it a delicate appetite teaser.

ITALIAN MINESTRONE

YIELD: 6 CUPS

1½ *cups kidney beans or pinto beans*
2 *quarts water*

2 *tablespoons unrefined sesame or*
   corn germ oil
2 *to 3 onions, sliced fairly thickly*
1 *to 2 cloves garlic, minced*
3 *stalks celery, sliced in ¼ to ½ inch*
   slices
3 *to 4 zucchini, cut in ¾ to 1 inch*
   rounds
2 *to 3 carrots, also cut in rounds*
1 *bunch swiss chard or other leafy green*
   vegetables, sliced

2 *teaspoons sea salt*
tamari soy sauce to taste

Garnish: grated parmesan cheese

☞ Wash beans and soak in the water overnight. The next day, bring the beans and water to a boil. Cover and cook until soft, about 1 hour. If you are in a hurry, pressure cook the beans without soaking about 45 minutes.
Meanwhile, heat a large skillet. Add the oil and vegetables in the order listed and sauté. Add the vegetables to the soft cooked beans. Add the salt and additional water if necessary. Bring to a boil and cook, uncovered, on medium heat for about 30 minutes until the soup is thick and creamy and the vegetables are tender.

Taste and correct seasoning, adding tamari about 5 minutes before serving.

Pass grated Parmesan cheese to sprinkle on top.

MISO SOUP

YIELD: 3 CUPS

1 cup dry wakame (sea vegetable)
1 cup water

1 tablespoon unrefined oil
3 onions, sliced

2 cups water

2 scallions, sliced in 1″ pieces

1 tablespoon miso soybean paste,
   or to taste

☞ Rinse the wakame briefly under running water and soak in 1 cup water for 15 minutes.

Heat a large saucepan. Add the oil and onions and sauté 5 minutes. Add the rest of the water and bring to a boil. Simmer 20 minutes. Cut the soaked wakame in ½″ pieces and add it to the soup. Simmer the soup 10 minutes more.

Add the chopped scallions and simmer 5 more minutes. Turn off the heat.

Dilute the miso in a small amount of the hot soup and add it to the soup. Stir well. Serve.

VARIATIONS:

Other vegetables may be included in the soup. Onions and wakame are traditional but almost any vegetable may be used, such as carrot, white radish, turnip, Chinese cabbage, or spinach.

Miso soup is excellent served at the beginning of a meal. Due to the natural fermentation process that occurs in making miso, this soup aids in the digestion of the meal.

MUSHROOM SOUP

YIELD: 6 CUPS

4 tablespoons unrefined oil
1 or 2 bunches green onions and green
   tops, washed and chopped
3 or 4 stalks celery, chopped
½ pound fresh mushrooms, washed and
   sliced

4 tablespoons whole wheat flour

sea salt
seasoned pepper
tamari soy sauce to taste
6 cups fresh milk

☞ Heat a large saucepan or dutch oven. Add the oil, onions, celery, and mushrooms and sauté until barely tender.
Stir in the flour.
Gradually add the seasonings and milk, stirring constantly. Simmer until slightly thickened.

This is a delicious party soup. Serve it on Christmas Eve or other special occasions.

FRENCH ONION SOUP

YIELD: 4 CUPS

2 tablespoons unrefined corn germ oil
2 large onions, thinly sliced

1 tablespoon whole wheat flour

4 cups hot tamari broth or
   vegetable stock

sea salt

Garnish: toasted croutons, grated cheese

Heat a large saucepan. Add the oil and onions and sauté until tender and golden brown.

Add the flour and cook over low heat for about 2 minutes, stirring constantly.

Add the hot broth and simmer 5 to 10 minutes.

Season to taste with sea salt. Serve hot with the garnish.

POTATO SOUP

YIELD: 6 CUPS

1 quart of potatoes, peeled and diced
3 cups leeks or onions, sliced
1 tablespoon sea salt
2 quarts of water, approximately

¼ cup heavy cream or
   3–4 tablespoons sweet cream butter

 Simmer vegetables in salted water until very soft.

Add butter or cream. Serve hot with crusty sourdough bread, buttered and warm.

V A R I A T I O N :
Substitute Jerusalem artichokes for the potatoes.

VICHYSSOISE

YIELD: 6 CUPS
potato soup

sea salt
white pepper
3 tablespoons tamari soy sauce
1 cup heavy cream

Garnish: chopped parsley or chives

Put potato soup through strainer or food mill.

Add salt, white pepper, and tamari; add 1 cup of heavy cream; chill thoroughly.

Serve in very cold soup cups. Sprinkle with chopped parsley or chives before serving.

SIMPLE BLENDER SOUP

YIELD: 6 CUPS

4 cups milk or broth
2 cups chopped fresh or
fresh frozen vegetables
4 tablespoons whole wheat flour
4 tablespoons unrefined oil or butter
seasoning to taste using sea salt,
tamari soy sauce, and pepper

 Blend all ingredients together in a blender and heat until slightly thickened.

One possible combination:

4 cups milk
2 cups fresh corn
4 tablespoons whole wheat flour
4 tablespoons unrefined corn germ oil
2 tablespoons chives
2 tablespoons tamari soy sauce
seasoned pepper

Use your imagination with this recipe. It's great for emergencies—those unexpected guests for lunch—or for a meal in summer when it's too hot to cook.

SPLIT PEA OR LENTIL SOUP

YIELD: 3 CUPS

4 cups water or soup stock
1 onion, sliced
2 stalks celery, sliced

¼ *green pepper, diced*
2 *carrots, chopped*

1 *cup split peas or lentils*

½ *teaspoon sea salt*
¼ *teaspoon celery seed*
1 *bay leaf*

2 *tablespoons tamari soy sauce or*
   additional sea salt to taste

Garnish: chopped parsley

☞ Bring the water or stock to a boil. Add the vegetables and bring
the water to a boil again. Add the split peas. Simmer 45 minutes.
Add the salt, celery seed, and bay leaf and simmer 15 more minutes.
Add the tamari or additional salt 5 minutes before soup is finished.
Remove bay leaf before serving.
Garnish with fresh parsley.

TAMARI BOUILLON

YIELD: 4 CUPS

1 *tablespoon unrefined safflower oil*
1 *small onion, thinly sliced*
1 *clove garlic, finely chopped*

5 *cups water*

1 *tablespoon parsley, chopped*
1 *carrot, thinly sliced*

2 *tablespoons tamari soy sauce*

☞ Heat a large saucepan. Add the oil, onion, and garlic and sauté.
Add the water and all the vegetables. Simmer 30 minutes.
Add the soy sauce and simmer 5 more minutes, and salt to taste.

Leave the vegetables in the broth or strain them out and use elsewhere.

Use this broth in place of beef broth or bouillon.

TODO EN LA CALDERA

YIELD: 2 QUARTS

3 tablespoons unrefined safflower oil
1 cup onions, chopped
1 ear of fresh corn, cut off cob
½ cup chopped carrots
½ cup chopped celery
½ cup chopped fresh mushrooms

1 cup chopped fresh tomatoes
1 cup cooked soybeans
3 or 4 whole peppercorns
5 or 6 sprigs of parsley
dash or two of cayenne pepper
2 cloves garlic
½ teaspoon each of summer savory,
    celery seed, basil, tarragon, oregano
¼ teaspoon each of thyme, rosemary,
    marjoram, sage
2 tablespoons tamari soy sauce
½ cup raw brown rice
2 quarts vegetable stock

1 heaping tablespoon miso soybean paste

Heat a large soup pot. Add oil and onions, corn, carrots, celery, and mushrooms and sauté briefly.
Add all the remaining ingredients, except the miso. Simmer slowly. Remove about ½ cup broth to make a paste with the miso and add this back to the soup. Cover and simmer 2 to 3 hours.

Todo en la caldera—all in the kettle—is a complete meal; serve it with warm sourdough bread and natural cheese.

VEGETABLE BROTH

YIELD: 3 CUPS

1 potato, washed, unpeeled, cut in cubes
1 carrot, washed, unpeeled, and
  coarsely chopped
12 fresh green beans, chopped
some mushroom stems if you have them
2 ribs celery, chopped
3 small yellow squash, unpeeled and
  coarsely chopped
1 onion, coarsely chopped
handful of spinach, watercress, or
  parsley
1 clove garlic
1 tomato, chopped

sea salt or tamari soy sauce to taste

 Cover vegetables with water and simmer until they are soft.
Strain; season with sea salt or tamari.
This is merely an outline. Use any vegetable, including the skins
of potatoes. It is good for everyone!

Some of the fashionable health spas keep this on hand at all times.
Hot or cold, it is an excellent midmorning or midafternoon drink
that provides lots of potassium, and is also good used in casseroles,
soups, and for seasoning.

NON-DAIRY CREAM OF VEGETABLE SOUP

YIELD: 4 CUPS
    2 tablespoons unrefined oil
    ½ cup rice flour

    4 cups water
    ¼ teaspoon sea salt (use ½ teaspoon of
        sea salt if you don't wish to add
        tamari)

    1 tablespoon unrefined oil
    2 onions, sliced
    3 stalks celery, sliced, or 1 cup chopped
        mushrooms, or vegetables of your
        choice

    Optional: 1 tablespoon tamari soy sauce

    Garnish: chopped parsley

☞ Heat a large saucepan. Add the oil and rice flour and sauté. Cool
and add the water and the salt and simmer for 30 minutes.
Heat a small skillet. Add the oil, onions, and celery and sauté.
Add them to the soup. Simmer for 15 more minutes.
Add the tamari if desired, and simmer 5 minutes more.
Garnish with chopped parsley.

If you prefer not to use dairy products, try making this "cream"
soup.

YOGURT SOUP

YIELD: 5 CUPS
    ⅓ cup raisins
    ⅔ cup cold water

3 *cups yogurt*
⅓ *cup milk*
⅓ *cup cucumber, chopped fine*
2 *tablespoons green onion, chopped fine*
¼ *teaspoon sea salt*
5 *or 6 ice cubes*

Garnish: 1 *tablespoon chopped parsley*
              1 *teaspoon fresh dill*

☞ Cover raisins with cold water and allow to plump, about ½ hour. Mix yogurt, milk, cucumbers, onions, and salt with ice cubes in a bowl, stirring until thoroughly mixed. Add water and raisins.
Cover and place in refrigerator until ready to serve. Serve in cups or cream of soup bowls, sprinkled with parsley and dill, with those delicious, thin, homemade wheat crackers.

Never tell your guests the ingredients of this soup until they ask for the recipe.

The Salad Bowl

VEGETABLE AND FRUIT SALADS

Fresh vegetable salads are a beautiful way to start a meal. They are light, nutritious, and easy to fix. Almost any fresh vegetable may be used in a salad. Raw vegetables straight from the garden are best, but they are not always available. As soon as you bring the vegetables in from the garden or home from the market, wash them quickly in cold water using a brush if needed, and whirl or towel dry. Place in plastic bags and chill thoroughly.

BASIC GREEN SALAD

Choose one or more of the following greens:
romaine lettuce	*spinach*
bibb lettuce	*swiss chard*
boston lettuce	*chicory*
red leaf lettuce	*tops of root vegetables*
escarole	*(best when young).*

Add color, beauty, and health to your salads with:

flowerets of raw cauliflower	*radishes*
or broccoli	*red cabbage*
slices of red and green bell	*celery*
peppers	*purple onions*
chopped or grated root	*or your own favorite crisp,*
vegetables	*fresh vegetables.*
fresh squash	*And remember the* sprouts!
avocado	

☞ When the ingredients are thoroughly chilled, tear the greens and slice or chop the other vegetables.

Immediately toss with enough unrefined oil, about 1 teaspoon per serving, to lightly coat all surfaces. The oil coat protects the nutrients in the vegetables against the leaching effects of moisture and vinegar.

Add tomato slices, artichoke hearts marinated in cider vinegar, crumbled blue cheese, or other grated cheeses.

Just before serving, add your own seasonings if desired—lemon or lime juice, cider vinegar, sea salt or kelp, pepper, herbs, or a handful of pumpkin or sunflower seeds.

If fresh green leaves are not available for underliners and garnishes, use red or white shredded cabbage, shredded carrots, or all three. Nothing adds more zest and beauty to mealtime than a crisp, colorful, freshly made salad accented with a complementary dressing.

AVOCADO-GRAPEFRUIT SALAD

SERVES 2

1 *red grapefruit*
1 *avocado*

☞ Cut a ruby red grapefruit in half. Remove alternate segments of the grapefruit and replace them with avocado wedges. Remove the core of the grapefruit and fill the cavity with poppy-seed dressing to dip the avocado and grapefruit segments.

The rich, smooth texture of avocado combines naturally with sweet 'n tart grapefruit sections. This pretty salad is often served in the Rio Grande Valley of Texas, where grapefruit of the finest quality is grown.

FRUIT BASKET WITH LIME SAUCE

> *4 firm ripe papayas*
> *1 box strawberries, washed, hulled,*
>   *and sliced*
> *2 bananas, peeled and sliced*

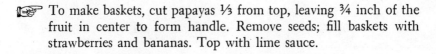 To make baskets, cut papayas ⅓ from top, leaving ¾ inch of the fruit in center to form handle. Remove seeds; fill baskets with strawberries and bananas. Top with lime sauce.

LIME SAUCE

> *½ cup raw honey*
> *¼ cup water*
> *6 tablespoons lime juice*
>
> *1 teaspoon grated lime rind*
>
> *Garnish: sprigs of fresh mint*

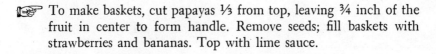 Combine all ingredients, except rind, in a small saucepan and simmer for 5 minutes. Add rind. Ladle sauce over fruit in baskets. Cover with plastic wrap and chill for several hours.
Garnish each basket with a sprig of fresh mint before serving.

Papayas are becoming a year-round fruit. This luscious fruit is very rich in natural vitamins and minerals, and provides almost four times the minimum daily requirement of Vitamin C and 87 percent of the minimum daily requirement of Vitamin A. It is also rich in potassium and contains a natural sugar which aids digestion. All this and a low 78 calories per half, for dieters, puts papaya in a tie for first place with grapefruit.
They are wonderful for breakfast with just a squeeze of fresh lime juice, but also make luscious salads and desserts. Papaya fruit baskets are appropriate at any meal.

PECOS BEAN SALAD

SERVES 4–5

>2 cups cooked beans (pinto, kidney,
>   garbanzo, or mixed beans)
>1 onion, sliced thin
>2 cloves garlic, crushed
>½ green pepper, sliced
>⅓ cup unrefined oil
>¼ cup cider vinegar or lemon juice
>1 teaspoon sea salt

☞ Place the beans in a bowl. Add the onion, garlic, green pepper, oil, vinegar, and sea salt.
Toss the ingredients together and allow the beans to marinate in the other ingredients at room temperature for 1 hour.
Toss again and serve.

RAW BEET SALAD

SERVES 6

>3 medium-size beets, washed, peeled,
>   and coarsely grated
>2 stalks celery, chopped fine
>½ medium-size onion, chopped fine
>1 grated carrot

>sour cream or yogurt dressing

>Optional: Jerusalem artichokes

☞ Mix all ingredients together with sour cream or yogurt dressing.

Now don't say, "My children won't eat *that*." This salad is a great favorite at Girl Scout camp.

CAESAR SALAD

SERVES 6

2 tablespoons unrefined olive oil
2 cloves garlic, minced
1 cup whole wheat bread cubes

1 head romaine lettuce
½ teaspoon sea salt

2 tablespoons unrefined olive oil

1 egg
1 tablespoon cider vinegar
⅛ cup grated cheddar cheese
⅛ cup crumbled blue cheese

☞ Heat a skillet. Add the oil and garlic and sauté 1 minute. Add the bread cubes and sauté until browned. Cool.
Tear the lettuce leaves and place in a salad bowl. Season with the sea salt.
Pour the oil over the lettuce and toss.
Break a raw egg into the salad and toss again.
Add the vinegar and toss again.
Add the cheese and bread cubes. Toss lightly and serve.

This famous salad originated on the West Coast.

SUNSHINE CARROT SALAD

SERVES 6

2 cups grated carrots
1 cup pineapple chunks
1 cup mandarin orange sections or
   tangerine sections
½ cup raisins
½ cup grated coconut
½ cup raw or toasted sunflower seeds
4 tablespoons homemade yogurt, sour
   cream, or mayonnaise

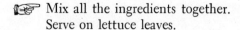 Mix all the ingredients together.
Serve on lettuce leaves.

This salad is best when it is refrigerated an hour or two before serving.

CAULIFLOWER PECAN SALAD

SERVES 4–6
> 1½ cups cauliflower flowerets
> 1 cup coarsely grated carrots
> ¾ cup green pepper
> 1 cup chopped celery
> 1 cup toasted whole pecan halves

Garnish: radish rose and carrot curls

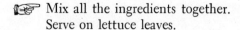 Blanch flowerets in hot, salted water for 2 minutes; drain, then chill.
Keep all ingredients separate until time to serve. Then toss together with the following dressing.

HORSERADISH MUSTARD DRESSING

> ¾ cup homemade mayonnaise
> freshly ground pepper
> 4 tablespoons drained horseradish
> ½ cup homemade sour cream or yogurt
> sea salt to taste
> ½ teaspoon prepared mustard

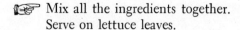 Mix well and correct seasoning according to taste. Serve on a lettuce leaf with the garnish.

CAULIFLOWER COLESLAW

SERVES 6

>2 cups shredded raw cauliflower
>¼ cup chopped fresh onion
>¼ cup chopped fresh green pepper
>2 tablespoons chopped fresh parsley
>1 cup sliced celery
>2 tablespoons homemade mayonnaise
>½ teaspoon sea salt
>
>Optional: ⅛ teaspoon black pepper

☞ Wash cauliflower and separate into flowerets. Shred and combine with remaining ingredients. Toss lightly.
Serve as any other coleslaw.

COMPLETE MADNESS COLESLAW

SERVES 6

>1 medium green cabbage (about 3 cups)
> sliced thin
>½ cup diced green pepper
>¾ cup soy nuts
>2 tablespoons caraway seeds
>1 teaspoon sesame seeds
>1 carrot, diced

☞ Combine all ingredients and toss together lightly. Make the following dressing:

HALF MAD DRESSING

>½ cup skim milk
>3 tablespoons unrefined sesame oil
>3 tablespoons cider vinegar
>sea salt and pepper to taste

Optional: Homemade cottage cheese

☞ Mix all the dressing ingredients together. Add dressing to salad and chill.

CUCUMBER SALAD OR ZUCCHINI SALAD

SERVES 4
> 1 *cup of a mixture of finely chopped*
> *parsley, dill weed, and green onions*
> 1 *cup homemade yogurt*
> 1 *tablespoon lemon or lime juice*
> 1 *tablespoon raw honey*
>
> 2 or 3 *fresh cucumbers or zucchini,*
> *sliced thin*

☞ Mix first 4 ingredients together. Fold in vegetables. Chill several hours.

> VARIATION:
> 2 *cucumbers sliced very thin*
> ½ *teaspoon sea salt*
>
> 1 *cup homemade yogurt*
> 2 *tablespoons lemon juice*
> 1 *tablespoon finely chopped onion*
> ⅛ *teaspoon pepper*
> *parsley, chopped*
> *chives, chopped*

Sprinkle the sliced cucumber with the sea salt. Chill and drain the cucumbers.
Mix all the other ingredients together and add them to the cucumbers.
Chill 1 hour or more to blend the flavors.

To add a fancy touch to your cucumbers, run a fork down the outside of the whole cucumber, all the way around, and then slice it.

JERUSALEM ARTICHOKE SALAD

SERVES 4

> *5 to 6 Jerusalem artichokes, grated*
> *2 carrots, grated*
> *3 stalks of celery, strung and chopped fine*
> *⅓ cup chopped parsley*
> *homemade mayonnaise or other dressing*
>
> *Garnish: carrot curls and black olives*

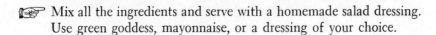 Wash and grate or chop the vegetables. Mix lightly with desired dressing. Serve on a lettuce leaf.
Garnish individual plates or the salad bowl before serving.
Other raw vegetables may be added. If desired, add a little spicy or hot sauce or seasoned sea salt to the mayonnaise.

MACARONI SALAD

SERVES 4–5

> *2 cups cooked macaroni*
> *1 head lettuce, torn in small pieces*
> *¼ cup sprouts*
> *1 stalk celery, sliced*
> *1 tablespoon finely chopped scallions*
> *1 tablespoon finely chopped parsley*

Mix all the ingredients and serve with a homemade salad dressing. Use green goddess, mayonnaise, or a dressing of your choice.

This makes a nice and easy salad for lunch and is quite filling. Noodles may be used in place of the macaroni.

ELLEN'S POTATO SALAD

SERVES 4

2 pounds white potatoes

1 onion, sliced paper thin

6 to 8 hard-boiled eggs, chopped coarse
1 green pepper, seeded and chopped fine
2 stalks celery, chopped medium fine
2 tablespoons pimento, chopped fine
½ cup parsley, chopped fine

homemade mayonnaise

☞ Boil potatoes in salted water with skins on for 25 to 30 minutes or until fork inserts easily. Peel while warm and slice into ¼ inch slices. Save water and skins for broth.
Add onion to warm potatoes.
Mix together eggs, pepper, celery, pimento, and parsley. Add to potatoes and onions.
Add enough mayonnaise to moisten. Season to taste.

GREEK HOT RICE SALAD

SERVES 4–6

2 cups hot, cooked brown rice

1 teaspoon sea salt
¼ teaspoon pepper
1 onion, chopped fine

¼ cup unrefined olive oil
1 tablespoon lemon juice

oregano

Garnish: parsley sprigs, ripe olives

While rice is still hot, add the salt, pepper, and chopped onion.
Blend the oil and lemon juice and pour over the rice.
Sprinkle with oregano and toss lightly.
Garnish and serve at once.

RICE AND ALMOND SALAD

SERVES 4–6

>2 cups cooked brown rice, chilled
>¼ teaspoon curry powder
>½ cup homemade mayonnaise
>½ cup celery, finely chopped
>½ cup toasted almonds, slivered

 Place the chilled rice in a chilled bowl and add the rest of the
ingredients.
Toss lightly and serve at once on lettuce.

SIM-SIM COS

SERVES 4

>3 unpeeled apples, diced
>3 stalks celery, diced
>2 to 3 tablespoons lightly toasted
> sesame seeds
>3 tablespoons homemade mayonnaise

 Combine all ingredients. Toss lightly.
Serve on lettuce leaves.

VAL VERDE SALAD

SERVES 4
> 1 pound fresh spinach leaves,
>   rinsed and thoroughly dried
> ½ pound fresh mushrooms, sliced
> 1 small red onion, sliced thin
> ¼ cup piñon nuts (pine nuts)

☞ Mix all the ingredients together. Toss lightly with French dressing.

TABOOLIE

SERVES 6
> 1 cup warm water
> 2 cups raw cracked wheat cereal or bulgur
>
> 1 cup chopped parsley
> ½ cup chopped onions
> 2 tomatoes, chopped
> 2 tablespoons fresh mint or 1 teaspoon
>   dried mint
> 1 cup lemon juice
>   (if you want less kick, use less juice)
> ½ to 1 cup unrefined oil
> sea salt and pepper to taste

☞ Soak the cracked wheat in the warm water for 1 hour.
Add the other ingredients and toss together lightly.
Refrigerate before serving to allow the wheat to absorb the moisture.

VARIATION:
Tomatoes may be omitted.
Use whole grain wheat that has been cooked and chilled instead of cracked wheat.

This delicious salad is unfamiliar to American tastes but is a staple in the Middle East. Serve on a bed of lettuce leaves and garnish with parsley.

WALDORF SALAD

SERVES 6

4 apples, diced, with a pinch of salt added
4 stalks celery, cut in small pieces
1 cup walnut meats, chopped
1 cup homemade mayonnaise

☞ Mix apples, celery, and nuts together with dressing. Serve in pretty salad bowl or on lettuce leaves.

Waldorf salad, made famous almost a century ago by a chef at the Waldorf Astoria Hotel in New York City, fits perfectly into our natural foods salads. Pineapple cubes, fresh grapes, and other fruits can be added, but this is the original recipe.

GELATIN SALADS

Gelatin salads are convenient and easy to prepare. Make them ahead of time and make them colorful. A bright, jellied salad adds beauty to a family meal or party buffet.

Agar-agar, a vegetable gelatin, or plain gelatin may be used to make these salads.

CITRUS ALMOND MOLD

SERVES 6

>2 tablespoons plain gelatin
>1½ cups boiling water
>
>⅛ teaspoon sea salt
>¼ cup raw honey
>
>½ cup fresh lemon juice
>¾ cup mixed orange and grapefruit juice
>grated rind of 1 lemon
>
>1 cup orange sections
>1 cup grapefruit sections, seeds and
>   membrane removed, cut in halves
>1 cup slivered, blanched almonds

☞ Dissolve gelatin in boiling water.
Add salt and honey and let cool.
Add fruit juices and grated lemon rind; let thicken slightly.
Add orange and grapefruit sections and almonds and pour into
individual molds. Chill.
Serve in a crisp lettuce cup with poppyseed dressing.

GAZPACHO ASPIC

SERVES 6

>2 tablespoons unflavored gelatin
>¼ cup water
>
>¾ cup water
>
>1 pound ripe tomatoes
>½ cup chopped bell pepper
>juice of 2 garlic cloves
>½ cup finely chopped onions
>2 tablespoons watercress leaves, no stems

2 tablespoons chopped parsley
2 tablespoons fresh lemon juice
2 tablespoons cider vinegar
sea salt, black pepper, and cayenne to taste

☞ Soak gelatin in ¼ cup water.
Bring other ¾ cup water to boil; add gelatin and stir well to dissolve. Let cool.
Add all the remaining ingredients. Pour into 6 individual molds. Refrigerate. Serve on lettuce leaf with orange whip dressing.

LIME-AVOCADO MOLD

SERVES 8 OR MORE
4 tablespoons gelatin
2 cups hot water
¾ cup raw honey

2 cups homemade cottage cheese
juice of 1 orange
1 cup lime juice, or the juice of 5 limes
½ teaspoon sea salt
½ cup homemade mayonnaise

2 cups unsweetened pineapple chunks,
   canned or fresh-cooked
1 large avocado, peeled and cubed
¼ cup pimento stuffed olives,
   thinly sliced

☞ Dissolve the gelatin in the hot water. Add honey and stir. Put homemade cottage cheese, orange juice, lime juice, sea salt, and mayonnaise into blender and blend until creamy.
Blend the cheese and the gelatin mixture and chill until partially set.
Add remaining ingredients. Turn into an 8-cup mold. Chill until firm. Unmold on greens. Garnish with ripe olives.

An excellent salad to serve with tamale soy pie.

SPROUTS

Sprouting is a simple process and greatly increases the nutritional value of grains, beans, and seeds. Not only do the seeds increase in food value, but they also develop nutrients that were not present before in measurable quantities, such as vitamin C. In addition, the starch in these foods changes to simple sugar, which makes sprouts easier to digest and a delight to eat raw. Wheat sprouts are particularly sweet when they first start to sprout and can be made into a grain honey. Some of the larger sprouts, such as soybeans, require some cooking. Steam or sauté them a few minutes.

Add sprouts to salads, soups, casseroles, and sandwiches. Cook them with vegetables or eggs or grind them and use them in breads. Sprouts will quicken the leavening action in yeast breads and will help unleavened breads rise. When fresh sprouts are included, unleavened bread dough will rise in half the time it normally takes.

Almost all whole seeds, grains, and dried beans will sprout. Alfalfa seeds and mung beans are favorites, but try some of the following: sunflower, radish, lettuce, carrot, fenugreek, rye, wheat, oats, lentil, soybean. Buy only untreated seed for sprouting to avoid the poisons often used in seed treatment. Untreated seeds often have a better germination rate, too. Do not eat potato sprouts; they are toxic.

Grow your sprouts in any container suitable for keeping food or in a commercial sprouter, but sprouting is simplest in a wide-mouth glass jar. Sprouting is easy and fun when you can watch the sprouts grow. Put one tablespoon of seed in a pint jar. Cover the seed with water—spring water if available. Place a piece of cheesecloth or nylon netting over the top and secure it with a rubber band. After soaking overnight, drain off the water. (This is excellent for watering your plants). Leaving the cheesecloth intact, run warm water in the jar. Rinse off the seeds, invert the jar at an angle, and let the seeds drain until evening when you should rinse them once again. Continue rinsing the seeds—morning and night—more often in a dry climate, until the sprouts have reached the desired length.* At this point, put the sprouts in cold water briefly and separate them so they will be easier to use later. Use the sprouts immediately or store them in a tightly covered jar in the refrigerator. Eat them as soon as possible, for they start losing nutritional value a few days after they are stored.

* Consult the Sprouting Chart (below) for the optimum length for each variety of sprout.

Sprouts will grow in the dark or in the light, but keep them out of direct sunlight. They will be greener and prettier if allowed to grow in the light. In either case, when they are almost ready, place them in direct sunlight for a few hours to develop the chlorophyll and a nice green color.

Sprouting is a great activity for children. One 10-year-old won first place in her school's science contest with her "Sprouting for Food" project.

SPROUTING CHART

Seeds	Sprouting Time in Days	Optimum Length of Sprout in Inches
Alfalfa	3 to 4	¾ to 1
Buckwheat	3 to 5	1 to 1½
Clover	3 to 4	¾ to 1
Garbanzo beans	3	½ to ¾
Lentils	2 to 3	length of the seed
Mung beans	2 to 3	¼ to ½
Oats	2	length of the seed
Peas	2 to 3	¼ to ½
Radish	3 to 4	½ to 1
Rye	2	length of the seed
Sesame	2	1/16 to ⅛
Sunflower	2	1/16 to ⅛
*Soybeans	3	¼ to ½
Turnip	3 to 4	½ to 1
Wheat	2	length of the seed

Other seeds to sprout: barley, beet, caraway, celery, cress, dill, fenugreek, flax, kale, lettuce, lima, millet, mustard, onion, parsley, peanut, pinto, pumpkin.

* Rinse soybean sprouts very, very thoroughly each time, for they mold quickly. Do not crowd them in the jar.

BEAN SPROUT SALAD

SERVES 4

¼ cup unrefined oil
2 tablespoons lemon juice or
  cider vinegar
2 tablespoons tamari soy sauce
¼ teaspoon sea salt
¼ cup scallions, finely chopped
2 tablespoons sesame seeds
1 clove garlic, minced
1 tablespoon chopped chives
2 tablespoons chopped parsley

Optional: ⅛ teaspoon grated ginger

2 cups fresh bean sprouts

☞ Mix together the oil, lemon juice, tamari, salt, scallions, sesame
seeds, garlic, chives, parsley, and ginger (if desired).
Pour over the sprouts and toss lightly.
Chill before serving.

SPROUTS AND COTTAGE CHEESE

SERVES 4

¼ cup lentil sprouts
¼ cup mung bean sprouts
4 green onions, chopped
2 cups cottage cheese

☞ Mix all ingredients.
Serve on lettuce leaf or use to stuff tomatoes.

ORIENTAL SPROUTS

SERVES 4
> 2 *cups mung bean sprouts*
> 1 *cup sliced fresh mushrooms*

 Toss sprouts and mushrooms together.
Serve on romaine lettuce leaves.
Sprinkle with Sendai Salad Dressing or another soy sauce dressing.

Sweet 'n' Sour Dressings and Sauces

SALAD DRESSINGS

Keep a variety of homemade salad dressings in the refrigerator. Serve your green salads lightly oiled so that each person may add his favorite dressing at the table. Salad dressings also complement grain dishes. One cup of dressing is usually ample for 4 people.

Use unrefined oils in salad dressings. They add flavor as well as valuable nutrients. Refer to pp. 332–333 for a discussion of these oils.

FERNANDO DRESSING

YIELD: 1½ CUPS

    1 cup homemade yogurt or
      sour cream
    ½ cup homemade mayonnaise
    ½ teaspoon sea salt
    1 teaspoon paprika
    1 clove garlic, minced
    1 tablespoon lemon juice or cider vinegar
    1 teaspoon whole dill seed, crushed
    1 tablespoon each chopped parsley,
      chives, and olives

☞ Mix all the ingredients well.
Chill.

FRENCH DRESSING

YIELD: 1½ CUPS

    1 cup cider vinegar
    1 tablespoon unrefined peanut oil
    ½ teaspoon basil
    ½ teaspoon oregano
    1 tablespoon raw honey
    1 tomato, chopped fine
    1 teaspoon chopped chives
    sea salt to taste

☞ Combine all ingredients in a jar, cover, and shake well.

GREEN GODDESS SALAD DRESSING

YIELD: 1 CUP

    3 scallions, chopped
    ½ cup unrefined corn germ oil
    2½ tablespoons lemon juice or 2 table-

spoons cider vinegar or 7 umeboshi
plums
⅓ *cup tamari soy sauce*

☞ Blend all the ingredients together in a blender.
This dressing is best with umeboshi plums, but it is good with lemon juice or vinegar too.

MAYONNAISE AND VARIATIONS

YIELD: 1 CUP
1 *egg*
2 *tablespoons fresh squeezed lemon juice*
¼ *cup unrefined oil*
½ *to 1 teaspoon dry mustard*
¾ *teaspoon sea salt*

Optional: ¼ *teaspoon white pepper*

¾ *cup unrefined oil*

☞ Combine egg, lemon juice, ¼ cup oil, dry mustard, sea salt, and pepper in electric blender jar. Cover and blend at low speed until mixed.
Increase speed to high, uncover or remove center cap, and add remaining oil in a thin, slow, steady stream. Blend until all the oil is added and mayonnaise is smooth and creamy. If necessary, turn motor off and stir occasionally. Always replace cover before turning motor back on.
Keep mayonnaise refrigerated, and use within 7 to 10 days.
Delicious plain or in one of the following dressing variations:

Thousand Island: Combine ½ cup mayonnaise with 1 tablespoon chili sauce, ½ tablespoon sweet pickle relish, ½ teaspoon fresh grated lemon peel, and enough lemon juice to thin to desired consistency.

Louis Dressing: Combine 1 cup mayonnaise with ¼ cup chili sauce, 2 tablespoons snipped fresh parsley, and 1 tablespoon minced green onion. Fold in ¼ cup heavy cream, whipped. Yield: about 1⅔ cups.

Horseradish Mayonnaise: Combine ½ cup mayonnaise with 1 tablespoon prepared horseradish, ½ teaspoon fresh grated lemon peel, and a dash of sea salt.

Tarragon Mayonnaise: Combine ½ cup mayonnaise with ¼ teaspoon dried tarragon leaves and ¼ teaspoon celery seed until thoroughly blended. Serve with vegetables, especially tomatoes.

Nut-naise: Add ¼ cup old-fashioned peanut butter to 1 cup mayonnaise. Add ½ clove minced garlic, ½ teaspoon chili powder, and a pinch of cayenne if desired.

Roquefort Mayonnaise: Add ¼ cup crumbled roquefort cheese to 1 cup mayonnaise.

MINT DRESSING

YIELD: 1½ CUPS
> 1 *cup unrefined oil*
> ½ *cup cider vinegar*
> 1 *cup fresh mint leaves, finely chopped*
> 1 *garlic clove, crushed*
> ½ *to 1 teaspoon cracked black pepper*
> 1 *teaspoon sea salt*
> 1 *teaspoon raw honey*

☞ Place all ingredients in a jar. Cover with a lid and shake vigorously.

This dressing is especially good on vegetable salads—or on cold asparagus or artichoke hearts.

ORANGE WHIP
(Fruit Salad Dressing)

YIELD: 1½ CUPS
> 1 *cup thick, homemade yogurt*
> ⅓ *cup non-instant milk powder*

⅓ *cup fresh orange juice*
1 *tablespoon raw honey*
1 *teaspoon vanilla*

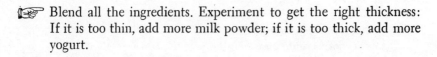 Blend all the ingredients. Experiment to get the right thickness: If it is too thin, add more milk powder; if it is too thick, add more yogurt.

PAUL'S SALAD DRESSING

YIELD: 1½ CUPS
¾ *cup unrefined sesame oil*
juice of 1 orange, about ⅓ *cup*
1 *tablespoon tamari soy sauce*
1 *heaping tablespoon tahini*

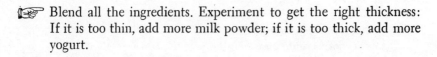 Blend all the ingredients together in a blender.
If the oil separates blend in one tablespoon of cold water.

Children will surprise you with the amount of salad they can eat with this dressing.

POPPY-SEED DRESSING

YIELD: 4 CUPS
1 *cup raw honey*
2 *teaspoons dry mustard*
2 *cups unrefined oil*
3 *tablespoons poppy seed*
2 *teaspoons sea salt*
¾ *cup cider vinegar*
3 *tablespoons onion juice*
1 *tablespoon lemon juice*
1 *teaspoon grated lemon peel*

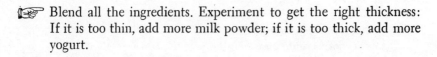 Combine all ingredients in blender and spin for one minute.

SENDAI SALAD DRESSING

YIELD: 1¼ CUPS
> ½ cup cider vinegar
> ⅓ cup raw honey
> ⅓ cup unrefined sesame oil
> 2 tablespoons tamari soy sauce
> ½ teaspoon sea salt
> dash of cayenne pepper

☞ Mix ingredients well. Chill. Stir before serving.

Use on tossed salad or spoon on individual servings of cooked or raw sliced zucchini, cauliflower, cucumbers, turnips, etc.

SAUCES

Sauces are especially flavorful when made with natural ingredients. Make vegetables and casseroles more attractive with the addition of interesting sauces.

BECHAMEL SAUCE

YIELD: 4 CUPS
> ¼ cup unrefined sesame oil
> 1 cup whole wheat flour
>   (use pastry flour for a lighter sauce)
>
> 4 cups water
> ¼ teaspoon sea salt
>
> ¼ cup tamari soy sauce

☞ Heat a skillet. Add the oil and the flour. Roast the flour until it gives off a nutty odor. Cool. If not cool, it will lump when the water is added.
Add the water and mix well with a whisk. Add the salt. Bring to

a boil. Cover and simmer on low heat for 30 minutes, stirring occasionally.

Add the tamari, mix, and simmer 5 more minutes.

This sauce is delicious on grains or in casseroles.

CHEESE SAUCE

YIELD: 1½ CUPS

1 cup fresh milk

1 or 2 cups diced cheese
(any natural hard cheese)
2 tablespoons stone-ground
whole wheat flour

½ teaspoon sea salt or 1 tablespoon
tamari soy sauce

☞ Heat the milk on low heat until very warm.
Add the cheese dusted with the flour.
Add salt or tamari. Cook on low heat, stirring occasionally until thick.

VARIATION:
Mornay Sauce: Add 2 beaten eggs and ¼ cup Parmesan cheese to the cheese sauce.

There is no easier sauce than this. Vary the seasoning any way you like. Incorporate the sauce in casseroles or serve over steamed broccoli or asparagus.

MOCK HOLLANDAISE SAUCE

YIELD: 1½ CUPS

> ¾ cup homemade mayonnaise
> ½ cup milk
> 1 tablespoon lemon juice
> ½ teaspoon sea salt or 2 teaspoons
>   tamari soy sauce
> 2 tablespoons chopped parsley

☞ Mix all ingredients in a sauce pan. Cook over very low heat until just heated through.

LEMON SAUCE

YIELD: 1½ CUPS

> 2 tablespoons arrowroot powder
> ½ teaspoon sea salt
> 1 cup water
>
> 2 tablespoons unrefined corn germ oil
> 2 tablespoons lemon juice
> 1 teaspoon grated lemon rind

☞ In a 1 quart saucepan, stir the arrowroot, salt, and water together over a medium flame. Stir the mixture constantly until it thickens. Lower the heat. Cover and simmer for 10 minutes. Remove from heat.
Add the oil, lemon juice, and lemon rind. Beat well.
Serve hot on vegetables.

MISO SAUCE

YIELD: 1 CUP

> 1 heaping tablespoon miso soybean paste
> 5 tablespoons tahini
> 1 cup water
>
> 1 teaspoon grated orange peel

Mix all the ingredients except the orange peel together and cook over low heat for 15 minutes.
Add the orange peel and mix.
Serve over vegetables or grains.

THICK TAMARI SAUCE

YIELD: 1 CUP
> 2 tablespoons unrefined corn germ oil
> 4 tablespoons tamari soy sauce
>
> ¾ cup water
>
> 1 tablespoon arrowroot powder dissolved
>   in 2 tablespoons water

 Pour oil into a small saucepan. Add the tamari and bring to a boil.
Add the water and boil 3 to 4 minutes.
Add the dissolved arrowroot and stir constantly until the sauce thickens.
Serve on artichokes, millet purée, grains, and casseroles.

SIMPLE TOMATO SAUCE
(Pizza and Chili Variations)

YIELD: 3 CUPS
> 2 tablespoons unrefined oil
> 1 large onion, chopped
> 2 or 3 cloves garlic, finely chopped
>
> 8 large tomatoes, cut in large chunks and
>   blended until smooth
>
> 1 teaspoon sea salt
> ¼ teaspoon pepper
> 1 tablespoon tamari soy sauce or
>   1 more teaspoon sea salt
> 1 tablespoon raw honey
>
> Optional: 1 tablespoon each chopped
>   chives and parsley

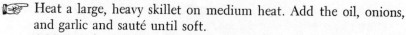 Heat a large, heavy skillet on medium heat. Add the oil, onions, and garlic and sauté until soft.

Add the blended tomatoes and then all the other ingredients.

Simmer, uncovered, over a low heat until bright red and thick. If too thin, cook a little longer or sprinkle 1 tablespoon arrowroot powder over the sauce. Let soften, stir, and simmer 5 minutes more.

VARIATIONS:

1. *Pizza Sauce:* While sautéeing, add ½ cup chopped mushrooms. Add 2 tablespoons oregano to other ingredients.
2. *Chili Sauce:* While sautéeing basic recipe, add 1 chopped green pepper and 2 or 3 chopped chili peppers or jalapenos. Add to the other ingredients:
     1 teaspoon dry mustard
     juice of 1 lemon
     Optional: 1 teaspoon cinnamon

BASIC WHITE SAUCE AND VARIATIONS

YIELD: 1 CUP

3 tablespoons unrefined oil
3 tablespoons whole wheat pastry flour

1 cup milk

½ teaspoon sea salt or 2 teaspoons
     tamari soy sauce or to taste
pepper

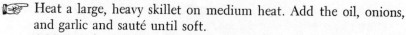 Heat the oil over low heat in a small saucepan.

Stir in the flour. Cook 1 minute, stirring constantly.

Slowly add the milk, stirring constantly. Continue to cook and stir until the sauce thickens.

Add salt or tamari and pepper to taste.

For a really thick sauce, use 4 tablespoons oil and 4 tablespoons flour.

This sauce is called "off-white sauce" by a friend because it is made with whole wheat flour.
Try the following variations:

Brown Sauce: Brown the flour lightly in a dry saucepan before adding the oil.

Mushroom Sauce: Sauté ¼ cup chopped mushrooms in the oil before adding the flour.

Onion Sauce: Sauté 2 tablespoons chopped onion and/or 1 clove minced garlic in the oil before adding the flour.
Use vegetable cooking water, or apple juice or cider, for all or part of the liquid.

OTHER VARIATIONS:
Additions to the sauce after cooking:
1. 1 or 2 sliced or chopped hard-boiled eggs.
2. 2 teaspoons dried dill and 4 tablespoons yogurt.
3. 1 tablespoon minced parsley, 1 teaspoon dry mustard, 1 tablespoon minced chives.
4. 1 tablespoon lemon juice, ½ teaspoon dry mustard.
5. to sauce made with apple juice or cider, add 1 cup chopped raisins. Simmer.

SIDE DISHES AND CONDIMENTS

YOGURT FOR BAKED POTATOES

YIELD: 1½ CUPS
    1 cup homemade yogurt
    ¼ to ½ cup chopped chives
      and/or parsley

Optional: 1 small clove garlic, minced

herbs to taste

☞ Mix all ingredients together. Chill and serve with baked potatoes.

CATSUP

YIELD: 1 QUART
　　2 quarts tomatoes, quartered
　　1½ teaspoons sea salt

　　½ cup cider vinegar
　　¼ cup raw honey
　　1 to 2 cloves garlic, minced
　　½ teaspoon basil
　　1 teaspoon nutmeg
　　½ teaspoon dry mustard
　　1 teaspoon ground celery seeds
　　pinch cayenne

　　Optional: arrowroot powder

☞ Set tomatoes in large saucepan and mash them in the pot to squeeze out the juice. Add salt, and mix. Cover and cook until the tomatoes are soft, stirring occasionally.

Put tomatoes through a Foley food mill. The juice will drain through first. Set it aside to use as a drink, for soup, etc. Continue to purée the tomatoes and return the purée to the stove. Add the remaining ingredients and simmer 30 minutes. If catsup is too thin add a small amount of arrowroot powder dissolved in cold water and continue simmering until the catsup thickens, about 5 minutes.

SWEET PEPPER RELISH

YIELD: 6 PINTS
　　12 sweet green peppers
　　12 sweet red peppers
　　8 green or red hot peppers,
　　　the small variety

　　10 medium onions

> 4 *cups vinegar*
> 3 *cups raw honey*
> 2 *tablespoons sea salt*

☞ Grind all the peppers in a food grinder. Place them in a saucepan and bring to a boil in their own juice. Let stand 10 minutes, then drain.
Grind the onions.
Add the onions, vinegar, honey, and sea salt to the peppers. Boil for 20 minutes or a bit longer.
Place the relish, while boiling, into clean, scalded pint jars and seal while hot.

Note: If you are short on green peppers, you may substitute, or even add, ground green tomatoes or apples. The red peppers, in the right proportions, make the relish much more attractive, although green peppers alone may be used if desired.

This relish is particularly delicious with dried bean dishes.

SESAME SALT

YIELD: 1½ CUPS
> 1 *tablespoon sea salt*
> 8 *to* 10 *tablespoons sesame seeds*

☞ Heat the salt in a heavy cast-iron skillet until it sparkles. Set it aside.
Wash the sesame seeds in a fine mesh strainer. Roast them in a skillet until they start popping and can be crushed easily between the thumb and first finger when rubbed together.
Grind the roasted seeds and the salt with a mortar and pestle or in a suribachi until most of the seeds are crushed. A blender can be used if you have no other equipment, but this is the least desirable method.
Store in an air-tight container to retain freshness.

Sesame salt is excellent on all grain dishes and vegetables.

YOGURT AND BEAN CURD

YOGURT

Yogurt is the most digestible form of milk. Many people who are allergic to milk can easily digest and tolerate yogurt. The beneficial bacteria in yogurt multiply at body temperature and help produce B vitamins. Yogurt helps to soothe the digestive tract and to counteract many mild upsets. Without these friendly bugs we couldn't survive. Since antibiotics often destroy the good guys as well as the bad, yogurt is especially important during illness.

Make your own yogurt. Yogurt is simple to make and is usually much better-tasting than the commercial product. Make it plain and add fruits and a little honey as desired. Use it in sauces, dressings, and even desserts.

YOGURT

YIELD: 1 QUART
1 quart fresh milk
3 tablespoons or more of yogurt, or
1 package of dried yogurt culture

Optional: ½ cup non-instant milk powder

☞ Be sure all the utensils you use are clean.
Heat the milk to scalding. Cool to lukewarm.
Blend some of the milk with the milk powder if thicker yogurt is desired. Then add this back to the rest of the milk.
Stir in the yogurt or the culture.
Pour the mixture into clean glasses. or jars. Set the jars in a large pan of warm water. Cover jars with clear plastic wrap. Place in warm oven. Maintain the temperature of water between 100° and 120° F. Or, set the pan over a pilot light on the stove. Cover with a towel or blanket. The yogurt will take 3 to 5 hours to thicken; dried yogurt culture takes longer. Refrigerate when thickened. However, the yogurt can be left to sit overnight and refrigerated in the morning.

Beneficial bacteria in yogurt multiply between 90° and 120° F. Therefore, they multiply at body temperature. Cooking destroys the beneficial bacteria in yogurt, but cooked yogurt still provides excellent, easily digestible protein.

Yogurt bacteria change milk sugars into lactic acid.

HOMEMADE SOUR CREAM

YIELD: 1 PINT
> 1 scant pint sweet cream
> 2 tablespoons yogurt

☞ Place sweet cream in a clean jar.
Add yogurt.
Mix and set in a warm place overnight or until thickened.
Refrigerate.

QUICK SOUR CREAM

YIELD: 1 CUP
> ½ cup creamed cottage cheese
> ½ cup plain yogurt
> 1 tablespoon lemon juice

☞ Blend all the ingredients in a blender until smooth.
Add about 1 tablespoon chopped chives or 1 teaspoon chopped green onions if desired.

HOMEMADE YOGURT CREAM CHEESE OR COTTAGE CHEESE

YIELD: 1 PINT
☞ Hang yogurt in a double cheesecloth overnight.
Save the whey for use in bread, pancakes, etc.

Use like cottage cheese or cream cheese. (This cheese will not have large curds like commercial cottage cheese.)

COTTAGE CHEESE SPREAD

YIELD: 1 PINT

☞ Mix pot cottage cheese from the recipe above with chopped pecans and/or chopped green pepper.

TOFU
(Soybean Cheese or Bean Curd)

YIELD: 1 PINT FOR EACH CUP OF SOYBEANS

  1 cup dry soybeans
  3 cups water

  1½ tablespoons cider vinegar or
    lemon juice

☞ Soak the soybeans in the water overnight. Drain off the water and rinse the beans well. Take 1 cup of the soaked beans at a time. Put them in a blender with 2 cups of water and blend for 20 seconds. Repeat until all the beans are blended.

Line a strainer or colander with a dish towel or muslin. Pour in the blended beans. Strain through the cloth into a 4 quart pot. Squeeze the mash left in the cloth to get all the liquid out and set the mash aside.

Measure the liquid and add enough water to make 10 cups. Place over medium-low heat and bring to a boil. Watch closely so that the mixture doesn't boil over. (It probably will the first time!)

Turn off the heat. Add the vinegar or lemon juice. Stir and let sit 5 minutes until the milk curdles. Pour the curds into cheesecloth. Tie a string around the top and rinse in cold water to wash off the excess acid.

Hang up for 3 or 4 hours or overnight. Take the tofu out of the cloth and put it in a container with water. Refrigerate. It will keep several days.

  Uses of tofu: Sauté in oil. Serve with tamari.
    Dip in whole wheat flour or cornmeal, mixed with a pinch of salt, and deep fry.
    Cook with eggs.

Serve cold with a little tamari.
Cook with vegetables.
Use in almond chop suey.

Uses of soy mash: Place mash in the top of a double boiler and cook over boiling water for 1 hour. Then use it in breads, casseroles, or soup.

The Garden Basket

VEGETABLES

Vegetables are extremely important in every diet. Unfortunately, government and university surveys tell us that Americans are consuming fewer vegetables and whole fruits and more refined carbohydrates. Perhaps these recipes will help reverse that trend.

Correct storage and cooking is necessary if vegetables are to provide maximum nutrition. Wash vegetables quickly in cold water. Rinse and dry them immediately. Chill them quickly unless they are to be used immediately. Once vegetables and fruits are mature, enzymes begin to break down the nutrients. Chilling stops or slows this process. Never soak vegetables to crisp them; many vitamins and minerals are water soluble. Chop vegetables (preferably chilled) as quickly as possible to prevent oxidation of vitamins through the cut surfaces. If the vegetables are to be eaten raw, quickly coat the surfaces with a little oil to block out oxygen.

While raw vegetables are the most valuable in vitamins and minerals, we can learn most about cooking vegetables from the Chinese. The golden rule of vegetable cookery is *do not overcook*. Vegetables should be cooked only until tender. Almost every vegetable is delicious

101

either when stir-fried lightly or steamed in a vegetable steamer. Brief cooking is the only way to retain the full natural flavor and vitamins. Fresh vegetables can be very popular additions to the family diet—if they are properly cooked.

SAUTÉING VEGETABLES

Heat a heavy pan on moderate heat. Add the unrefined oil to thinly coat the bottom, which heats immediately if the skillet is hot. Do not allow the oil to smoke. Quickly add the chopped, chilled vegetables, stir lightly to coat with the oil, and heat through. Reduce the heat. Cover and cook in the oil and the vegetables' own juices until barely tender. Vegetables that cook quickly need not be covered. If tougher vegetables are used, such as green beans, add a few tablespoons of water, cover, and steam until tender. When sautéing several vegetables, add the onions first, then the tougher vegetables, and finally the more tender ones.

Use wooden spoons because they do not bruise and tear the vegetables so easily.

BOILING

Drop chilled, chopped vegetables into a small amount of boiling water. (Most greens need no water because the leaves contain so much liquid.) Heat the vegetables quickly. Then reduce the heat. Cover and cook until barely tender. There should be little or no liquid left in the pan. Save every drop for sauces or soup stock.

STEAMING

Steam vegetables quickly until just tender in a foldable steam basket or metal colander above boiling water.

If using a pressure cooker, cook the vegetables the *minimum* amount of time.

OLD-FASHIONED BAKED BEANS

SERVES 6–8

> *2 cups dry pinto beans, kidney beans, or*
>   *navy beans*
> *5 cups boiling water*
>
> *2 tablespoons unrefined oil*
> *1 onion, thinly sliced*
>
> *¼ cup unsulphured molasses*
> *1½ teaspoons sea salt*
> *1 teaspoon dry mustard*
> *1 teaspoon chili powder*
>
> *Optional: ¼ cup homemade*
>   *tomato sauce*

☞ Pick through and rinse the beans. Add the beans slowly to the boiling water. Reduce the heat.

Cover and simmer the beans 2 to 3 hours until tender.

Heat a small skillet. Add the oil and onion and sauté. Add to the beans after the beans are cooked.

Add all other ingredients after the beans are tender. Simmer the beans 5 to 10 minutes, until desired thickness is reached. This is much faster than baking in the oven.

The beans may be pressure cooked. Then add other ingredients and simmer a few minutes.

Serve with a cauliflower salad and Boston brown bread.

A favorite Southwestern lunch consists of a green salad, baked beans, and hot cornbread.

BLACK BEANS

SERVES 4

  2 *cups cooked black beans with liquid*

  1 *tablespoon unrefined oil*
  1 *green pepper, chopped*
  2 *onions, chopped*
  1 *clove garlic, minced*

  2 *bay leaves*
  1 *teaspoon sea salt*
  ¼ *teaspoon marjoram*

  1 *clove garlic, minced*

 Heat a saucepan. Add the oil, pepper, onions, and garlic and sauté. Add the beans and mash them partially.
Add the bay leaves, salt, and marjoram. Cover and simmer 15 minutes.
Add the second garlic clove and simmer 5 more minutes.
Remove the bay leaves and serve the beans over hot cooked rice.

BEETS AGLOW

SERVES 6

  4 *cups of cooked beets, sliced or*
    tiny whole ones

  1 *teaspoon arrowroot powder*
  ¼ *cup beet juice*

  ¾ *cup orange juice*
  ¼ *cup lemon juice*
  2 *tablespoons cider vinegar*
  1½ *tablespoons raw honey*
  ½ *teaspoon sea salt*

2 tablespoons butter
1 tablespoon grated orange peel
  (orange part only)

☞ Mix arrowroot with beet juice and stir until smooth.
Add orange juice, lemon juice, vinegar, honey, and sea salt. Cook until clear and thickened.
Add butter, orange peel, and beets. Serve hot.

CARROTS IN CIDER

SERVES 4–6
3 cups sliced carrots
1 cup apple juice

½ teaspoon sea salt

Optional: 1 tablespoon butter
    1½ teaspoons grated orange
      peel
    1½ teaspoons grated lemon
      peel

☞ Cover the carrots with the apple juice in a saucepan. Cover saucepan and simmer until tender. Add a little water if necessary.
Uncover. Simmer until any extra moisture is absorbed and liquid is syrupy.
Add sea salt to taste. Melt butter. Add lemon and orange peel. Pour over carrots and heat through.
For glazed carrots, add 2 tablespoons raw honey.

CAULIFLOWER BOUQUET

1 head cauliflower
sea salt
½ cup milk

broccoli spears
glazed carrots
pimento, chopped
parsley, chopped
cheese sauce

☞ Trim leaves and wash head of firm white cauliflower under running cold water. Place in kettle of boiling water, enough to cover. Add sea salt to taste and ½ cup milk. Cook uncovered until tender (approximately 20 minutes). Drain and place in center of vegetable platter.
Place broccoli spears and glazed carrots around the cauliflower. Add chopped pimento and chopped parsley to a cheese sauce and pass to put on top.

INDIAN VEGETABLES

SERVES 4

2 tablespoons unrefined oil
2 onions, chopped
½ pound cauliflower, broken into
   flowerets
½ pound broccoli, chopped
curry powder to taste

¼ cup roasted peanuts
¼ cup raisins

☞ Heat a skillet. Add the oil, onions, cauliflower, broccoli, and curry powder. Sauté until the vegetables are tender.
Add the roasted peanuts and raisins.
Serve over steamed millet or steamed rice flakes. Top with sour cream or yogurt.

Other vegetables may be added to or substituted for the onions, cauliflower, and broccoli.

WONSAN CELERY

SERVES 6

>2 tablespoons unrefined oil
>4 cups diagonally sliced 1-inch-wide
>   celery pieces

>½ cup chopped water chestnuts or
>   Jerusalem artichokes

>1 cup white sauce
>1 tablespoon tamari soy sauce
>¼ cup diced pimiento

>½ cup whole wheat bread crumbs
>¼ cup toasted slivered almonds or
>   2 tablespoons toasted sesame seeds
>1 tablespoon melted homemade
>   safflower butter

Heat a large, heavy skillet on medium heat. Add the oil and celery. Cover and sauté about 10 minutes, stirring occasionally.
Add the water chestnuts.
Make 1 cup of plain white sauce and season it with the tamari. Add the sauce and pimiento to the vegetable mixture in a 1½ quart casserole.
Toss the bread crumbs, almonds, and safflower butter together. Sprinkle the crumb mixture over the celery mixture.
Bake 30 minutes at 350°.

CORN PUDDING

SERVES 4

>   2 cups milk or soy milk
>   2 cups fresh, uncooked corn,
>   cut from the cob
>   2 tablespoons unrefined corn germ oil
>   1 teaspoon sea salt
>   3 beaten eggs
>
>   Optional: 1 cup grated cheese

☞ Mix all the ingredients together, except the cheese. Bake in an oiled 8 inch round casserole dish for 45 minutes at 350°. Sprinkle grated cheese on top if desired.

VARIATION:
Add ½ cup green pepper or one onion, chopped, or about ¼ cup of both, sautéed lightly.

EGGPLANT ORLÉANS

SERVES 6–8

>   3 medium eggplants
>
>   ½ cup onions, minced
>   2 teaspoons sea salt
>   2½ cups boiling water
>
>   4 eggs, slightly beaten
>   1 teaspoon sea salt
>   dash of pepper
>   4 tablespoons butter
>   4 tablespoons heavy cream
>
>   1 cup buttered bread crumbs
>   1 cup sharp cheese, grated

☞ Peel eggplants, cut in cubes.

Mix together eggplant, onion, and 2 teaspoons sea salt. Cover and simmer in 2½ cups boiling water until tender but not soft, about 10 minutes. Drain. Save liquid for soups.

Add eggs, 1 teaspoon salt, pepper, butter, and cream. Pour into buttered 10 x 6 x 2 inch Pyrex baking dish.

Cover with bread crumbs and cheese.

Bake, uncovered, 45 minutes at 350°.

For a party dish, do not peel eggplants. Split them in half, retain shell, and fill with the cooked mixture.

ENDIVES
(Belgian)

SERVES 4–6

1 tablespoon unrefined oil

8 endives, split in half lengthwise

¼ cup water

2 tablespoons tamari soy sauce

☞ Heat a skillet. Add the oil and endive. Sauté until transparent. Add the water. Cover and simmer 5 minutes.

Add the tamari and simmer uncovered until all the liquid is absorbed.

Endives are a special treat. Don't miss them.

FRESH GREEN BEANS ITALIENNE

SERVES 4

>1 pound green beans
>
>4 tablespoons butter
>1 small onion, sliced thin
>1 clove garlic
>
>½ cup parsley, chopped fine
>
>Optional: 1 tablespoon toasted
>   sesame seeds

☞ Cut beans on slant in approximately 1 inch pieces. Place in vegetable steamer with 1 cup water. Cook 10 to 15 minutes or until tender.
Melt butter in skillet, add onions and stir constantly for 1 minute. Crush garlic and add to onion. Add beans and stir lightly until coated with the butter. Remove garlic.
Add parsley and sesame seeds and toss lightly. Serve at once.

SOUTHERN SAUTÉED OR STEAMED GREENS

>Any kind of greens—cabbage, kale,
>   endive, spinach, mustard greens, chard,
>   collard greens, tops of radishes or
>   turnips or beets, or wild greens.

☞ Heat a large, heavy skillet. Add 1 or 2 tablespoons water or unrefined oil. Peanut or corn oil are best, the South being the homeland of peanuts and rich corn.
Drop in chilled, chopped greens. Stir quickly.
Cover with a tight-fitting lid. Reduce the heat as low as possible. Cook 2 to 10 minutes, depending on the toughness of the greens, until barely tender.
Strong-tasting greens lose their strong taste when cooked in a little milk.
When cooking bitter vegetables such as mustard or dandelion

greens, salt should be added at the end of cooking; otherwise, the greens retain their bitterness.

Top with lemon or lime juice, cider vinegar, yogurt or sour cream, salad dressings, nuts or seeds, or grated cheese.

GREEK SPINACH

SERVES 4

2 pounds fresh spinach

1 tablespoon unrefined olive oil
½ cup pine nuts

1 clove garlic, minced
1 small onion, finely chopped
2 tablespoons cider vinegar
sea salt or tamari to taste

☞ Wash and tear the spinach, removing heavy stems.

Heat a large skillet. Add the oil and nuts and sauté until golden. Add all the other ingredients. Stir, cover, and cook 2 minutes, until the spinach is barely tender.

VARIATION:
Use ¼ cup sesame seeds instead of pine nuts.

CREAMED MUSHROOMS

SERVES 4–6

1 pound mushrooms, sliced fairly thin .
2 tablespoons butter

¼ teaspoon sea salt
2 tablespoons whole wheat pastry flour

1 cup cream

pinch of marjoram
paprika

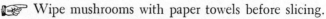 Wipe mushrooms with paper towels before slicing.
Heat a skillet and quickly sauté mushrooms in butter until done.
Add salt and sprinkle with flour.
Gradually stir in cream and bring to boil.
Add seasonings.

The mushrooms go naturally with the rice ring. Creamed mushrooms might also be used with other grains or on toasted wheat bread for a light supper.

FRIED OKRA

SERVES 4

　　1 pound okra
　　stone-ground yellow corn meal
　　sea salt

　　unrefined safflower oil

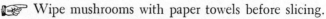 Cut okra in ½ inch thick rounds. Rinse the okra so it is slightly wet. Shake the okra pieces in a bag with stone-ground yellow corn meal and a little sea salt.
Fry in unrefined safflower oil over medium heat. The heat has to be watched carefully in order to fry the okra crisp but not burn the corn meal.

This is a great way of fixing okra for those who claim not to like it.

BAKED PINEAPPLE

SERVES 4–6

　　2 cups canned, drained pineapple chunks
　　　or fresh pineapple chunks
　　1 cup grated cheddar cheese

　　¾ cup pineapple juice, water, or other
　　　fruit juice (orange juice is good)
　　¼ cup raw honey

⅛ *teaspoon sea salt*
1 *tablespoon whole wheat flour made*
   into a smooth paste with 2 tablespoons
   of the above juice

1 *cup whole wheat bread crumbs*
2 *tablespoons butter*

☞ Mix the pineapple and cheese in a 2 quart casserole.
Mix the juice, honey, salt, and flour mixture in a saucepan. Stir and heat just until well blended. Pour over the pineapple and cheese.
Top with bread crumbs. Dot the crumbs with butter.
Bake 30 minutes at 350°.

Serve baked pineapple with vegetable or grain dishes or try it as an unusual dessert.

MILLET PURÉE
(Mock Mashed Potatoes)

SERVES 4

1 *tablespoon unrefined oil*
1 *cauliflower, cut up in small pieces*

1½ *cups millet*

7 *cups water*
½ *teaspoon sea salt*

☞ Heat a large saucepan. Add the oil and cauliflower and sauté until golden.
Add the millet and sauté until lightly browned.
Add water and salt and bring to a boil. Reduce heat and simmer 1 hour.
Put the mixture through a food mill.
Serve with bechamel sauce or thick tamari sauce.

For those who don't eat potatoes, this purée makes a wonderful substitute.

BAVARIAN POTATOES

SERVES 8

>4 cups hot, mashed, cooked potatoes
>3 cups homemade cottage cheese
>¾ cup homemade yogurt
>one onion, finely chopped
>2½ teaspoons sea salt
>pepper
>
>Garnish: slivered almonds

☞ Mix all ingredients with potatoes. Pour into a 2 quart oiled dish.
Brush top with oil.
Bake 30 minutes at 350°.
Sprinkle top with chopped or slivered almonds and brown lightly
under broiler.

OVEN-FRIED POTATO STICKS

SERVES 8

>½ cup unrefined safflower oil
>6 to 8 large potatoes, cut in fourths or
>   eighths, lengthwise
>1 teaspoon sea salt

☞ Pour oil in a large, shallow baking dish.
Arrange the potato sticks, 1 layer deep, in the dish, turning once
to coat with oil.
Sprinkle with salt.
Bake 30 minutes to 1 hour at 400°. Length of time depends on
the thickness of the sticks.

PARTY POTATOES AU GRATIN

SERVES 8

>4 tablespoons butter
>1 large onion, thinly sliced

6 medium potatoes, thinly sliced
2 cups grated swiss cheese
sea salt
pepper
1½ cups sweet cream

☞ Dot the bottom of a shallow baking dish with half the butter.
Cover the bottom with a layer of thinly sliced onions.
Then add a layer of potatoes, followed by a layer of half the cheese. Salt and pepper each layer of potatoes.
Repeat all layers again, starting with the butter.
Pour the cream over all.
Cover and bake 1½ to 2 hours at 350°. Uncover and bake until browned.
The long cooking makes a very creamy dish.

HOLIDAY SWEET POTATOES

SERVES 6

3 large sweet potatoes or yams

2 tablespoons homemade safflower butter
½ cup milk
½ teaspoon sea salt
2 egg yolks, beaten

2 egg whites, stiffly beaten

Optional: ½ teaspoon cinnamon and
½ teaspoon nutmeg

☞ Wash, dry, and oil the skins of the potatoes.
Bake the potatoes about 1 hour at 400° or until tender. Cool until easy to handle.
Slice the cooked potatoes in half lengthwise. Scoop out the soft potatoes and mix with the butter, milk, salt, spices if desired, and egg yolks. Beat one minute.
Fold the stiffly beaten egg whites into the mixture.
Refill the potato shells. Place these filled shells in an oiled dish. Bake 10 minutes at 450° or until hot through.

SAUERKRAUT

YIELD: 1½ QUARTS

>   1 head cabbage
>   3 to 5 tablespoons sea salt
>   water

☞ Wash, quarter, core, and shred the cabbage.
Thoroughly mix the cabbage with the salt. Firmly pack into crock or tight keg. Add water to cover.
Cover the cabbage with a plate to hold the cabbage under water. Fill a quart jar with water and place this on the plate to hold the plate down.
Remove the fermentation each day if necessary.
The kraut will be ready in 1 to 2 weeks.
When properly cured, sauerkraut is yellow-white and free of white spots.
Refrigerate.

If you have your own garden, this is a wonderful way of preserving cabbage when you have too much.

SAUTÉED SPROUTS

SERVES 4–6
>   2 tablespoons unrefined oil
>   1 large onion, sliced thin
>
>   4 cups mung bean sprouts
>   1 tablespoon tamari soy sauce, or to taste

☞ Heat a skillet on medium heat. Add the oil and the onions. Sauté for 5 minutes.
Add the mung bean sprouts and sauté until heated through.
Season with tamari to taste.

VARIATIONS:

1. Omit the onion. Sauté 4 to 6 stalks chopped celery. Add the sprouts, seasoning, and ½ cup stock. Cover and simmer 2 minutes.
2. Add some chopped red bell pepper to the sauté before adding the mung bean sprouts.

BAKED SQUASH WITH CHEESE

SERVES 6

> 6 medium yellow squash
> 1 large onion, chopped
> 1 pound cheese, grated
> 1 cup dry bread crumbs
>   (or seasoned crumbs)

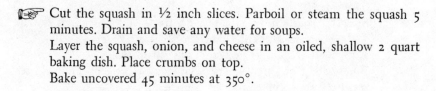 Cut the squash in ½ inch slices. Parboil or steam the squash 5 minutes. Drain and save any water for soups.

Layer the squash, onion, and cheese in an oiled, shallow 2 quart baking dish. Place crumbs on top.

Bake uncovered 45 minutes at 350°.

YELLOW SQUASH WITH CORN AND TOMATOES

SERVES 6

> 6 young yellow squash
>   (uniform in size), halved lengthwise
>
> 1 tablespoon unrefined oil
> 1 tablespoon chopped onion
> 1 medium-sized tomato, chopped,
>   with seeds removed
> ¾ cup whole kernel corn
> 1 egg yolk, beaten
> sea salt and pepper to season
>
> buttered whole wheat toast crumbs
> 3 very thin pimento strips
> 1 big sprig parsley

Parboil or steam squash.

When tender, but not soft, scoop out centers and place shells in colander to drain. Turn cut side down to drain well.

In a skillet, sauté the onion in the oil. Mash the centers of squash and add to the onion. Add tomato, corn, and egg yolk. Season with sea salt and pepper.

Fill cavity of squash with skillet mixture and sprinkle buttered toast crumbs on top.

Bake 20 minutes at 350°. Remove and garnish with pimento strips and parsley sprig.

SQUASH IDEAS

1. Dip squash slices in beaten egg and then into wheat germ. Sauté in oil.
2. *Sweet 'n Sour:* Steam squash with fruit. Add a little raw honey and cider vinegar.
3. Add small crisp pieces of fresh squash to salads.
4. Finely chop or shred squash. Sauté in a little oil and add to spaghetti sauce or grain and bean dishes.
5. Use very thinly sliced squash on homemade pizza. Put squash on before tomato sauce and cheese.
6. Use squash in soups. Creamed squash soup is especially delicious. Also try the recipes for other cream soups.
7. Sauté chopped or grated squash with the onions in the omelet recipe.
8. Substitute eggplant for squash in any recipe. Especially good on pizza, as suggested in number 5 above.

TOMATOES WITH SPINACH VERA CRUZ

SERVES 4

2 *cups of cooked, chopped spinach*

6 *medium-sized firm tomatoes*
sea salt

1 tablespoon unrefined oil
¼ cup chopped onion

1 cup sour cream
dash of Tabasco
freshly ground black pepper
5 slices mozzarella cheese

☞ Drain spinach. Save liquid for stock.
Cut out centers of tomatoes, leaving firm outside wall. Sprinkle with sea salt and turn open side down to drain. Chop the part of the tomato removed from center and drain also.
Heat a skillet. Add oil and onion and sauté on low heat.
Squeeze the spinach to dry it completely, then add to the onion. Also add the chopped, well-drained tomatoes and sour cream. Season with sea salt, Tabasco, and freshly ground pepper. Stir well and add 2 slices of the cheese, finely chopped.
When heated through, fill cavity of tomatoes. Place in lightly oiled baking dish. Top each tomato with a triangle of cheese.
Just before time to serve, place in 350° oven long enough to melt cheese and heat through (about 15 minutes).

HOT TOMATO CASSEROLE

SERVES 6

12 to 15 large tomatoes, cut in chunks
2 or 3 jalapeno peppers, blistered,
    peeled, and chopped, or
    uncooked chopped jalapenos

1 teaspoon sea salt, or to taste
pepper to taste
3 or 4 thick slices of whole wheat bread,
    crumbed

1 cup grated cheese

☞ Put all the tomatoes and peppers in a deep saucepan. Bring to a boil. Reduce the heat. Simmer until the tomatoes are reduced to

a thick sauce, about 30 minutes.
Salt and pepper to taste.
Stir in the bread crumbs.
Pour the tomato mixture into a 2 quart casserole.
Bake 30 minutes at 350° or until the mixture is fairly firm and not soupy. Top with grated cheese.

This is a very old recipe, handed down for several generations.

SWEET TOMATO CASSEROLE

YIELD: 3–4 CUPS
4 to 5 cups diced fresh tomatoes

Optional: 2 teaspoons arrowroot powder

juice and grated rind of ½ orange
(about ½ cup) or ½ cup lime juice
1 tablespoon lemon juice
½ cup raw honey

3 cups whole wheat bread cubes,
lightly toasted
3 tablespoons melted homemade
safflower butter

☞ Bring the tomatoes to a boil in a saucepan. Simmer uncovered about 30 minutes or until thick. If needed, add 2 teaspoons arrowroot powder to thicken. Blend the cooked tomatoes until smooth. This makes about 2½ cups purée.
Add the juices and honey to the tomato purée.
Toss the toasted bread cubes with the melted butter. Add the cubes to the tomato mixture in a 1½ quart casserole dish. Stir lightly.
Bake 30 minutes at 375° or 45 minutes at 325°.

This is an unusual twist for a tomato dish. Serve it hot or cold.

PIES

CARROT PIE

YIELD: 1 LARGE PIE

1 9 inch or 10 inch whole wheat pie shell,
*   partially cooked*

1 tablespoon unrefined corn germ oil
2 large onions, chopped

10 fairly large carrots, cut in chunks

¼ teaspoon sea salt
3 tablespoons cinnamon, or less

topping

☞ Heat a pressure cooker on medium-low heat. Add the oil and onions and sauté until very soft.

Add the carrots and 1 cup water. Bring up pressure and cook for 20 minutes at lowest possible pressure. Reduce the pressure. Drain excess liquid, but save it for soups or sauces.

Blend the carrots, onions, salt, and cinnamon until smooth in a blender.

Pour all into the partly cooked pie shell. Sprinkle with topping. Bake about 15 minutes at 350°.

VARIATIONS:

Substitute any sweet vegetable—such as butternut squash, sweet potatoes, or pumpkin—for the carrots.

Carrot pie is a delicious and different vegetable dish or a delightful and healthy dessert.

This pie tastes just like pumpkin pie. Just don't tell them what's in it until they've eaten it.

PINTO PIE

YIELD: 1 LARGE PIE

Follow the carrot pie recipe above, but omit the carrots.

Substitute 2 cups well-cooked, unseasoned mashed pinto beans for the cooked carrots. Do not pressure cook.

You may wish to add 2 to 4 tablespoons raw honey because pinto beans are not as sweet as carrots. However, organically grown pinto beans are amazingly sweet.

OTHER VARIATIONS:

You may wish to substitute some other vegetable purée in this recipe. Remember, the trick is in sautéing the onions until they are very soft and sweet.

ONION PIE

SERVES 4–6

1 pastry-lined pie dish
onions
sea salt

2 tablespoons flour
1 cup cream, sweet or sour
butter
pepper

☞ Peel and slice, very thin, enough onions to fill a pastry-lined pie dish evenly. Salt the onions—mix well and set aside for about 15 minutes. Drain onions and put into pie shell.

Add about 2 tablespoons flour, 1 cup cream (sweet or sour). Stir with a fork. Dot with butter and sprinkle with pepper.

Bake in oven 45 minutes at 400° until nice and brown.

This pie should be eaten while warm. It is excellent with cheese or with beans.

WINTER SQUASH OR PUMPKIN PIE

YIELD: 1 9 INCH PIE
1 uncooked 9 inch whole wheat pie shell

3 cups cooked winter squash or pumpkin
1 cup milk
¼ cup tamari soy sauce
½ onion, chopped
3 cloves garlic, minced
2 eggs, beaten
4 tablespoons butter or unrefined
   corn germ oil
4 tablespoons chopped parsley

☞ Mix all the filling ingredients together until fairly smooth. Pour into the pie shell.
Bake 45 minutes at 375° or until the pie is firm in the center.

SOUFFLÉS

A vegetable soufflé adds elegance to an otherwise plain meal. The combination of eggs and whole milk with vegetables contributes greatly to the nutrition of the dish. Soufflés are an excellent means of converting vegetable haters. This basic recipe can be used for chopped carrots, chopped broccoli, mashed squash, chopped spinach, or chopped asparagus.

BASIC SOUFFLÉ

SERVES 4

    ¼ *cup butter*
    ¼ *cup whole wheat pastry flour*

    1 *teaspoon sea salt*
    1 *tablespoon raw honey*
    1½ *cups milk, heated*

    5 *egg yolks*
    2¾ *cups of cooked vegetables,*
        chopped fine, drained
    5 *egg whites*

☞ Melt butter, add flour; simmer 3 or 4 minutes without browning. Add sea salt, raw honey, and heated milk. Whip with wire whip until smooth; cool slightly.

Add beaten egg yolks and cooked vegetables and continue to cool. Beat egg whites until stiff. When vegetable mixture is cool, fold in egg whites. Pour into a 1½ quart buttered casserole. Place in pan of hot water (2 inches deep), in 325° oven. Bake for approximately one hour, or until inserted knife comes out clean.

Broccoli soufflé is especially good with soyburger patties. One good topping for this soufflé is Fernando dressing; another is:

INDIAN SAUCE

    ½ *cup homemade mayonnaise*
    ½ *cup homemade sour cream*
    1 *teaspoon lemon juice*
    ¼ *teaspoon curry powder (dissolved in*
        the lemon juice)

☞ Mix all ingredients together.

BUTTERNUT SQUASH SOUFFLÉ

SERVES 6

 3 tablespoons unrefined corn germ oil
 ¼ cup whole wheat pastry flour

 ¾ cup milk
 ¼ cup pure maple syrup
 ½ teaspoon sea salt
 ¼ teaspoon ground cinnamon
 dash of nutmeg

 4 eggs, separated

 1 medium-size butternut squash,
   cooked and puréed

☞ Heat a small saucepan on low heat. Add the oil and the flour. Cook 1 minute, stirring constantly. Cool slightly.
Add the milk, maple syrup, salt, cinnamon, and nutmeg. Cook and stir until thick and smooth. Remove from the heat.
Add the egg yolks, one at a time, beating after each addition. Stir in the squash.
Beat the egg whites until stiff. Fold the squash mixture into the egg whites.
Turn into an oiled 1½ quart casserole. Bake 35 to 40 minutes at 375°.

VARIATION:
Use 1½ cups cooked, puréed yams instead of the squash.

This soufflé is quite sweet and could be served as a dessert.

TEMPURA

Tempura should be cooked quickly and eaten while warm. To avoid being in the kitchen after the guests arrive, heat the oil in a fondue pot at the table. Make an attractive arrangement with the fondue pot, a bowl of batter, and a plate of fresh, crisp, sliced zucchini or other vegetables. Dip the vegetables in the batter and deep fry them before your guests' eyes.

This is also a good way to get your children to eat vegetables. Like most adults, children love almost anything that has been tempura'd.

TEMPURA OR FRITTERS

½ cup whole wheat flour
½ cup corn meal or part corn meal and
   part rice flour
½ teaspoon sea salt
1 to 1¼ cups water

unrefined safflower oil for deep frying

☞ Mix first 4 ingredients lightly. Lumps don't matter. Chill for half an hour or more before using. When ready to use, mix again.
Tempura any of the following vegetables or those of your choice. However, watery vegetables do not work well:
   sliced carrots
   onion rings
   cauliflower flowerets
   broccoli flowerets
   string beans
   sliced eggplant
   sliced squash
Dip vegetable pieces into the batter. If the batter does not stick, dip the vegetable in flour first. Deep fry in hot oil (350–400°) until golden and crisp. Drain on paper towels. If the oil smokes, it is too hot.

Fritters: Use a little less water and make a thicker batter. Dice the vegetables. Mix them with the batter and drop by the spoonful into the hot oil. If using corn, run a fork down the kernels to pop them before removing them from the cob, or they will burst while frying and spatter hot oil. Corn and diced onion are delicious together.

VARIATION OF BATTER:
1 cup whole wheat flour
½ teaspoon sea salt
1 to 1¼ cups water or milk
1 egg, beaten, or 1 tablespoon
   arrowroot powder

Serve the following as a dip for the tempura or fritters: tamari diluted with a little water with grated or powdered ginger mixed in.

ZUCCHINI TEMPURA

SERVES 6
1⅓ cups whole wheat pastry flour
1 teaspoon sea salt
⅓ teaspoon pepper
1 tablespoon unrefined safflower oil
2 beaten egg yolks

¾ cup flat beer

Optional: 2 egg whites, stiffly beaten

1 pound chilled fresh zucchini,
   thinly sliced

unrefined safflower oil for deep frying

☞ Mix the flour, salt, pepper, oil, and egg yolks.
Gradually add the beer, stirring constantly.
Allow batter to rest, covered, in refrigerator for 3 to 12 hours. Just before using you may add stiffly beaten egg whites for a puffier crust.
Dip zucchini slices into the batter and drop into deep, hot safflower oil. When the crust is golden brown and puffy, remove the zucchini from the oil. Drain on paper towels. Cool slightly and serve.

Gather 'Round

MAIN DISHES

Main dishes need not be your only source of protein, but they are traditionally the major source in our culture. These recipes are offered as a change from standard dishes, to be used alone or in combination with other protein foods. These recipes also offer a wide variety of whole grains, beans, nuts, and vegetables.

PROTEIN EFFICIENCY

Proteins are made up of many amino acids, some of which are essential to human health. A complete protein contains all the essential amino acids in near-perfect balance. The body must have all the essential amino acids at the same time and in the correct proportions in order to use them fully. If one amino acid is missing or deficient, the utilization of that particular protein is severely limited. Complete protein balance may be obtained in different ways. In using vegetable proteins the general rule is to combine two or more such proteins at the same meal. Between them, the complete list of essential amino acids will be provided. Another good practice is to combine vegetable proteins with each other and with some other protein—particularly milk, eggs, or cheese.

129

COOKING WHOLE GRAINS, FLAKES, AND CEREALS

Grain (1 cup dry)	Regular Cooking		Pressure Cooking	
	WATER (CUPS)	TIME (MIN.)	WATER (CUPS)	TIME (MIN.)
Barley	2½	60	2	40
Porridge	4-5	90	NO*	
Buckwheat Groats	2-2½	20-25	NO	
Corn meal, yellow	4	30	NO	
Corn meal, white	4	30	NO	
Millet	3½	30	3	25
Porridge	5	60	NO	
Oats	3	60	2½	45
Porridge	5	2½ hrs.	NO	
Flaked, Rolled, Oatmeal	3	30	NO	
Rice				
Short grain	2½	50	2	40-60
Medium grain	2	50	1½	40-60
Long grain	1½	40-50	1¼	30-40

Porridge	5	90	NO	
Rice cream	4	30	NO	
Flaked	2	20	NO	
Rye	2½	60	2	45
Flaked	2	20	NO	
Wheat Berries	2½	60	2	45
Porridge	5½	2½ hrs.	NO	
Cracked wheat	3	20–25	NO	
Bulgur	2	15–20	NO	
Flaked	2	20	NO	

SEASONING: ¼ teaspoon sea salt per cup of dry grain.

OPTIONAL: 1 tablespoon lemon juice may be added to cooked whole grains for a bright taste.

YIELD: 1 cup of dry whole grain makes approximately 2½ cups of cooked grain.

COOKING CEREALS: Cereals, grains that are cracked, ground, or flaked, may be lightly roasted before cooking for a nuttier flavor.

In a saucepan, boil the water, add the salt, and then slowly add the cereal. Simmer the cereal for the recommended time, on an asbestos pad.

* Do *not* pressure cook cereals or porridges; they may clog up the vent on the top of the pressure cooker.

131

COOKING DRY BEANS AND BEAN FLAKES

Beans (1 cup dry)	Soaking Time	Regular Cooking		Pressure Cooking (15 lbs.)	
		WATER (CUPS)	TIME (MIN.)	WATER (CUPS)	TIME (MIN.)
Azuki	unsoaked	4	90	2½–3	45
	1 hr.	4	60	2½–3	30
Black	overnight	4	2–3 hrs.	2½–3	60*
Black-eye Peas	unsoaked	3	60	2½	45
	1 hr.	3	45	2½	40
Chick-peas (Garbanzos)	overnight	4	2–3 hrs.	2½–3	60
Kidneys	unsoaked	3	90	2½	60
	1 hr.	3	60	2½	45
Lentils	unsoaked	3	60–90	2½	30
	1 hr.	3	45	2½	25
Navy beans	unsoaked	3	90	2½	50
	1 hr.	3	60	2½	40
Pintos	unsoaked OR soaked overnight	3	2–2½ hrs.	2½–3	60
Flaked	unsoaked	2	45		NO

132

	Soaking				
Soybeans	overnight	4	3 hrs.	2½–3	90–150*
Flaked	unsoaked	2	60–90	NO	
Split peas	unsoaked	3	45	2½	20

ALTERNATIVE TO OVERNIGHT SOAKING: Bring the beans and water to a boil. Cover and remove from stove. Let sit 1 hour. Then cook by the method of your choice.

SEASONING: ½ teaspoon sea salt.

Do not add salt until the beans are soft or until after the pressure has come down.

2–3 teaspoons unrefined oil

Do not add until beans are soft.

tamari soy sauce

Add tamari to taste during the last 5 minutes of cooking.

YIELD: 1 cup of dry beans makes approximately 2½ cups of cooked beans.

OPTIONAL: garlic, minced onion, diced green pepper, diced carrots, diced celery, 1 small section

kombu, 3" strip (sea vegetable)

Vegetables should be added during the last ½ hour of cooking. If pressure cooking, add vegetables after pressure has come down and continue cooking until vegetables are soft.

Lime juice may be added to soybeans or flakes while they are cooking.

Kombu may be cooked with beans to add flavor and minerals. It also helps keep beans from foaming up.

Millet or wheat berries may be substituted for up to ¼ of the azuki beans. If using wheat berries, cook additional time until berries are soft.

* When pressure cooking black beans or soybeans, be very careful; they tend to foam up and clog the vent. These beans must be cooked over a very low flame, preferably on an asbestos pad.

The use of vegetable proteins is a relatively inexpensive way of obtaining high-quality protein. Nuts and beans are particularly good sources of vegetable proteins. Soybeans are the basis for many protein foods because they are one of the few complete vegetable protein foods, containing 34 percent protein (dry weight). For further information regarding vegetable proteins, refer to *Diet for a Small Planet* by Frances Moore Lappé (New York: Ballantine, 1971).

EGGS AND CHOLESTEROL

There is a huge controversy over the cholesterol in eggs. Some doctors, noting the cholesterol content of eggs, automatically rule them out, particularly if the patient has heart disease or a high cholesterol count. Other doctors and researchers point out that while eggs are high in cholesterol they are also one of the best sources of other nutrients that foster healthy metabolism and keep cholesterol from depositing in arteries. Since the body itself produces cholesterol, the problem seems to be its proper disposition and use, not cholesterol itself. Refined carbohydrates and other dietary and nondietary factors can raise cholesterol levels more quickly than fats. In a large group of doctors, on whom very detailed health records were kept, 50 percent avoided eggs completely, and yet a disturbing number had dangerously high cholesterol levels. When all were encouraged to eat eggs during the next year, cholesterol levels fell.*

It is preferable to use barnyard eggs. Usually roosters are kept with the hens, so the eggs are also fertile. Barnyard hens are allowed to run loose in the yard, to scratch and to eat a more varied diet. Tests at the University of Texas have shown that eggs laid by barnyard hens are significantly more nutritious than eggs laid by caged hens.†

BURGERS AND LOAVES

Sprout and nut burgers are delicious and high in protein. Make the best "hamburgers" you ever ate with homemade buns and all the trimmings.

* Dr. E. Cheraskin, M.D., D.M.D., University of Alabama Medical Center.
† Dr. Roger Williams, Ph.D., University of Texas, Clayton Foundation Biochemical Institute.

NUT BURGERS

SERVES 4–6
½ pound cashews, ground in a blender
½ pound walnuts, ground in a blender
1 cup cooked brown rice
1 cup grated colby cheese
  (or any mild cheese)
1 egg
½ onion, chopped
1 teaspoon sea salt
Chili powder, hot sauce, other seasonings

whole wheat flour or bread crumbs
unrefined safflower oil for frying

☞ Mix first 7 ingredients together and season to taste with chili powder, hot sauce, or other seasoning.
Shape into patties. Roll in whole wheat flour or bread crumbs. Chill. Fry in hot oil (not deep).
When forming patties, dip hands in cold water before shaping each one to keep them from sticking to your hands.

SOY SESAME BURGERS

YIELD: 4 SMALL PATTIES
1 cup dry soybeans
1 cup cracked wheat

2–3 tablespoons tamari soy sauce or
    2–3 teaspoons sea salt
3 tablespoons unrefined oil
½ medium onion, finely chopped
⅓ cup sesame seeds
⅓ cup whole wheat flour
2 tablespoons water

whole wheat flour
unrefined safflower oil for frying

Rinse the soybeans in cold water. Cover the beans and wheat with water and soak them separately 12 to 24 hours, adding more water if needed to keep the beans covered. Drain both.

Grind the soaked beans in a hand grinder or ⅓ cup at a time in a blender.

Mix all the ingredients together, adjusting the amount of flour and water as needed to bind the ingredients together.

Shape into patties. Dip in flour. Fry in a little oil.

Serve with homemade buns and all the trimmings.

RICE PANCAKE WITH TOFU

SERVES 4

2 cups cooked brown rice
2 cups tofu, chopped
½ cup chopped walnuts or pecans,
    toasted
2 tablespoons lemon juice
1½ teaspoons sea salt
whole wheat flour to hold patties together
unrefined safflower oil for frying

 Mix all the ingredients except oil, and form into 4 small burger-like cakes.

Heat skillet. Add oil and fry patties until brown on one side. Turn and brown on the other side.

NUT LOAF DE LUXE

YIELD: 9 X 5 INCH LOAF

3 tablespoons unrefined oil
1 medium onion, chopped
1 green pepper, chopped

⅓ cup tomatoes, chopped and drained
2 tablespoons chopped parsley or
    celery tops

1 cup cooked brown rice
⅓ cup whole wheat bread crumbs
1 cup walnuts, chopped
1 egg, well beaten
¾ teaspoon sea salt
¼ teaspoon paprika
1 teaspoon grated lemon peel

2½ cups mashed potatoes
paprika

Garnish: parsley and cherry tomatoes

☞ Heat a skillet; add oil, onion, and pepper and sauté. Mix sautéed vegetables with next 9 ingredients. Place in oiled, 1 quart baking dish and bake 30 minutes at 350°. Remove from oven. Cover with seasoned mashed potatoes, sprinkle with more paprika, and return to oven until potatoes are browned (approximately 15 minutes). Garnish with bunches of parsley and whole cherry tomatoes.

Serve with Beets Aglow and a tossed green salad.

PECAN LOAF

SERVES 4–6

2 cups finely chopped pecans
¼ teaspoon sage
1 medium onion, chopped fine
1 cup chopped tomatoes
1 cup whole wheat bread crumbs
2 well-beaten eggs
½ cup light cream
¾ teaspoon sea salt, or to taste

Optional: black pepper to taste

pecan halves
melted butter

Garnish: parsley

☞ Mix first 8 ingredients together with pepper, if desired. Place in 1 quart oiled baking dish. Score top with handle of table knife. Place a pecan half in each scored square. Brush with melted butter. Bake 35 minutes at 350°. If pecans on top begin to brown too much, lay sheet of foil lightly over the top. Remove from pan to warm platter. Garnish with bouquets of parsley.

Serve with broiled tomatoes filled with Spinach Vera Cruz, cider carrots, and small buttered new potatoes.

SOYBEAN LOAF

YIELD: 9 X 5 LOAF

2 cups dry soybeans

3 tablespoons unrefined oil

½ cup chopped onion
2 celery stalks, chopped fine
1½ cups dry whole wheat bread crumbs
1 egg
1 teaspoon sage
2 tablespoons raw honey
2 teaspoons sea salt
2 cloves garlic
¼ teaspoon cayenne pepper
1 cup homemade tomato sauce

Optional: grated cheese

☞ Soak soybeans overnight and then cook until tender. Drain. Save the liquid for stock. Put beans through food chopper (using coarse knife) or blend ⅓ cup at a time in a blender.
Heat a large frying pan. Add oil and chopped soybeans. Sauté until brown.
Add other ingredients, tomato sauce last, saving ¼ cup. Mix lightly.

Shape into a loaf in a greased 9 x 5 loaf pan. Bake 1 hour at 350°.
Pour remaining sauce over loaf. Add grated cheese if you like and
bake 5 more minutes.

Serve with tomato sauce or gravy.

ALMOND CHOP SUEY

SERVES 6
> *3 tablespoons unrefined oil*
> *2 large onions, thinly sliced*
> *4 carrots, sliced diagonally,*
>   *⅛ inch thick*
>
> *4 stalks celery, sliced diagonally*
> *1 green pepper, chopped*
>
> *Optional: mushrooms*
>   *zucchini*
>   *turnip*
>   *water chestnuts*
>   *Jerusalem artichokes*
>   *soybean curd*
>
> *2 cups soy or mung bean sprouts*
> *1 cup whole blanched almonds*
>
> *1 to 2 tablespoons tamari soy sauce*

☞ Heat a large, heavy skillet on medium heat. Add oil, onions, and
carrots and sauté 5 minutes.
Add the other vegetables, bean sprouts, and almonds. Cover and
continue sautéing on low heat, stirring occasionally, until the
vegetables are barely done but still crisp.
Add the tamari and just heat through.
Serve over hot, cooked rice, millet, noodles, or other whole grains.
More tamari may be added at the table.

VARIATIONS:
For a thick sauce, pour 1 cup boiling water over the vegetables after sautéing them lightly. Cover and simmer 5 minutes.
Add 2 tablespoons of arrowroot powder dissolved in 2 tablespoons of cold water. Cook, stirring constantly, until the sauce thickens. Garnish with deep-fried whole wheat noodles. (Cook noodles 2 minutes in water, drain, and deep fry until crisp.)

This makes a good party dish. Seat your guests on pillows around a low coffee table and provide them with chop sticks. Festive oriental lanterns will also add to the occasion. Be sure to have plenty of hot tea and, of course, almond gems.

BAKED CHESHIRE

SERVES 6–8

3 cups water
1½ to 2 teaspoons sea salt

1½ cups yellow stone-ground corn meal

4 eggs, beaten
4 cups grated cheese

½ teaspoon hot pepper sauce
paprika, as desired
garlic, one clove, finely minced

☞ Bring the water and salt to a boil.
Stir in the meal slowly so that it does not lump. Lower heat.
Simmer 3 to 5 minutes until thick, stirring constantly.
Remove from heat. Stir in the beaten eggs and cheese.
Add other seasonings to taste.
Bake in a deep oiled 2 quart dish 45 minutes to 1 hour at 325°.

Serve a crisp green salad with this variation of cheese grits.

BLINTZES

SERVES 4

BLINTZ BATTER
2 eggs
1 cup water
⅓ cup whole wheat pastry flour

☞ Beat eggs, flour, and water with a wire whisk until the batter is
smooth.

Heat a 6 inch skillet (cast iron works best) over medium-high
heat. Put 1 teaspoon oil in the pan. Add 2 to 3 tablespoons of
batter, tilting the pan so that the batter spreads evenly over the
entire pan. Cook 2 minutes or until the bottom starts to brown.
Flip the blintz out onto a counter so that the cooked side is facing
down. Make one blintz after another in this manner until the
batter is used up.

Put 1 or 2 tablespoons of one of the following fillings into the
center of the cooked side of each blintz. Roll up and brown in a
little hot oil or butter.

VEGETABLE FILLING
1 tablespoon unrefined oil
1 cup chopped carrots
½ cup chopped mushrooms
2 green onions, sliced
1 cup chopped zucchini
1 tablespoon chopped parsley
1 tablespoon tamari soy sauce

☞ Sauté the vegetables in the oil. Add the tamari.

CHEESE FILLING
1½ cups ricotta or small-curd cottage
*   cheese*
½ cup chopped strawberries or cherries or
*   2 tablespoons honey and a dash of*
*   nutmeg*

☞ Mix well.

STUFFED CABBAGE LEAVES

SERVES 4
> 2 cups water
> ½ teaspoon sea salt
> 1 cup buckwheat groats
>
> 1 head cabbage
>
> 1 tablespoon unrefined oil
> 1 onion, finely chopped
> 1 small carrot, finely chopped
>
> 1 tablespoon tamari soy sauce
>
> *Optional: 1 egg, beaten*

☞ Bring water and salt to a boil. Add the buckwheat groats. Cover, lower heat, and simmer for 15 minutes.
Meanwhile, drop the head of cabbage into a pot of boiling water and boil for 3 minutes. Drain. Carefully peel off the 8 outer leaves.
Heat a skillet on medium heat. Add the oil, onion, and carrot. Sauté until tender.
Add 1 tablespoon tamari and the cooked buckwheat.
Stir in an egg, if desired.
Put 2 to 3 tablespoons of this mixture into each cabbage leaf. Wrap the leaf snugly around the filling and place in an oiled casserole dish.
Cover and bake for 20 minutes at 350°.

If leaves are small and wrapped securely, they may be eaten with the fingers.

CORN MEAL SPOONBREAD

SERVES 4–5
> 3 cups milk

2 tablespoons butter
1 teaspoon sea salt
1 cup stone-ground yellow or white
   corn meal

4 eggs, separated

Scald the milk.
Add the butter and salt. Slowly add the meal, stirring constantly.
Cook one minute after adding the last of the meal, still stirring.
Add the beaten egg yolks.
Beat the egg whites until stiff and fold into the corn meal mixture.
Pour into an oiled 2 quart casserole.
Bake 35 to 40 minutes at 350°.

This is a delicious, custardy soufflé.

BAKED DEVILED-EGG CASSEROLE

YIELD: 4 SERVINGS

6 hard-boiled eggs
2 teaspoons prepared mustard
3 tablespoons homemade sour cream
¼ teaspoon sea salt

2 tablespoons butter
½ cup chopped green pepper
⅓ cup chopped onion

¼ cup chopped pimento
1½ cups mushroom sauce
¾ cup homemade sour cream

½ cup shredded cheddar cheese

Halve eggs lengthwise; remove yolks. Mash yolks, mustard, 3 tablespoons sour cream, and sea salt together. Fill whites with yolk
mixture.

Melt butter in large skillet; sauté green pepper and onion until tender. Remove from heat.

Stir in pimento, ¾ cup mushroom sauce, and remaining sour cream. Place half of this mixture in a 1½ quart shallow baking dish; arrange eggs, cut side up, in a single layer in the dish. Pour remaining sauce mixture over the top; sprinkle with cheese.

Bake 20 minutes at 350° or until heated through. Casserole may be assembled in advance; refrigerate until ready to bake.

EGG FOO YUNG

SERVES: 4

1 tablespoon unrefined oil
1½ cups bean sprouts

4 eggs
2 teaspoons tamari soy sauce
¼ cup grated onion

Optional: ½ cup sautéed chopped celery
½ cup mushrooms,
finely chopped and sautéed

1 tablespoon unrefined oil for each
serving

Heat a skillet. Add the oil and sprouts. Sauté the sprouts until just heated through.

Beat the eggs until light. Add the tamari, onion, and bean sprouts, and other chopped vegetables if desired, and mix well.

Heat 1 tablespoon oil in a 6 inch skillet. Pour ¼ cup of the egg mixture into the skillet and brown on both sides. Repeat until the egg mixture is used up.

Serve with cooked brown rice.

STUFFED GREEN PEPPERS

SERVES 4

4 green peppers

1 tablespoon unrefined oil
2 onions, diced
½ cup bean sprouts
1 stalk celery, sliced

Optional: chopped green chilis

2 tablespoons tamari soy sauce
¾ cup grated cheese
1½ cups cooked brown rice

 Slice across the top of the peppers and remove the seeds. Steam the peppers on a rack above boiling water for 10 to 15 minutes.
Heat a skillet, add the oil, onions, sprouts, celery, and green chilis, if desired, and sauté 5 minutes.
Add the tamari, the grated cheese, and the rice. Mix well and heat through.
Stuff the peppers with this mixture. Bake 15 to 20 minutes at 350°.

VARIATION:

Steam whole cabbage leaves or Chinese cabbage leaves until slightly softened. Fill with the pepper stuffing. Roll. Place on oiled foil. Puncture air holes in the foil. Fold the foil around the rolls. Place on a rack over hot water in a baking dish. Bake 10 minutes at 350° until steamed through.

SAUERKRAUT PIZZA OR REUBEN SANDWICH

YIELD: ALLOW ½ CUP SAUERKRAUT FOR EACH PERSON

sauerkraut
pizza sauce with cooked soy flakes
grated cheese

☞ Cover the bottom of a baking dish ½ inch thick with sauerkraut.
Spread pizza sauce thickly over kraut.
Sprinkle with grated cheese.
Bake at 350° until heated through. Add more grated cheese and
serve.

Reuben sandwich: Sauerkraut and the sauce mixture make an
excellent Reuben sandwich when served with plenty of cheese between slices of whole wheat toast.

This is a good recipe to utilize leftovers.

POLENTA PIE

SERVES 4–6
    1 cup stone-ground yellow corn meal
    1 teaspoon sea salt
    ½ teaspoon crumbled dry sage
    ¼ teaspoon black pepper

    3½ cups cold water

☞ Mix the dry ingredients in a 2 quart saucepan. Stir in the cold
water. Cook, stirring constantly, until very thick. This recipe does
not lump.
Pour into an oiled, flat 1½ quart baking dish. Bake until firm,
about 15 to 20 minutes, at 425°. Cover the meal crust with the
following mixture:

Filling
    1 pound cheese, cubed
    ¼ to ½ cup chopped ripe olives
    2 cloves garlic, minced
    2 onions, chopped
    ½ cup chopped, cooked chili peppers
    1 cup homemade tomato sauce
    1 tablespoon unrefined oil
    1 tablespoon oregano

Optional: 1 egg

Mix all the ingredients. Spread over hot corn meal crust. Bake in 425° oven until the cheese melts.

QUICHE AVON

YIELD: 1 8 INCH PIE

1 8 inch pie pan lined with flaky pie crust
and baked for 10 minutes

3 eggs, beaten
1 cup light cream, heated
1 teaspoon sea salt
¼ teaspoon dry mustard
dash of nutmeg

6 thin slices of onion, sautéed
1½ cups grated natural swiss cheese

☞ Mix eggs, cream, sea salt, mustard, and nutmeg. Add sautéed onions and grated cheese. Pour into baked pie shell. Bake 45 minutes at 350°.

VARIATIONS:
   ½ cup fresh mushrooms
         or
   1 cup fresh chopped spinach

Miniature quiches made in small muffin tins are excellent hot hors d'oeuvres.

VEGETABLE QUICHE

SERVES 6

>   2 tablespoons unrefined oil
>   1 onion, thinly sliced
>   1 clove garlic, finely minced
>   1 green pepper, chopped
>   4 cups broccoli and cauliflower pieces
>
>   4 to 6 eggs, beaten
>   2 cups cubed or grated sharp cheese
>   ½ teaspoon sea salt
>   ½ teaspoon each of cumin and marjoram
>   or crushed basil
>
>   Optional: sprinkle of curry powder

☞ Heat a skillet on medium heat. Add the oil and vegetables and sauté lightly. Cover and steam the vegetables in their own juices for 2 minutes.
Fold in the eggs, cheese, salt, and herbs.
Pour in an oiled 1½ or 2 quart baking dish.
Bake 30 to 40 minutes at 325° or until set.

VARIATIONS:
Fold in toasted bread cubes and bake.
Or line the oiled dish with lightly toasted whole wheat bread. Pour the vegetables and cheese mix over the bread and bake.

CREPES

SERVES 4

>   3 eggs
>   2 tablespoons whole wheat pastry flour
>   1 tablespoon water
>   1 tablespoon milk
>   pinch of salt
>
>   4 tablespoons unrefined oil, 1 per crepe

Beat the eggs, flour, water, milk, and salt until smooth. The batter will be quite thin.

Heat the skillet. Add 1 tablespoon oil and heat. Cover the bottom of the skillet with a thin coating of batter, tilting the pan as you pour in the batter.

Cook 1 minute. Turn the crepe. Brown the other side. Fold the crepe twice to form a triangle.

Serve with apple butter or pure maple syrup.

These are as close as you can come to the crepe the street vendors sell in Paris.

Crepes can be made and kept in the refrigerator. To use them for exotic desserts, fill with fruits and creams. For an impressive luncheon dish, fill with creamed vegetables.

With crepes, you can let your imagination run wild!

BAKED RICE

SERVES 4

2 cups cooked brown rice
2 eggs, beaten
2 cups milk
2 tablespoons butter
1 tablespoon tamari soy sauce, or
* 1 teaspoon sea salt, or to taste*
1 cup chopped almonds

 Mix all ingredients. Bake immediately or let sit an hour first to increase almond flavor.

Pour into oiled 1½ quart casserole.

Bake 20 to 30 minutes at 350° until set and lightly browned.

GREEN RICE CASSEROLE

SERVES 6

    3 tablespoons unrefined sesame oil
    1 onion, minced
    1 clove garlic, minced

    ½ cup fresh chopped parsley
    1 cup grated sharp cheese
    2 eggs, beaten
    2 cups milk
    1 teaspoon sea salt
    2 cups cooked brown rice

☞ Heat a skillet. Add the oil, onion, and garlic. Sauté 5 minutes.
Mix the parsley, cheese, eggs, milk, and salt with the cooked rice.
Add the sautéed onions and garlic.
Pour into a 2 quart baking dish. Bake at 350° 30 to 40 minutes,
or until firm.

PHILIPPINE RICE

SERVES 4

    1 tablespoon unrefined oil
    2 onions, diced

    3 cups cooked brown rice
    2 tablespoons tamari soy sauce

    2 tablespoons unrefined oil
    4 eggs
    4 bananas, cut in half lengthwise

    Garnish: parsley

☞ Heat a skillet. Add 1 tablespoon of oil and the onions. Sauté 5
minutes. Then add the rice and tamari and fry together.
Heat another pan. Add the remaining oil and fry the eggs. Remove
the eggs. Cover and set aside while you fry the bananas.

Place one serving of the rice on a round dish. Make an indentation in the center of the rice. Fill with one egg. Arrange 2 slices of banana around the egg.

Garnish with fresh parsley.

RICE RING

SERVES 4–6
    1 cup wild rice or brown rice
    1 teaspoon sea salt
    ½ clove garlic, minced
    4 cups boiling water

    ¼ cup butter
    ¼ teaspoon sage
    ¼ teaspoon thyme
    pinch marjoram
    pinch nutmeg
    1 cup onions minced
    1 cup pine nuts

☞ Combine rice, sea salt, garlic, and boiling water in a double boiler; steam until tender, about 45 minutes. Stir frequently.
Melt butter; add seasonings, minced onions, and pine nuts. Cook over low heat 3 or 4 minutes. Put in buttered, 8 inch ring mold. Stir in rice mixture. Set mold in a pan of hot water and bake 20 minutes at 350°.
To serve, loosen edges with a knife; invert on serving dish and fill with Creamed Mushrooms.

SWISS BROWN RICE

SERVES 8

>2 tablespoons unrefined sesame oil
>2 cups onions, sliced
>3 stalks celery, sliced
>½ pound mushrooms, sliced
>½ cup watercress or parsley, chopped
>
>1 clove garlic, minced
>1½ teaspoons paprika
>1 teaspoon sea salt
>½ teaspoon black pepper
>¼ teaspoon ground ginger
>
>3 cups cooked brown rice
>
>1 pound swiss cheese, coarsely grated
>
>Garnish: chopped parsley or
>   chopped watercress

☞ Heat a large skillet. Add oil and sauté the onions, celery, mushrooms, and watercress or parsley. Add garlic, paprika, salt, pepper, and a little ginger to taste.

Layer the brown rice, vegetables, and grated swiss cheese in a shallow casserole. Repeat layers. If it seems dry, sprinkle with ¼ cup water before adding last layer of cheese.

Bake for 20 to 25 minutes at 350°.

VARIETY WITH RICE

SERVES 6

>2 tablespoons unrefined oil
>2 cups chopped green onions,
>   including tops
>3 stalks celery, chopped
>
>½ cup sunflower seeds
>¼ cup sesame seeds

3 cups cooked brown rice
1 cup mixed dried fruits, chopped

2 cups cubed cheese

☞ Heat a large skillet. Add the oil and vegetables and sauté 5 minutes. Add the seeds and sauté 2 or 3 minutes more.
Add the cooked rice and fruits. Add a little water or stock if needed to heat rice. Heat through.
Pour all into 2 quart baking dish. Add the cubes of cheese and poke them into the mixture.
Cover and bake just until the cheese melts—5 to 10 minutes at 350°.

The seeds and fruits give this simple dish a surprising and delicious flavor.

CHEESE SOUFFLÉ

SERVES 4
3 tablespoons butter or
*   unrefined corn germ oil*
3 tablespoons whole wheat flour
dash of cayenne

1 cup milk
1 teaspoon sea salt
1 teaspoon prepared mustard
½ pound sharp cheddar cheese, diced

6 eggs, separated

☞ Melt the butter over low heat. Stir in the flour. Cook 1 minute. Add a little cayenne pepper, salt, and mustard to taste.
Slowly add the milk, stirring constantly. Cook until smooth and thick. Add the cheese. Stir until it is melted. Remove from the heat.
Beat the egg yolks. Stir them into the cheese sauce. Beat until well blended. Cool until lukewarm or cooler.

Beat the egg whites until stiff. Mix a large spoonful into the sauce. Now fold the sauce into the remaining whites.
Pour gently into a buttered 1½ quart soufflé dish. Bake 20 to 25 minutes at 350°.

VARIATION:
1 cup creamed cottage cheese may be used instead of the cheddar. Reduce the number of eggs to 3 or 4.

MUSHROOM SOUFFLÉ

SERVES 4–6
5 eggs, separated

½ pound fresh mushrooms

2 tablespoons butter
½ cup diced onion

2 tablespoons whole wheat pastry flour
½ cup water
½ teaspoon sea salt
¼ teaspoon ground thyme
⅛ teaspoon ground white pepper

3 tablespoons butter
3 tablespoons flour

1½ cups milk

¼ teaspoon cream of tartar

Separate eggs, putting whites in large bowl, yolks in small bowl. Keep at room temperature 1 hour.
Rinse, pat dry, and chop mushrooms (makes about 2½ cups); set aside.
In a large skillet heat 2 tablespoons of the butter. Add the onion and sauté 2 minutes; add the mushrooms and sauté 5 minutes, stirring occasionally.

Meanwhile, mix 2 tablespoons of the flour with water. Add to the mushroom mixture along with salt, thyme, and white pepper. Cook 2 minutes, stirring constantly; set aside.

In a medium saucepan melt remaining 3·tablespoons butter. Stir in remaining 3 tablespoons flour and cook until lightly browned. Gradually stir in milk. Cook and stir until thickened; cool.

Beat egg whites with cream of tartar until stiff but not dry. Beat egg yolks until pale yellow.

Stir egg yolks into sauce mixture. Blend in sautéed mushrooms. Fold mushroom mixture into beaten egg whites. Turn into a well-buttered 2 quart soufflé dish. Bake in a preheated, moderate oven (375°) for 1 hour. Serve at once.

WELSH RAREBIT DELIGHT

YIELD: ENOUGH FOR 12 SERVINGS

6 tablespoons butter
1 teaspoon sea salt
½ teaspoon red pepper
1 teaspoon paprika
1 teaspoon prepared mustard
1 tablespoon tamari soy sauce
1 pound grated natural cheddar cheese

1 cup flat beer

½ cup flat beer
3 eggs, beaten

Garnish: 6 large black pitted olives

☞ Melt butter in top of double boiler, add seasonings and cheese, and stir with wooden spoon until cheese is melted.

Add 1 cup of beer slowly, stirring constantly.

Mix remaining beer with eggs and add to cheese mixture. Stir until smooth.

Serve on triangles of rye or wheat toast. Garnish with black olives split in half.

Serve with stir fry spinach and sliced tomatoes.

COOKING WITH BEAN FLAKES

Some recipes call for dry, uncooked flakes. Others require cooked flakes. Whether cooking is needed depends on the type of bean flakes. Soybean and pinto bean flakes usually require precooking. However, even when flakes must be cooked, the necessary cooking time is always much less than for whole grains. Soy and pinto flakes cook in 45 minutes to 1½ hours instead of the several hours required to cook the dry beans. Always cook flakes *without* seasonings so that they may be added to anything from desserts to the spiciest casseroles. Cook up a quantity of flakes and freeze the excess for later use.

During cooking, the skins of the bean flakes separate and rise to the top. They are a nutritious part of the flakes and should be stirred back in. Sometimes, however, the skins may be skimmed off, leaving the beautiful meat of the beans. Save the skins and use them in mixed grain dishes or casseroles.

After studying the following recipes you will be able to incorporate flakes into many of your own dishes.

BLAZING STAR TIMBALES

SERVES 6

2 tablespoons unrefined oil
½ to 1 cup green onions, finely chopped
¾ cup tomatoes, chopped in small pieces

2 eggs, beaten
1 cup fresh milk beaten with ¼ cup
   non-instant dry milk powder

2 cups toasted whole wheat bread cubes
1 cup cooked soybean flakes
½ teaspoon sea salt or
   2 teaspoons tamari soy sauce

☞ Heat a small, heavy skillet on medium heat. Add oil, onions, and tomatoes and sauté 5 minutes.

Mix with the eggs and milk.

Fold in bread cubes, soy flakes, and salt.

Fill individual oiled custard cups. Bake 20 to 30 minutes at 350° or until set.

SLOPPY JOE MIX

SERVES 6–8

4 tablespoons unrefined oil
1 onion, thinly sliced
1 cup dry pinto bean flakes or
   soybean flakes or a mixture of both

1 cup raw brown rice
1 cup homemade tomato sauce
1 teaspoon dry mustard or
  2 teaspoons prepared mustard
1 teaspoon sea salt
dash of pepper
3 cups hot water

grated cheese

☞ Heat a large, heavy skillet on medium heat. Add the oil, onion, and bean flakes and sauté 5 minutes on low heat.

Add all other ingredients except cheese. Cover and simmer 45 minutes to 1 hour or until the rice is done. Check occasionally. Add 1 cup more water if necessary.

Serve as a thick stew or on buns. Top with grated cheese.

SUNFLOWER CASSEROLE

SERVES 4–6

>2 tablespoons unrefined oil
>2 cups whole grain flakes
> (wheat, rye, rice, triticale, oat, or a
> mixture)
>
>¼ teaspoon sea salt
>2½ cups water
>
>1 tablespoon unrefined oil
>2 onions, chopped
>1 green pepper, chopped
>1 stalk celery, sliced
>2 tablespoons chopped parsley
>2 cloves garlic, minced
>¼ cup hulled sunflower seeds
>
>1 teaspoon cumin, powder or ground seed
>2 tablespoons tamari soy sauce

☞ Heat a saucepan. Add the oil and flakes and sauté 5 minutes. Add the water and the salt. Cover and simmer for 20 minutes. Meanwhile, sauté the vegetables and sunflower seeds in oil in the order given.

Mix the vegetables with the cooked flakes. Add the cumin and the tamari.

Bake in a 2 quart casserole dish for 25 to 30 minutes at 350°.

Serve with thick tamari sauce.

This is reminiscent of a turkey dressing. It is really delicious with the tamari sauce.

PASTA

HOMEMADE NOODLES

SERVES 6

    4 cups whole wheat pastry flour
    2 teaspoons sea salt

    4 eggs
    4 tablespoons unrefined olive oil
    ⅓ cup cold water

    arrowroot powder

☞ Mix the flour and salt in a large bowl. Make a large depression in the center of the flour mixture.

Mix the eggs, oil, and water. Pour into the center of the flour.

Work flour into the liquids by hand to make a stiff dough. (The dough may not take every bit of the flour.)

Place dough on unfloured board. Knead 10 minutes. Wrap the dough. Let rest at room temperature 1 hour.

Sprinkle the board with arrowroot powder. Roll ¼ of the dough out into a very thin rectangle. Gently fold the rectangle in half lengthwise. Fold in half again. Repeat with the rest of the dough. Cut the folded strips of dough crosswise into ¼ inch wide pieces. Unwind the strips. Lay them out on clean towels to dry. Cook after drying an hour or dry several hours longer and store, in closed containers, in the freezer.

MUSHROOMS AND NOODLES AU GRATIN

SERVES 6
> 1 cup Mornay sauce
> 1 cup medium cream sauce
> 1 tablespoon dry sherry
> 3 cups cooked, fine whole wheat noodles
> ½ cup mushrooms, sliced and sautéed
>
> 8 whole fresh mushrooms, sautéed
> ½ cup Parmesan cheese
> ¼ cup buttered bread crumbs
> paprika

☞ Mix sauces, sherry, noodles, and sliced mushrooms. Pour into buttered 2 quart casserole.

Place whole mushrooms on top. Mix Parmesan cheese and crumbs and sprinkle on top. Sprinkle with paprika.

VARIATIONS:
Rice or spinach can be substituted for the noodles for a good casserole, too.

Thick tomato slices sprinkled with clear French dressing and chopped parsley are good accompaniments. Serve broiled fresh pears for dessert.

NOODLES AND VEGETABLES WITH LEMON SAUCE

SERVES 4–6
> 2 tablespoons unrefined corn germ oil
> 1 onion, chopped
>
> 2 cups diced carrots
> 2 cups fresh shelled peas
>
> Optional: other fresh vegetables

½ cup water

juice of 1 lemon
1 teaspoon grated lemon rind
1 teaspoon sea salt

Optional: ½ teaspoon lemon thyme

2 tablespoons arrowroot powder
2 tablespoons cold water

1 8 ounce package of
 whole wheat noodles, cooked

☞ Heat a large saucepan on medium heat. Add the oil and onion and sauté for 5 minutes.
Add the carrots, peas, other vegetables, if desired, and water. Cover and simmer until tender.
Add lemon juice, lemon rind, salt, and lemon thyme if desired.
Dilute the arrowroot powder in the water and stir into the vegetable sauce. Simmer until thickened.
Serve over cooked noodles.

SPAGHETTI CASSEROLE

SERVES 5

>2 *cups boiling water*
>1 *package whole wheat or*
>   *buckwheat spaghetti*
>
>1 *tablespoon unrefined corn germ oil*
>1 *large onion, chopped*
>
>1 *cup mushrooms, sliced*
>1 *green pepper, chopped*
>6 *tomatoes, diced*
>½ *cup sliced olives*
>1 *teaspoon sea salt*
>2 *tablespoons tamari soy sauce*
>
>2 *cups grated cheese*

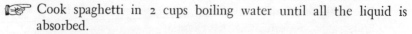 Cook spaghetti in 2 cups boiling water until all the liquid is absorbed.

Heat a skillet. Add the oil and onion and sauté until browned.

Mix all the ingredients except cheese and place in an oiled 2 quart casserole dish.

Cover and bake 30 minutes at 350°. Sprinkle the cheese on top and bake uncovered for 5 more minutes.

BAKED MACARONI AND CHEESE

SERVES 6

>4 *cups cooked whole wheat macaroni*
>   *tossed with 1 tablespoon unrefined oil*
>
>2 *eggs*
>1½ *cups milk or light cream*
>½ *teaspoon sea salt*
>1 *cup grated cheddar cheese*
>
>½ *cup grated cheddar cheese*
>½ *cup buttered bread crumbs*

Combine eggs, milk, salt, and ½ cup of cheese.
Toss with macaroni. Place in 1½ quart oiled baking dish.
Top with remaining cheese mixed with bread crumbs.
Bake 20 minutes at 350°.

MACARONI LAFAYETTE

SERVES 4–6
    2 cups boiling water
    2 cups whole wheat macaroni

    4 tablespoons unrefined oil
    4 tablespoons whole wheat flour
    1 small onion, finely chopped
    1 tablespoon tamari soy sauce
    2 teaspoons dry mustard
    1 teaspoon sea salt

    2 cups fresh milk

    1 pound cheddar cheese, grated (4 cups)
    3 or 4 ounces blue cheese, crumbled

    1 cup whole wheat bread crumbs
    (about 3 slices)

 Drop the macaroni into the boiling water. Cook until barely
tender, about 5 minutes. All the water should be absorbed. Place
the macaroni in a 2 quart baking dish.
Heat the oil in a saucepan. Stir in the flour, onion, tamari, mustard, and salt, stirring constantly until mixture simmers.
Slowly add the milk, stirring constantly. Cook until the sauce
thickens.
Add the cheeses. Stir until cheese melts. Pour the sauce over the
macaroni in the baking dish. Stir gently. Sprinkle the bread crumbs
over the top.
Bake 30 minutes at 350°.

GRAIN SIDE DISHES

Serve other protein foods with the following grain casseroles. These dishes are similar to pilafs and are excellent with vegetable protein dishes, egg and cheese dishes, or other proteins. Or serve them occasionally as main dishes accompanied by a crisp vegetable salad.

BARLEY WITH MUSHROOMS

SERVES 4
> 1 tablespoon unrefined sesame oil
> 1 onion, chopped
>
> 1 cup barley
>
> 3½ cups vegetable stock, or water
> ¼ teaspoon sea salt
>
> 2 tablespoons tamari soy sauce
>
> 2 tablespoons unrefined oil
> ¼ pound mushrooms, coarsely chopped
>
> Garnish: parsley sprigs

☞ Heat a skillet. Add the oil and the onion and sauté. Add the barley and sauté 5 minutes more.
Slowly add the stock and the salt. Cover and simmer about 1 hour until the barley is soft and most of the liquid is absorbed. Add the tamari and simmer 5 more minutes.
Sauté the mushrooms separately in 2 tablespoons oil. Then add them to the cooked barley. Mix and serve. Garnish with parsley.

CAJUN DELIGHT

SERVES 4–6

3 tablespoons unrefined oil
1 cup raw brown rice

3 cups boiling water

2 tablespoons unrefined oil
1 clove garlic, minced
1 onion, chopped
1 bell pepper, chopped
1 stalk celery, chopped
1 or 2 jalapeno peppers, finely chopped
½ to 1 cup sliced mushrooms

1 cup homemade tomato sauce
grated cheese, about ¼ cup

☞ Heat a heavy skillet. Add the oil and rice and sauté until rice is golden. Add the boiling water. Cover and simmer 25 to 30 minutes. Heat another skillet. Add the oil and chopped vegetables and sauté 5 to 10 minutes. Add the tomato sauce to the vegetables. Add the rice to the vegetables and simmer 5 more minutes. Top with grated cheese. Cover and steam until the cheese is melted.

COUNTRY PILAF

SERVES 6
> 2 tablespoons unrefined sesame oil
> 1 cup chopped fresh mushrooms
> 2 medium onions, chopped
> 1 cup chopped celery
> 3 cups cracked wheat or bulgur,
>   buckwheat, or millet
>
> ½ teaspoon cumin powder
> 5½ cups vegetable stock, or water
> 4 tablespoons tamari soy sauce
>
> Optional: ½ teaspoon coriander
>
> Optional: green pepper, parsley, scallion,
>   chopped carrots

☞ Preheat the oven to 300°. Heat the oil in a 2 quart casserole. Sauté the mushrooms, onions, celery, and wheat or other grains until the onion is transparent and the grain is lightly browned.
Stir in the spices, stock, and the tamari. Bring to a boil. Reduce heat, cover, and simmer 15 minutes. Add chopped vegetables if you wish.
Bake, uncovered, 30 to 40 minutes at 300°. The pilaf is done when all the grains are dry and separate.

ORANGE PILAF

SERVES 4
> ½ cup hulled millet
> juice of 2 oranges with added water,
>   to make a total of 1½ cups liquid
>
> ¼ teaspoon sea salt

⅓ *cup chopped peanuts or other nuts*
⅓ *cup raisins*
2 tablespoons raw honey
juice and grated rind of 1 orange
1 tablespoon unrefined sesame oil

Garnish: chopped, pitted dates

☞ Rinse the millet. Add orange juice and water to the millet and pour into a saucepan.
Bring to a boil. Reduce heat. Cover and simmer 30 minutes. Add the salt.
Chop peanuts and raisins together. Beat in honey, rind, orange juice, and oil. Add this mixture to the cooked millet. Toss. Garnish with chopped pitted dates.

VARIATION:
Brown rice may be used in place of the millet.

SESAME RICE

SERVES 4–6
    2 cups brown rice
    3 tablespoons roasted sesame seeds
    4 cups boiling water

    1 teaspoon sea salt or
     2 tablespoons tamari soy sauce

☞ Rinse rice. Add rice and sesame seeds to boiling water. Reduce heat. Cover and simmer 45 minutes to 1 hour.
Add salt or tamari to taste.

VARIATION:
Lightly roast the sesame seeds and add them to the cooked rice at the table.

RICE CROQUETTES

YIELD: 4 LARGE PATTIES

　　2 cups cooked brown rice, millet, or
　　　　buckwheat
　　½ cup leftover cooked cereal
　　½ teaspoon sea salt

　　1 egg, beaten
　　½ cup whole wheat flour

　　3 tablespoons unrefined safflower oil for frying

☞ Mix rice, cereal, and salt and form into patties.
Dip in beaten egg and then whole wheat flour.
Fry in hot oil in skillet until crisp on the bottom. Turn and fry
on the other side.
Serve with tamari.

VARIATIONS:
Diced, sautéed vegetables may be added, such as onions, carrots,
etc.
½ cup grated cheddar cheese may be added.

RYE BERRY CASSEROLE

SERVES 6

　　2 cups rye berries
　　3 cups water
　　½ teaspoon sea salt

　　1 tablespoon unrefined sesame oil
　　2 medium onions, diced
　　1 small purple cabbage, about 1 pound

☞ Wash the rye berries and drain. Place them in a pressure cooker, add the water and the salt, and bring to full pressure. Reduce heat and cook 45 minutes. Remove from heat and allow pressure to reduce to zero. Uncover and stir.

Heat a skillet. Add the oil and onions and sauté until transparent. Wash the cabbage and cut into 1″ square pieces. Add to the onions and sauté for 5 minutes. Cover and simmer until tender. Add water if necessary to prevent sticking.

Add the cooked vegetables to the cooked rye berries. Mix and place in an oiled 2 quart casserole. Season to taste with salt. Bake 15 minutes in a preheated oven at 350°.

A delicious combination.

LUNCH MENUS

Sunshine Carrot Salad
Mushroom Soufflé
Sautéed Sprouts
(Basic) Blueberry Muffins
Herb Tea
Carob Silk Pie

Quiche
Broiled Tomatoes sprinkled with Parmesan Cheese
Val Verde Salad tossed with Whole Wheat Croutons
and French Dressing
Apricot Soufflé
Herb Tea

W I N T E R
Vegetable Broth
Crab au Gratin in Whole Wheat Crêpes
Steamed Asparagus with Lemon Butter
Popovers
Apple Mousse
Hot or Iced Herb Tea

SUMMER
Cherry Fizz
Lime-Avocado Mold
Almond Chop Suey
Fruit Quartet

DINNER MENUS

French Onion Soup
Avocado and Grapefruit Salad
with Poppyseed Dressing
White Wine

Creamed Mushrooms in Rice Ring
Yellow Squash Stuffed with Tomatoes & Fresh Corn
Assorted Hot Breads
Hearts of Celery
Honey Peach Jam
Homemade Ice Cream

Cold Yogurt Soup
Grapefruit-Orange-Almond Salad Mold
Cheese Soufflé
Small Whole Wheat Pastry Shells
filled with Tiny Buttered Peas
Assorted Cookies
Herbed Tea

Cold Apple Juice with Fresh Lime
Pass: Olives Romano

Vichyssoise
Mixed Green Salad with French Dressing
Tomatoes filled with Spinach Vera Cruz
Stuffed Celery
Ruth's Rolls
Strawberry Ice Cream

Tengo Hambre

SOUTHWESTERN DISHES

The Southwestern and Western part of our country has great Spanish, Mexican, and Indian traditions. Many local dishes reflect these cultures. These dishes have universal appeal and are not limited to any region or nationality. Since indigenous Southwestern dishes have always included whole grains and beans, they are also a "natural" for the whole foods philosophy.

CHILI SAUCE

YIELD: 1½–2 CUPS

6 to 8 jalapeno peppers
1 onion, chopped
4 fresh tomatoes
2 teaspoons sea salt
½ teaspoon garlic powder or 1 clove garlic
dash of cumin powder

☞ Boil jalapenos until well done. Peel and remove stems. Blend or chop together the peppers and onions. Add tomatoes, salt, garlic, and cumin powder. Blend or chop together again.
Simmer the mixture until well done and thick.

Serve in a small dish with tostados for dipping. A little goes a long way since it is very hot.
Use sparingly on enchiladas or tacos.

ENCHILADA SAUCE

YIELD: 1½–2 CUPS
   ⅓ cup unrefined oil
   1 clove garlic, finely minced
   3 tablespoons whole wheat flour or
      corn meal

   2 tablespoons red chili powder
      dissolved in 4 tablespoons hot water

   Optional: 1 cup homemade tomato sauce

   water
   2 teaspoons sea salt

☞ Heat a deep sauce pan. Add the oil and garlic. Add the flour or corn meal and stir constantly until lightly browned.
Stir the dissolved chili powder into the flour mixture.
Continue stirring while adding the tomato sauce, if desired, and hot water to make the sauce as thick or thin as you wish. Add the salt.

COOKING GREEN CHILIS
   (Jalapenos)

☞ Roast the chilis over a low flame or on a hot griddle, turning them until most of the skin is loose. Plunge them into cold water. This will allow you to peel the skins off the chilis easily. Now they are ready to use, whole or chopped.

Another way to prepare chilis is to boil them in water about 3 to 5 minutes, or until the skin slips off easily.

Chilis may be broiled in the oven until blistered. Turn them often. Watch carefully to prevent burning. Drop in cold water. Peel.

If the chilis do not peel easily, they haven't been cooked long enough.

NIK'S GUACAMOLE

SERVES 4–6
> *2 to 3 avocados, quartered*
> *juice of 1 lemon*
> *1 clove garlic*
> *½ onion, sliced*
> *½ or 1 bell pepper*
> *½ cup homemade yogurt*
> *½ teaspoon chili powder*
> *1 teaspoon sea salt*

☞ Blend all the ingredients together in a blender. Chill.

Serve as a salad on lettuce leaves, a dip with corn munchies, or a garnish on chili. Also used in guacamole tacos.

MEXICAN SALAD

YIELD: ½ CUP OF BEANS WILL SERVE 1 PERSON
> *cooked pinto beans, drained*
> *chili powder to taste*
> *cumin powder to taste*
> *chopped onions*
> *grated sharp cheese*
> *homemade mayonnaise*
>
> *chopped lettuce*
> *corn chips*

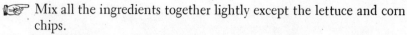 Mix all the ingredients together lightly except the lettuce and corn chips.

Just before serving, toss the bean mixture lightly with the lettuce and corn chips.

The amounts of all ingredients are up to you.

FRIJOLES
(Refried Beans)

YIELD: VARIES WITH THE AMOUNT OF BEANS
> 2 tablespoons unrefined oil
> 1 to 2 onions, chopped
> ½ green pepper, chopped
>
> leftover cooked beans, mashed
> ¼ to ½ cup grated cheese

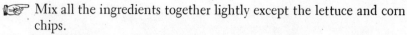 Heat a skillet. Add the oil, onion, and pepper and sauté. Add enough mashed beans to cover the bottom of the skillet. Cook 10 minutes, stirring occasionally.

Add the grated cheese and cover. Remove from heat when the cheese is melted.

RICE TORREÓN

SERVES 4
> 1 tablespoon unrefined oil
> 1 clove garlic, minced
>
> 1 cup raw long-grain brown rice
>
> 1 cup homemade tomato sauce
> 2 cups hot water
> 1 teaspoon sea salt

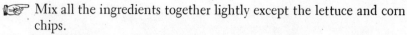 Heat a skillet. Add the oil and the minced garlic. Sauté briefly. Add the rice and roast until golden.

Add the tomato sauce, hot water, and salt.
Bring to a boil. Cover and simmer about 45 minutes until the rice
is tender.

DEEP FRIED SQUASH BLOSSOMS

SERVES 4
   8 squash blossoms

   Batter: ½ cup whole wheat flour
   *   ½ cup corn meal*
   *   ½ teaspoon sea salt*
   *   1 to 1¼ cups water*

   unrefined safflower oil for deep frying

☞ Mix batter ingredients lightly. Chill for half an hour.
   While batter is chilling, wash and pat dry squash blossoms. When
   ready to cook the blossoms, dip them in the batter and fry in
   hot oil until golden and crisp. Drain on paper towels.

CHILEQUILES

SERVES 6
   2 tablespoons unrefined oil
   2 medium onions, chopped
   1 clove garlic, minced

   4 cups tomatoes, chopped
   sea salt
   ½ cup green chili peppers, chopped

   ½ cup unrefined vegetable oil
   1 dozen tortillas cut in fourths

   2 pounds Monterey Jack cheese, grated

   1 pint homemade sour cream
   dash or two of paprika

☞ Heat a heavy skillet. Add 2 tablespoons oil, onions, and garlic and sauté.

Add tomatoes, salt, and green chili peppers and sauté 5 minutes more.

Heat ½ cup oil in heavy skillet. Dip tortilla strips in the hot oil. Remove immediately and drain on paper towel.

In a glass (2 quart) baking dish make alternate layers of tortillas, tomato mixture, and cheese until all ingredients are used, finishing with grated cheese.

Bake 15 to 20 minutes at 350° or until heated through. Top with sour cream and a sprinkle of paprika and watch this dish disappear.

BAKED CHILI RELLENOS

SERVES 4–6

8 to 10 long (5 or 6 inches) green chiles
  (mild)
10 ounces jack cheese, grated

5 eggs, well beaten
2 tablespoons butter
½ teaspoon sea salt
½ teaspoon pepper
½ teaspoon cumin powder

☞ Roast, peel, and seed the chili peppers. Layer them alternately with the grated cheese in a deep, buttered 1½ quart casserole dish. Mix the beaten eggs, butter, salt, pepper, and cumin powder. Pour this mixture over the peppers and cheese. Bake 35 to 40 minutes at 350°.

This is a spicy, soufflé-like dish.

ARROZ Y PINTOS ENCHILADAS

SERVES 6
YIELD: 20 ENCHILADAS

2 tablespoons unrefined oil
2 onions, chopped

1 *large green pepper, chopped*
1 *stalk celery, finely chopped*
1 *carrot, finely chopped*

1½ *cups cooked brown rice*
½ *teaspoon sea salt*

Optional: 1 *or* 2 *jalapeño peppers,*
              finely chopped

3 *teaspoons chili powder, or to taste*
sea salt to taste
3 *cups cooked pinto beans with*
  1 *to* 2 *cups bean juice*

½ *to* 1 *cup unrefined oil for*
    softening tortillas
20 *corn tortillas*
grated cheese

Garnish: *chopped fresh onions*
            more grated cheese
            chili and tomato hot sauce

☞ Heat a large, heavy skillet on medium heat. Add the oil and chopped vegetables and sauté 5 minutes.
Add the cooked rice and salt, mix well, and heat through. Add the jalapeños if desired or mix them with the beans if you'd rather.
Add the chili powder and salt to the beans and juice in a saucepan. Heat through.
Dip one tortilla in a skillet containing a small amount of very warm oil just until the tortilla softens.
Fill the tortilla with a heaping tablespoonful of the rice and vegetable mixture. Sprinkle on grated cheese. Roll the tortilla around the mixture. Place in a long baking dish. Continue until all the tortillas are filled.
Pour the seasoned bean mixture over the tortillas. Sprinkle with grated cheese. Bake at 350° until hot through.
Serve with lots of grated cheese and hot sauce or onions.

This delicious recipe was a happy accident—a combination of desperation and leftovers.

MAVERICK CHILI

SERVES 6

    1 cup soybeans
    1 cup whole grain wheat
    6 cups water

    2 tablespoons unrefined oil
    1 clove garlic, minced
    1 teaspoon chili powder
    ½ teaspoon cumin powder
    ¾ teaspoon ground red chili powder
    ¼ teaspoon oregano
    2 onions, chopped
    2 jalapeno green chilies, chopped
    4 tomatoes, chopped

    tamari soy sauce or sea salt, pepper

    Garnish: grated cheese
                  chopped green onions

☞ Soak beans and wheat overnight in the water. Next day, pressure cook them for 2 hours or pot cook them for 3 or 4 hours. (If you pressure cook them use very low heat and an asbestos pad to prevent their foaming up and clogging the vent.)
Stir the oil and seasonings into the beans. Add the vegetables to the beans. Simmer until the beans and wheat are tender.
Season with tamari or salt, and pepper.
Garnish with grated cheese and chopped green onions.

Serve this chili with guacamole salad, tostados, and plenty of extra cheese and chili sauce. Better serve a bowl of plain yogurt for those who want to "cool" their chili.

GUACAMOLE TACOS

MAKE 1 OR 2 PER PERSON
> *taco shells*
>
> *guacamole*
>
> *lettuce, shredded*
> *onions, chopped*
> *tomato, chopped*
> *cheese, grated*
>
> *Optional: sprouts*
>
> *hot chili and tomato sauces*

☞ Starting with the guacamole, layer the ingredients in the taco shells.
Add the hot sauce last.

TACOS

SERVES 6
> *2 cups simple tomato sauce with extra*
> *chopped onions*
> *2 cups cooked, drained soybean flakes, or*
> *cooked whole soybeans and/or pinto*
> *beans, or cooked lentils*
> *4 to 6 jalapeno peppers, chopped and*
> *sautéed in 1 tablespoon oil (or 1 small*
> *can chopped green chilis)*
> *2 to 4 teaspoons chili powder*
> *¼ teaspoon cumin powder*
> *1 teaspoon sea salt*
>
> *12 ounces cheese, grated*
> *20 taco shells*
> *4 cups salad greens, chopped*
>
> *grated cheese*
> *hot sauce*

Simmer the tomato sauce, bean flakes, peppers, and seasonings for 5 minutes.
Layer the bean mix and grated cheese in the shells.
Bake 5 minutes at 350°.
Add chopped fresh greens to the other ingredients in the shells.
Serve immediately with more grated cheese and hot sauce.

TAMALE SOY PIE

SERVES 8

FILLING
1 tablespoon unrefined corn germ oil
1 onion, chopped
2 cloves garlic, finely chopped

4 tomatoes, chopped
¼ cup green pepper, chopped
1 cup homemade tomato sauce
1 tablespoon chili powder
1½ teaspoons sea salt
¼ cup sliced, ripe olives

4 cups cooked soybeans or cooked
  soybean flakes

 Heat a heavy skillet. Add the oil, onion, and garlic and sauté.
Add the tomatoes, pepper, tomato sauce, chili, salt, and olives.
Simmer 10 minutes.
Add the soy beans and simmer on low heat while preparing the crust.

CRUST
¾ cup stone-ground corn meal
1 cup milk

2 cups milk
1 tablespoon unrefined corn germ oil
1 teaspoon sea salt

2 beaten eggs

Garnish: grated cheese

☞ Combine corn meal and 1 cup milk.
Bring 2 cups milk, oil, and salt to boil. Slowly add the corn meal mixture, stirring constantly. Simmer until thick. Cover and cook on lowest heat for 15 minutes.
Stir in beaten eggs.
Finally, line the bottom of an oiled 2 quart casserole with the crust mixture, reserving 1½ cups for topping.
Add the filling. Add the remaining corn meal mixture over the top. Sprinkle with ½ cup grated cheese.
Bake 30 minutes at 350°. Serve with more grated cheese.

This is a hearty party dish that teenagers will enjoy especially.

SOPA DE TORTILLA

SERVES 4–6

4 cups tamari bouillon or
* vegetable broth*
¼ teaspoon garlic powder
½ teaspoon oregano
1 small bunch fresh parsley, chopped
1 or 2 tomatoes, chopped

5 corn tortillas, cut in strips and toasted
2 to 4 green chili peppers,
* chopped and sautéed*

☞ Cover and simmer the bouillon, garlic, oregano, parsley, and tomatoes for 30 minutes.
Add the tortillas and green chilis and serve immediately.

Tortilla soup is tasty soup to serve before a Mexican dinner. Make a colorful centerpiece with a piece of pottery and bright paper flowers. Bring the soup to the table in a Mexican pottery tureen (available almost everywhere now at surprisingly low prices). Follow it with a "do-it-yourself" taco supper.

CHALUPAS

MAKE 1 OR 2 PER PERSON
   corn tortillas

   cooked pinto beans, mashed to a paste
      with sea salt and chili powder to taste

   finely chopped cooked green chilis
   tomatoes, chopped
   green onions, chopped
   lettuce or fresh greens, chopped
   sliced avocados

   grated cheese

☞ Brush the tortillas with oil. Bake them 5 minutes at 350° until crisp.
Spread the crisp tortillas with the bean paste.
Sprinkle the other foods on top, avocado slices last.
Add grated cheese.

NACHOS

MAKE 4 NACHOS (1 WHOLE TORTILLA) PER PERSON
   tortillas
   unrefined safflower oil for deep frying

   cheddar cheese
   jalapeno pepper, cut in strips

☞ Cut the tortillas in quarters and deep fry them.
Top each quarter with a piece of cheddar cheese and a strip of jalapeno pepper. Bake 8 to 10 minutes at 350°. Pass while hot.

Nachos are one of the most popular tidbits in the Southwest.

CORN TORTILLAS

YIELD: 12–15
   1 cup stone-ground corn meal
   (yellow, white, or blue)
   1 cup boiling water

2 to 2½ cups whole wheat flour
½ teaspoon sea salt

☞ Pour the boiling water over the corn meal. Let sit 10 minutes or more.
Mix salt and whole wheat flour. Add enough flour to the corn meal mixture to make a kneadable dough. Knead 5 to 10 minutes. Let sit 5 minutes.
Pinch off a piece of dough the size of a golf ball. Roll it out on a floured board to a more or less round shape about 4 inches in diameter. Cook on an unoiled hot griddle or in a skillet, about 2 minutes on each side. You can salt the griddle to keep the tortilla from sticking, but it is not really necessary.

FLOUR TORTILLAS

YIELD: 2 DOZEN
4 cups whole wheat pastry flour
1 teaspoon sea salt

⅓ cup unrefined oil
1 cup warm water (approx.)

☞ Mix flour and salt.
Add oil and work, mixing together with your fingertips.
Stir in enough water to make a firm ball of dough.
Knead until smooth. Let sit 20 minutes.
Follow directions in Corn Tortillas for rolling out.

PURÉ DE AGUACATE
(Avocado Cream)

SERVES 4
2 large avocados
juice of 1 lime
2 tablespoons raw honey
2 teaspoons milk or cream

Blend all ingredients to consistency of heavy mayonnaise.

Serve chilled in sherbet glasses (with topping if desired).

Follow a spicy dinner with this delightful, cool dessert.

PUDÍN

SERVES 8

> 1 cup sprouted wheat flour or
>   whole wheat pastry flour
> 4 cups water
>
> 8 ounces (2 cups) pitted dates
>
> 1 cup pecans
> ¼ teaspoon sea salt
>
> cinnamon
> sunflower or toasted sesame seeds

 Stir the water into the flour gradually. Simmer 30 minutes, stirring often.
Pour half the mixture into a blender with the dates and blend until the mixture is creamy. Pour into a bowl.
Blend the remaining mixture with the pecans and salt. Pour into a bowl with the first mixture. Stir well.
Pour into individual serving dishes. Dust with cinnamon and sprinkle with sunflower seeds or toasted sesame seeds. Chill.

SOPAPILLAS

YIELD: 1 DOZEN SMALL SOPAPILLAS

> ½ cup whole wheat pastry flour
> ¾ teaspoon sea salt

2 eggs
1 cup milk
1½ to 2 cups more flour

unrefined safflower oil for deep frying

☞ Sift the dry ingredients together.
Beat the eggs well and add milk. Stir in the dry ingredients and add as much more flour as the mixture will absorb. Roll out ¹⁄₁₆ to ⅛ inch thick. Cut in squares and fry in deep oil until golden brown.

When done the sopapillas will be nice and fluffy. Break open and serve with honey or jelly. Great as the final touch to a wonderful Mexican dinner!

A FIESTA PARTY

Let's have a South of the Border fiesta! Big paper flowers in vivid colors or clay pots of red geraniums like the ones which grow so prolificly south of the border can help set the mood. Mexican music on the stereo and a gay piñata suspended in a doorway provide a land of mañana atmosphere—and natural foods make up an authentic menu.

MOCK SANGRIA
GUACAMOLE *with* CORN CHIPS

CHILI CON QUESO *with* TOSTADOS
in chafing dish

TACO SHELLS—*on hot plate*
Choice of filling—Refried beans with onions,
Chopped lettuce and tomato, Grated natural
cheddar cheese, Spoon or two of guacamole
to make a super-taco

MINIATURE CHALUPAS *and* LITTLE NACHOS
can be passed piping hot.

BIG CASSEROLE OF CHILIQUILES *(kept hot)*

SOPAPILLAS AND SMALL CUPS OF GRAIN COFFEE
FOR DESSERT

The Bread Board

Why make bread? Because it's *so* good! And if you make it yourself, you know what you're getting. Homemade bread can be a tremendous plus in your family's nutrition. It can supply the rich variety of trace minerals and vitamins possessed by the complete whole grain plus the added bonus of other concentrated nutrients you may choose to include. You eat more bread and grain products than you realize. Why not make them nutritional assets?

A beautiful loaf of homemade whole wheat bread is guaranteed to garner you more compliments at your next dinner party than the most elaborate entrée or flaming crepes or whatever the *pièce de resistance* is. If you really want to make an indelible impression on your guests, serve homemade hamburger buns and all the fixings. There is something about homemade buns that excites the most jaded gourmet taste.

Fortunately, bread making is really easy once you learn the simple principles and realize that the whole process can be fitted around your schedule and not vice versa. If you're new at the game, perhaps you should start with quick breads. Soon you'll want to move on to yeast, sourdough, and unleavened breads, for they are truly creative ventures.

189

Remember, everything that is brown is *not* 100 percent whole grain flour. Many "whole wheat" flours are actually refined white flours with a little bran added to make them look "real." They may even be artificially colored. Bread made from that kind of flour is no better than white bread. Be sure the flour you buy is labeled "100 percent stone-ground." Try to find a store that will grind the whole grain fresh while you watch, or buy brands that are explicitly labeled.

QUICK BREADS

Quick breads are so named for the obvious reason that they can be made on the spur of the moment. They usually rise by virtue of the baking powder included, but "quick" yeast breads are also possible if you use enough yeast. You may wish to omit all leavening and fold in stiffly beaten egg whites for lightness.

When baking powder is called for, always use low-sodium baking powder—store bought or homemade—which is free of both sodium and aluminum compounds. Baking soda (sodium bicarbonate) destroys B vitamins and Vitamin C. And aluminum is toxic to the body. When using yeast in quick breads, omit the baking powder and dissolve 1 to 3 packages of dry active yeast in some of the liquid. The more yeast used, the less rising time required before baking.

Quick breads lend themselves to the addition of concentrated nutrients and fortifiers—noninstant milk powder, wheat germ, nutritional yeast—as well as fruits, nuts, and other goodies.

Important: Stir quick breads only enough to mix the ingredients well. Do *not* beat.

HOMEMADE BAKING POWDER
(Low Sodium)

1 part potassium bicarbonate
2 parts cream of tartar
2 parts arrowroot powder

☞ Mix well. Store in airtight jar so that baking powder will not lump. Sift into each recipe.

Use this baking powder in the same proportions as any other.
If potassium bicarbonate is not available at your drugstore, ask
your pharmacist to order it for you.
This baking powder is free of sodium and aluminum compounds.
Low-sodium baking powders are also available at natural food
stores.

FLAKY BAKING POWDER BISCUITS

YIELD: 12 BISCUITS

2 cups sifted whole wheat flour
3 teaspoons low-sodium baking powder
½ teaspoon sea salt

⅓ cup unrefined corn germ oil

⅔ cup fresh milk

☞ Sift dry ingredients together.
Rub in the oil.
Add the milk. Stir until dough cleans the bowl. Knead lightly 15
times. Roll out ½ inch thick on floured board. Cut with biscuit
cutter. Place the biscuits touching each other on an oiled cookie
sheet. Bake 12 to 15 minutes at 400°.

VARIATION:
Substitute yogurt for the milk.
Add 1 tablespoon grated Parmesan cheese, 2 tablespoons chopped
chives, and 1 clove garlic, finely minced.

BOSTON BROWN BREAD

YIELD: 3 LOAVES

    1 cup whole wheat flour
    1 cup rye flour
    1 cup stone-ground corn meal
    3 teaspoons low-sodium baking powder
    1 teaspoon sea salt

    ¾ cup unsulfured molasses
    1¾ cups sweet milk or 2 cups buttermilk

    1 cup raisins and/or 1 cup pecans

Mix the dry ingredients.

Blend the molasses and the milk. Add to the dry ingredients and mix well.

Add the raisins and the nuts.

Fill 3 well-oiled number 2 cans ¾ full. Cover with oiled foil and secure with string. Place on a trivet in a kettle with enough boiling water to cover cans half-way up. Place cover on kettle. Add boiling water when necessary. Steam for 3½ hours. To unmold, place in cold water for a few seconds before turning out of can. Cool on rack. Slice and serve with butter.

CRANBERRY BREAD

YIELD: 1 9 X 5 INCH LOAF

    2 cups whole wheat flour
    1½ teaspoons low-sodium baking powder
    ½ teaspoon sea salt

    Optional: ¼ cup non-instant milk powder

    juice of 1 orange
    2 tablespoons unrefined safflower oil
    enough hot water to bring liquid
       ingredients to ¾ cup mark

¾ *cup raw honey*
1 *egg, beaten*

1 *cup broken nut meats*
1 *cup whole, raw cranberries*

Optional: 1 *tablespoon grated orange rind*

☞ Mix the flour, baking powder, salt, and milk powder.
Mix the orange juice, oil, and water. Add the honey and egg to the liquid.
Stir the liquid ingredients into the dry mixture.
Add the nuts and berries and fold together.
Pour into an oiled loaf pan. Bake at 325° 50 minutes to 1 hour. Cool on a rack.

This is a delicious Thanksgiving or Christmas bread. Slice thinly and serve plain or lightly buttered.

JALAPENO CORNBREAD

SERVES 6–8
    1 *cup stone-ground corn meal*
    ½ *cup whole wheat flour*
    2 *teaspoons unsulfured molasses*
    2 *teaspoons low-sodium baking powder*
    ½ *teaspoon sea salt*
    2 *eggs*
    1 *cup milk*
    1 *onion, grated*
    2 *jalapeno peppers, chopped*
    ¼ *cup unrefined corn germ oil*
    1 *cup corn (kernels from 3 ears)*
    1 *cup grated sharp cheese*

☞ Mix all the ingredients and pour into an oiled, hot 8 x 8 inch pan. Bake at 375° for 40 minutes or until brown and crisp on top. Eat hot.

SOUTHERN CORNBREAD

SERVES 6–8
> *3 cups stone-ground corn meal*
> *1 teaspoon sea salt*
> *3 tablespoons unrefined corn germ oil*
>
> *2 cups boiling water*
>
> *1 cup milk*
>
> *1 egg, beaten*
> *3 teaspoons low-sodium baking powder*

☞ Mix the corn meal, salt, and oil together.
Pour boiling water over the corn meal mixture and stir until well mixed.
Add the milk to the mixture and set aside to cool, about 40 minutes.
When cool, stir in the egg and baking powder. Pour into a hot, well-oiled 8 x 8 inch pan or muffin tins.
Bake at 425° for 30 to 40 minutes. Eat hot.

DATE NUT BREAD

YIELD: 1   9 x 5 INCH LOAF
> *2 cups whole wheat pastry flour*
> *2 teaspoons low-sodium baking powder*
> *1 teaspoon cinnamon*
> *½ teaspoon sea salt*
>
> *4 tablespoons butter*
> *⅓ cup raw honey*
>
> *½ teaspoon vanilla*
> *2 eggs, beaten*
>
> *½ cup milk*
> *1 cup chopped dates*

½ cup chopped and lightly roasted
   walnuts
2 teaspoons grated orange rind

☞ Sift the flour, baking powder, cinnamon, and salt together.
Cream the butter and the honey together.
Add the vanilla and beaten eggs to the butter and honey.
Alternately add the flour mixture and the milk to the butter mixture. Fold in the dates, nuts, and orange rind. Pour into an oiled loaf pan and bake at 325° for 1 hour and 15 minutes. Cool on rack.

OATMEAL-HONEY LOAF

YIELD: 1   9 X 5 INCH LOAF
   1 cup oat flakes
   1 cup boiling water

   2¼ cups whole wheat pastry flour
   2½ teaspoons low-sodium baking powder
   1 teaspoon sea salt
   5 tablespoons non-instant dry milk powder

   ¼ cup melted butter or
      unrefined corn germ oil
   3 tablespoons raw honey

   1 egg
   ⅔ cup water

☞ In a large bowl, combine the oats and boiling water, stirring until well mixed. Cool for about 2 hours.
In another bowl sift together pastry flour, baking powder, salt, and dry milk.
Add the butter and honey to the oatmeal mixture. Mix well with a wooden spoon.
In a small bowl, beat 1 egg with ⅔ cup water. Add the flour mixture. Then add this mixture to the oatmeal mixture until combined. Do not overmix.

Turn into an oiled loaf pan. Bake at 350° for 70 minutes, until the crust is golden. Turn onto rack to cool. Eat while warm or toasted with honey butter.

SWEET 'N SIMPLE LOAF

YIELD: 1   9 X 5 INCH LOAF
   1 or 2 eggs
   1 cup milk
   1 tablespoon melted butter or
      unrefined oil
   ½ cup pure maple syrup, raw honey, or
      unsulfured molasses

   3 cups whole wheat flour, or a mixture of
      whole wheat flour and rye flour, or
      whole wheat pastry flour
   2 teaspoons low-sodium baking powder
   1 teaspoon sea salt

   ½ cup raisins, chopped dried fruits, or
      chopped nuts or seeds

☞ Beat eggs, milk, butter, and syrup together.
   Mix flour, baking powder, and salt and stir into the liquids.
   Fold in fruit or nuts.
   Pour into an oiled loaf pan. Bake at 350° for 1 hour. Cool on rack.

APPLE MUFFINS

YIELD: 24 LARGE MUFFINS
   1 cup raw honey
   1 cup unrefined oil
   4 eggs

   2½ cups whole wheat flour
   2 teaspoons low-sodium baking powder

½ *teaspoon sea salt*
1 *teaspoon allspice*
1 *teaspoon nutmeg*
1 *teaspoon cinnamon*
½ *cup noninstant dry milk powder*

1¾ *cup grated apple, including peel*
   (2 *large apples*)
1 *teaspoon vanilla*

Optional: 1 *cup raisins and chopped nuts*

☞ Beat the honey, oil, and eggs.
Mix all dry ingredients. Add to honey mixture. Stir well.
Add and fold together the apple and vanilla, and the raisins and nuts.
Bake at 400° for 12 to 15 minutes. Remove from tins to cool.

These moist muffins were introduced by a favorite baby sitter. They delight adults as well as children.

STARR MUFFINS

YIELD: 3–4 DOZEN MUFFINS
   2 *cups stone-ground yellow corn meal*
   1¼ *cups whole wheat pastry flour*
   1 *cup soy flour*
   3 *tablespoons wheat germ*
   2 *tablespoons low-sodium baking powder*
   1 *teaspoon sea salt*

   2 *cups milk*
   1 *cup unrefined safflower oil*
   1 *cup raw honey*
   4 *eggs*

☞ Mix the dry ingredients.
Beat all the liquid ingredients together. Stir the 2 mixtures to-

gether. Refrigerate overnight. The batter should be "loose"—some-what thin.

Pour into oiled muffin tins. Bake 15 to 20 minutes at 400°. Remove from tins to cool.

This recipe was developed by a professional baker. These muffins are better than cake.

WHOLE GRAIN MUFFINS

YIELD: 10–12 MUFFINS

    1 cup mixed whole grain flours
    (⅓ cup buckwheat flour,
    ⅓ cup soy flour, and
    ⅓ cup rice flour or ½ cup
    whole rye flour and ½ cup
    whole wheat flour)
    1 rounded teaspoon low-sodium baking
    powder
    ½ teaspoon sea salt

    1 tablespoon unrefined safflower oil

    1 egg, beaten
    1 cup buttermilk
    1 tablespoon unsulfured molasses

☞ Mix dry ingredients.
Work in oil with fingers or pastry blender.
Add beaten egg, buttermilk, and molasses and stir well.
Fill oiled muffin tins a little more than half full. Bake at 450° for 17 minutes. Serve hot.

VARIATIONS:
1. Use fresh orange juice for the liquid. Add ½ cup chopped nuts.
2. Use the grated rind and juice of one lemon in place of part of the liquid. Increase the sweetening if desired.
3. Add ½ cup drained blueberries or raisins to the batter.

HERB DUMPLINGS

YIELD: 18 DUMPLINGS
   soup stock, simmering

   2 cups sifted whole wheat flour
   2 or 3 teaspoons low-sodium
      baking powder
   1 teaspoon sea salt

   2 eggs
   enough milk over eggs to make
      1 cup liquid

   2 tablespoons unrefined corn germ oil
   1 tablespoon chopped parsley

   Optional: ½ teaspoon thyme,
              ¼ teaspoon marjoram

☞ Sift flour, baking powder, and salt together.
Break eggs in measuring cup. Add milk to 1 cup mark. Add oil, parsley, and other herbs, if desired.
Mix all ingredients well.
Have soup stock simmering. Drop dumplings by spoonful into stock. Don't let them touch. Cover tightly and cook 2 minutes. Turn the dumplings and cook 2 minutes longer. Serve hot.

LIGHT BREADS WITHOUT LEAVENING

The following breads and muffins do not contain baking powder or yeast. They depend on stiffly beaten egg whites or whole eggs for lightness.

BANANA NUT BREAD

YIELD: 1   9 X 5 INCH LOAF
   2 cups whole wheat pastry flour
   ¼ teaspoon sea salt

   ½ cup unrefined oil
   ½ cup pure maple syrup

   4 eggs, separated

   2 tablespoons milk
   3 ripe bananas, mashed
   ½ cup chopped walnuts

☞ Mix flour and salt.
Blend in oil and maple syrup.
Beat in egg yolks and mix well.
Add milk and mashed bananas and fold in chopped nuts.
Beat egg whites until stiff and fold in.
Turn into an oiled loaf pan.
Bake at 350° for 50 minutes. Cool on rack.

POPOVERS

YIELD: 8–10 POPOVERS
   1 cup whole wheat pastry flour
   ¼ teaspoon sea salt
   2 eggs
   1 cup milk
   1 tablespoon unrefined oil

☞ Preheat oven to 425°. Heat glass, earthenware, or cast iron muffin pan.
Combine all ingredients in a bowl, beat with a rotary beater until smooth.
Remove pan from oven and oil well. Immediately, while pan is still very hot, fill cups a little less than half full and return to oven at once.

Bake about 35 minutes in preheated oven, until sides are rigid to the touch. Serve immediately.

SAVANNAH SPOON BREAD

SERVES 4

½ cup soy flour
1½ cups stone-ground corn meal

3 cups water

1 teaspoon sea salt
3 tablespoons unrefined corn germ oil
3 eggs, separated

☞ Mix the corn meal and soy flour together in a saucepan.
Stir the water in slowly to prevent lumping, and cook over a medium heat, stirring constantly, until boiling. Remove from heat and cool to lukewarm.
Add salt, oil, and egg yolks.
Beat egg whites until stiff and fold them in gently.
Pour into an oiled 2 quart casserole. Bake 40 to 45 minutes at 400°.
Serve hot.

YEAST BREADS

The thought of homemade bread always brings back memories of that good yeasty odor coming from the kitchen and the sight of a high crusty loaf cooling on a rack. That thing of beauty is the result of the expansion of gases released by the yeast's action and the stretching of the gluten in the wheat. Mixing the ingredients is very simple and the rising is self-starting, but things really start to happen when you dig in with both hands and "work" the dough.

There *is* a proper way to knead bread dough. But if you're not proper don't worry too much—just do the best you can. To knead correctly, place the dough on a floured board; fold a big corner of dough toward you and push down and away with the heels of your hands. Give the dough a quarter turn and repeat the motion. Continue until the dough is smooth and elastic. Kneading is one of those things you have to gain a feel for, so have a friend show you how. Bread making just can't be described clinically.

Your first attempt may look pretty sad, or it may turn out beautifully. Try *not* to overcook the bread, and it will probably taste great.

The breads included here will work with little or no kneading. However, the texture of your breads will always be better if the dough is kneaded—even 5 minutes will help.

HINTS FOR BREAD MAKING

Bread making's easy when you know the tricks.

Beginners often have trouble getting whole grain breads to rise. If this is your problem, use a little extra yeast. After you get the feel of kneading these breads, reduce the amount of yeast. Kneading should not be a time-consuming affair. Five minutes is usually sufficient.

Every flour and every bag of flour has a slightly different moisture content, so you may have to increase or decrease slightly the amount of flour kneaded into the dough.

If you can't be at home during the day, let the dough rise in the refrigerator. It will rise very slowly and will be ready to shape into loaves when you get home.

Cool breads before slicing unless you can't resist that first loaf hot out of the oven. Slice the loaves before freezing. When you need fresh bread, frozen slices pull apart easily and thaw quickly. Always save the crumbs when you slice homemade bread. Store them in a covered container in the freezer until you need them.

Save work and don't wash the bread pans. Bread pans used only for baking bread don't need washing. Or do without bread pans altogether by shaping free-form loaves on cookie sheets.

CHALLAH
(Jewish Egg Bread)

YIELD: 1 LOAF

4 teaspoons dry yeast or
1⅓ cakes fresh yeast
½ cup water, warm
1 teaspoon pure maple syrup

3 to 3½ cups whole wheat flour
1 teaspoon sea salt

3 eggs
¼ cup unrefined corn germ oil

poppy or sesame seeds

☞ Have all ingredients at room temperature.

Dissolve the yeast in water; add the maple syrup and mix well. Sift the flour and salt into a bowl.

Separate yolk from 1 egg and reserve. Then add the white to remaining eggs and corn oil. Beat well and add to the yeast mixture. Add ½ of the flour to the liquid and mix. Add remaining flour and mix well. Knead on lightly floured board for 10 to 15 minutes until dough is soft and pliable.

Then form dough into a ball and place in an oiled bowl. Turn dough to coat with oil. Cover bowl with a plate and let dough rise in warm place for about 45 minutes, until double. Punch down and let rise 30 minutes.

Punch down again and divide into 3 equal pieces. Roll each piece into a ball, then into strands of equal length. Sprinkle the strands with flour and braid them, tucking the ends neatly under the braid. Place the bread on a cookie sheet sprinkled with corn meal or in an oiled bread loaf pan.

Add 1 teaspoon water to the reserved egg yolk, mix, and brush the top of the loaf. Sprinkle with seeds before the bread starts to rise.

Cover and let rise 45 to 60 minutes, until not quite fully risen. Bake in preheated oven at 375° 30 to 40 minutes or until golden brown.

CHEESE BATTER BREAD

YIELD: 1   9 X 5 INCH LOAF
   ¾ cup warm milk or water
   ¼ cup unrefined oil
   1 tablespoon raw honey
   3 eggs, beaten

   2½ cups whole wheat flour
   1 package (1 tablespoon) active dry yeast
   1½ teaspoons sea salt
   ¼ cup toasted sesame seeds
   2 cups (8 ounces) grated cheddar cheese

☞ Mix the milk, oil, honey, and eggs.
Mix half the flour, the yeast, salt, sesame seeds, and cheese. Add to the liquid mixture. Beat 3 or 4 minutes. Work the remaining flour in by hand.
Cover the dough and let rise 45 minutes to 1 hour.
Shape into a loaf and place in a well-oiled 9 x 5 inch loaf pan. Press extra sesame seeds into the top of the loaf. Bake 45 minutes at 350°. Cool on a rack.

CUMIN BREAD

YIELD: 2   9 X 5 INCH LOAVES
   ¼ cup unrefined oil
   ¼ cup raw honey
   2 teaspoons sea salt
   2 cups hot milk
   ½ cup apple juice

   ¼ cup warm water
   1 teaspoon raw honey
   2 tablespoons dry yeast

   1 egg, beaten

6 cups whole wheat flour
1 cup rye flour
1 tablespoon ground cumin, or more
to taste

☞ Combine oil, honey, salt, milk, and juice. Cool to lukewarm.
Dissolve the yeast and honey in warm water and let sit 5 minutes.
Add to the milk mixture.
Add the egg.
Mix the flours and cumin and beat into the liquids.
Turn the dough out on a floured board and knead in more flour
for 5 minutes to make a smooth dough.
Put the dough in a well-oiled bowl. Turn the dough to coat with
oil. Cover. Let rise until double, about 1 hour.
Punch the dough down. Knead 1 more minute. Place in the oiled
bowl again and turn to coat. Cover and let rise 30 minutes.
Divide and shape into two loaves. Place in oiled loaf pans. Cover
and let rise until double.
Bake 10 minutes at 425°. Lower the heat to 350° and bake 25 to
30 minutes more. Cool on a wire rack. Brush the crust with oil.

DILLY BREAD

YIELD: 2   9 X 5 INCH LOAVES
2 tablespoons dry yeast
½ cup warm water

2 cups creamed cottage cheese with a
little milk to fill in the spaces
2 tablespoons raw honey
2 tablespoons unrefined oil
4 tablespoons minced onion, or more
to taste
2 teaspoons dill seed
2 teaspoons sea salt
2 eggs, beaten

5 cups whole wheat flour (approximately)

☞ Dissolve the yeast in the warm water in a large bowl.

Mix the cottage cheese, milk, honey, oil, onions, dill, salt, and eggs in a saucepan. Heat all to lukewarm. Add to the yeast mixture. Stir well.

Add the flour, adding a little more water or a little less flour if necessary to make a soft dough.

Allow the dough to rise 1 hour. Knead down to about ½ the amount. Shape into 2 loaves. Place in 2 oiled pans. Allow to rise 40 minutes more.

Bake 30 to 40 minutes at 350°. Cool on rack.

A great party bread. Try it with herb spreads.

PEASANT BREAD

YIELD: 2   9 x 5 INCH LOAVES
(no shortening or oil in this bread)

2 cups milk
1 cup water
2 teaspoons sea salt
3 tablespoons unsulfured molasses

2 tablespoons dry yeast
1 cup stone-ground yellow corn meal
6 cups whole wheat flour

1 cup whole wheat flour

☞ Mix the liquids, salt, and molasses. Heat them to lukewarm.

Add the yeast and flours. Mix well and let rest 10 minutes.

Knead the dough in 1 more cup of flour for 5 minutes. Place in an oiled bowl. Cover. Let rise until double.

Knead again for a short time. Shape into 2 loaves.

Place in oiled loaf pans. Let rise again until doubled.

Bake 15 minutes at 375°. Lower the temperature to 350°. Bake 30 minutes more. Place on a rack to cool. Brush the crusts with oil. Cover with a towel while cooling.

The corn meal gives this bread a slightly crunchy texture.

PHYLLIS' BREAD

YIELD: 2   9 x 5 INCH LOAVES
2½ cups warm water
2 tablespoons dry yeast

3 tablespoons unrefined corn germ oil
4 tablespoons raw honey or
  unsulfured molasses

5½ to 6 cups whole wheat flour
1½ teaspoons sea salt

☞ Dissolve the yeast in the warm water.
Add the oil and honey.
Mix the flour and salt. Add the liquids. Mix well with hands, adding a little more flour if needed.
Cover and let rise until double (about 1½ hours). Knead down. Shape the dough into 2 loaves. Place in oiled loaf pans. Allow to rise again until nearly doubled.
Bake 10 minutes at 400°. Reduce the heat to 350° and bake 20 minutes more. Cool on rack.

VARIATION:
Substitute 1 cup cracked wheat for 1 cup flour.

This is a simple, delicious bread. It works well for beginners or old hands.

MORGAN COUNTY RYE BREAD

YIELD: 2   9 X 5 INCH LOAVES
1½ *cups boiling water*
¾ *cup stone-ground corn meal*

1 *cup cold water*
1 *teaspoon sea salt*
3 *tablespoons unsulfured molasses*
4 *tablespoons unrefined corn germ oil*

1 *tablespoon dry yeast for heavy rye bread*
   or 2 tablespoons dry yeast for a lighter
   bread
¼ *cup warm water*

2 *cups mashed cooked potatoes*

3 *cups rye flour*
1 *cup coarsely ground rye meal or*
   1 *additional cup rye flour*
4 *to 5 cups whole wheat flour*
2 *tablespoons caraway seeds*

☞ Pour boiling water over the corn meal and mix. Let stand 10 minutes.
Add cold water, salt, molasses, and oil. Cool to lukewarm.
Dissolve the yeast in the water and let sit for 5 minutes.
Add the mashed potatoes and yeast to the corn meal and let sit 5 minutes more.
Add the rye flour, rye meal, caraway seeds, and enough whole wheat flour to make the dough kneadable.
Knead on a floured board, adding more flour if the dough is too sticky.
Place in a well-oiled bowl and let the dough rise until it doubles in bulk, about 1½ hours.
Divide the dough into 2 parts. Shape into loaves and place them in oiled pans or make free-form loaves on oiled cookie sheets. Let rise 30 minutes.
Bake 1 hour at 375°. Cool on rack.

SWEDISH RYE BREAD

YIELD: 1   1LB. LOAF
> 1 tablespoon dry yeast or
>   1 cake fresh yeast
> 1 cup warm water
> 3 tablespoons unrefined safflower oil
> 3 tablespoons unsulfured molasses
>
> 1½ cups whole wheat flour
> 1 tablespoon orange rind
> 1½ teaspoons fennel seed, ground
> 1 tablespoon anise seed, ground
> 1 teaspoon sea salt
>
> 1¼ cups stone-ground rye flour

☞ Have all ingredients at room temperature.

Dissolve the yeast in water. Stir in the oil and molasses and set aside.

Blend seasonings with the wheat flour and mix with the yeast liquid.

Add the rye flour and mix together well.

Knead on a lightly floured board until the dough is pliable and soft (about 10 to 15 minutes). Shape into a ball and place in an oiled bowl. Turn to coat the dough. Cover the bowl with an airtight lid and let rise in a warm place for 1 hour.

Punch down, form into a tight ball, and place on a cookie sheet sprinkled liberally with corn meal. Cover with a large bowl and let rise in a warm place (30 to 45 minutes). After 10 minutes of rising slash the top of dough with a knife to allow it to rise better. Bake in preheated 375° oven 30 to 35 minutes. Cool.

SHELLEY'S SURPRISE BREAD

YIELD: 2   9 X 5 INCH LOAVES OR 2 ROUND 6 INCH LOAVES
1 *cup warm water*
2 *cakes fresh yeast or 2 tablespoons*
   dry yeast

¾ *cup milk*
¾ *cup water*
1 *tablespoon sea salt*
½ *cup raw honey*

3 *eggs, beaten*
½ *cup unrefined corn germ oil*
7 *cups stone-ground whole wheat flour*

Optional: ½ *cup wheat germ*
          ½ *cup cracked wheat*
          (Pour 1½ *cups hot water*
          over the wheat and soak for
          1 *hour or more. Drain the*
          wheat before using. Save
          the water and use for part
          or all of the water listed.)
          ¼ *cup non-instant milk*
          powder, mixed with the
          dry flour

☞ Dissolve the yeast in the warm water.
Stir in milk, water, salt, and honey.
Add the eggs, oil, and half the flour. Mix well, then add remaining flour by working with hands.
Turn the dough on to a lightly floured board. Allow dough to rest for about 10 minutes (while you clean up). Knead for 5 minutes. Place in oiled bowl. Cover the dough with a damp cloth and allow it to rise until doubled. Punch down and let rise again for 30 minutes more.
Divide dough in half. Shape the dough into 2 loaves. Place in oiled loaf pans or shape into round loaves and place on oiled

baking sheets. Cover the loaves with a damp cloth and let rise until double.

Optional: Oil loaves lightly or glaze with 1 egg yolk beaten with 2 tablespoons of cold water.

Bake 30 to 40 minutes at 350°. Cool on rack.

The crusts will stay soft if you wrap the loaves in plastic or wax paper as soon as they are cool enough to touch, or wrap them in dish towels after removing from the oven.

According to Shelley, the surprise is that Shelley can cook at all.

SPROUTED WHEAT BREAD

YIELD: 2   9 X 5 INCH LOAVES
   3 cups lukewarm water
   1 tablespoon dry yeast

   ¼ cup unsulfured molasses or raw honey
   4 tablespoons unrefined oil
   1 teaspoon sea salt
   4 cups whole wheat flour

   2 cups wheat sprouts (more can be used)
   3 to 4 cups whole wheat flour

Dissolve the yeast in the water.

Add the molasses, oil, salt, and flour. Beat well. Let rise for 1 hour.

Add the wheat sprouts (ground in a food grinder or hand grain mill) to the raised sponge.

Add additional flour to make the dough kneadable. Knead well on a floured board.

Place the dough in an oiled bowl. Cover with a damp cloth. Let rise until double in bulk, about 1 hour.

Punch down and form into 2 loaves and place in oiled loaf pans. Let rise about 30 minutes.

Bake 1 hour at 350°. Cool on rack.

SUNFLOWER BREAD

YIELD: 2   9 X 5 INCH LOAVES
   2 tablespoons dry yeast
   2 cups whole wheat flour

   2½ cups milk
   1 tablespoon sea salt
   2 tablespoons unrefined oil
   ¼ to ½ cup raw honey

   4 cups whole wheat flour
   1 cup sunflower seeds, or chopped
      pumpkin seeds, or raisins.

☞ In a large bowl mix 2 cups of the flour with the yeast.
Heat the milk, salt, oil, and honey to lukewarm. Add the liquid to
the flour-yeast combination and beat 2 minutes.
Add the remaining flour and the seeds or raisins, and work in by
hand. Knead the dough 5 to 10 minutes on a floured board.
Place the dough in an oiled bowl, turning to coat the dough.
Cover and let rise until doubled, about 2 hours.
Punch the dough down. Divide it in half and shape into 2 loaves.
Place in oiled loaf pans. Cover and let rise until double, about 1
hour.
Bake 40 to 45 minutes at 375°. Cover loosely with foil during the
last 15 minutes of baking. Turn loaves out on a rack to cool.

VARIATIONS *(Fruit Breads)*:
Prune bread: Add 1 cup chopped, pitted prunes to dough.
Apricot bread: Soak or cook dried apricots before chopping. Then
                add 1 cup chopped, drained apricots to the dough.

TRITICALE BREAD

YIELD: 2   9 X 5 INCH LOAVES
   1 tablespoon dry yeast or 1 cake fresh
      yeast
   ¼ cup warm water

¼ *cup raw honey*
4 *tablespoons unrefined oil*
1¾ *cups milk*

1 *tablespoon sea salt*
3 *cups whole wheat flour*
3 *cups triticale flour*

☞ Dissolve the yeast in warm water and let sit for 5 minutes.
Combine the yeast, honey, oil, and milk.
Mix the salt and the flour and sift into the liquids. Stir until
smooth. The dough should be soft to the touch. Handle as little
as possible. Let the dough rise until double in bulk. Knead and
let rise again.
Shape into 2 loaves. Place in oiled loaf pans. Bake 50 to 60
minutes at 350° to 375° or until browned. Cool on rack.

VEGETABLE BATTER BREAD

YIELD: 1 ROUND LOAF 7 INCHES IN DIAMETER
    4 *cups whole wheat flour*
    1 *tablespoon dry yeast*
    2 *teaspoons sea salt*

    ¼ *cup raw honey or*
        unsulfured molasses
    2 *tablespoons unrefined oil*
    1 *egg, beaten*
    1½ *cups hot water or vegetable stock*

    1 *cup cooked buckwheat or*
        other cooked whole grain
    1 *large carrot, grated*
    ¼ *cup fresh chopped parsley*

    Optional: 2 *cups fresh alfalfa sprouts*

☞ Combine the flour, yeast, and salt in a large mixing bowl. Mix
well.

Add the honey, oil, egg, and water. Stir well until all ingredients are thoroughly mixed.
Let the dough rest 10 minutes.
Stir in the cooked grain and the vegetables.
Place the dough in an oiled 2 quart casserole. Let rise in a warm place until almost doubled—about 45 minutes to 1 hour.
Bake 45 minutes to 1 hour at 350°. Cover loosely with foil for the last half hour of baking. Turn out on a rack to cool.

BUCKWHEAT MUFFINS

YIELD: 12 MUFFINS
> 1½ cups buckwheat flour
> ½ cup whole wheat pastry flour or
>   whole wheat flour
> 1½ teaspoons cinnamon
> ½ teaspoon sea salt
>
> 1 egg
> ¼ cup unrefined corn germ oil
>
> 2½ cups water
> 1 teaspoon dry yeast dissolved in
>   ½ cup warm water
> ½ cup raisins

☞ Mix the flours, cinnamon, and salt together.
In a separate bowl beat the egg in the oil. Add to the flour mixture.
Add yeast and water and raisins to the flour mixture. Mix well.
Let sit for 15 minutes or more.
Fill oiled muffin tins ¾ full. Bake 20 to 30 minutes at 400°.

Serve hot with honey, apple butter, or jelly.

MAPLE NUT ROLLS

YIELD: 2 DOZEN ROLLS

1½ *cups lukewarm water*
1 *tablespoon dry yeast*
¼ *cup pure maple syrup or raw honey*

3½ *to* 4 *cups whole wheat flour*

1 *teaspoon sea salt*
¼ *cup unrefined corn germ oil*

1 *cup raisins*
1½ *cups whole wheat pastry flour*

1 *cup chopped walnuts*
½ *cup pure maple syrup*

☞ In a large bowl, combine the water and the yeast. Stir until it dissolves and add ¼ cup maple syrup or honey.

Stir in the whole wheat flour, beating with "fold-in" strokes. Try not to tear the dough, but try to incorporate air into it. Beat about 50 strokes. Cover the bowl with a cloth and set in a warm place to rise for 1 hour.

Fold in the salt and oil until thoroughly mixed.

Add the raisins and the pastry flour. Knead on a floured board until smooth and elastic. Place the dough in an oiled bowl, oil the top, and cover. Set in a warm place to rise for 40 minutes. Punch down.

Roll out ¾ inch thick. Cut in 2 inch rounds. Put maple syrup and nuts into 2 small bowls and dip each roll first into the maple syrup and then into the nuts. Place them nut side down on a cookie sheet about ¼ inch apart. Cover with a cloth and let rise for 20 minutes.

Bake 25 minutes at 350°. When done, turn over to serve.

SUNDAY ROLLS

YIELD: 2 DOZEN ROLLS
  2 tablespoons dry yeast
  1 cup lukewarm water

  1 cup hot water
  ¼ cup to ½ cup raw honey
  ¾ cup unrefined oil
  2 teaspoons sea salt
  2 eggs, beaten

  6 cups whole wheat flour

☞ Dissolve the yeast in the warm water. Let sit 5 minutes until bubbly.
Mix the hot water, honey, oil, and salt until the honey is completely dissolved. Add the eggs. Stir well. Add the yeast.
Add the flour. Mix well.
If the dough is to be used immediately, add ½ cup more flour. Shape the dough into any type rolls. Allow to rise. Bake 10 to 12 minutes at 425°.
This dough is more easily handled after chilling until firm. Then shape the dough into rolls. Allow to rise. Bake 10 to 12 minutes at 425°.

After shaping, the raw rolls may be frozen. Allow 3 hours from freezer to oven.

ENGLISH MUFFINS

YIELD: 14–18 MUFFINS
☞ Use dough for Sunday Rolls.
Roll out the chilled dough ½ inch thick on a board sprinkled with cornmeal.
Cut into 3 inch rounds. Let rise 20 to 30 minutes.
Transfer the muffins with a spatula to a hot, ungreased griddle.
Bake 5 to 7 minutes on each side, or until brown, over medium to hot heat.

"HAMBURGER" BUNS

YIELD: 14–18 BUNS

☞ Use Sunday Rolls dough or any good roll dough.
Roll the chilled dough out to a thickness of ½ inch (not thinner).
Cut the dough with a 6 ounce baking custard cup.
Place the buns on an oiled cookie sheet allowing room for sideways expansion. Allow to rise.
Bake 10 to 12 minutes at 400°.

SWEET ROLLS

YIELD: 2 DOZEN ROLLS
chilled Sunday Roll dough

raisins
chopped nuts
cinnamon

raw honey
butter

☞ Roll the chilled dough into fairly thin large rectangles.
Sprinkle the dough with raisins, chopped nuts, and cinnamon.
Heat the honey and butter until well blended. Drizzle over the dough.
Roll like a jelly roll. Cut in 1 inch slices. Place close together and let rise on oiled cookie sheet or long pan.
Bake 15 minutes at 400°.

CINNAMON DOUGHNUTS

YIELD: 30–40 LARGE DOUGHNUTS
8 cups whole wheat pastry flour
1½ tablespoons cinnamon
½ teaspoon sea salt

2¾ cups lukewarm water
1 tablespoon dry yeast

¼ cup unrefined corn germ oil
½ cup unsulfured molasses or
    raw honey

2 cups whole wheat pastry flour

unrefined safflower oil for deep frying

☞ Mix the flour, cinnamon, and salt in a large bowl.
Sprinkle the yeast into warm water and stir gently until the yeast is dissolved.
Add the corn germ oil and molasses or honey to the yeast mixture, stirring constantly.
Add the liquids to the flour in the bowl. Stir with a long wooden spoon until the ingredients are very well blended.
Spread 2 cups more pastry flour on a board and place the dough on it. Scrape remaining dough from sides of bowl and add to dough on board. Oil the bowl.

Knead the dough for 15 minutes or until it is very smooth.

Place the dough in the oiled bowl. Cover with a damp cloth and allow to rise in a warm place for 1 hour. Punch the dough down and let rise 30 minutes more.

Roll the dough out on a lightly floured board and cut with a doughnut cutter.
Heat 3 inches of safflower oil in deep pan for 5 to 10 minutes over a medium-high flame. If the oil starts to smoke, it is too hot.

Fry the doughnuts about 1 minute on each side. Drain on paper towels.

FROZEN BAKED GOODS:

HOT BREADS AND CAKES EVERY DAY

Have flavorful, nutritious hot yeast breads every day. Enjoy more free time and save energy by using yeast dough prepared especially for the freezer. You can anticipate holidays and company dinners happily when you know that there will be enough freshly baked loaves, rolls, coffee cakes, fruit rolls, etc., that need only to be taken from the freezer and baked. Another advantage—frozen dough takes less space than baked items.

WHOLE WHEAT BREAD

YIELD: 3 9 X 5 INCH LOAVES OR 3 DOZEN ROLLS
   2 tablespoons dry yeast
   3 cups warm water

   ½ cup unrefined corn germ oil
   ½ cup unsulfured molasses
   2 teaspoons sea salt
   1 beaten egg

   8 cups whole wheat flour

☞ Sprinkle yeast into warm water and stir until dissolved.
Add the oil, molasses, salt, and egg. Blend well.
Add half the flour and beat with a wooden spoon until smooth.
Work the remaining flour in with the hands.
Turn dough out onto a lightly floured board and knead until smooth and elastic.
Place in an oiled bowl and turn to oil all sides of the dough. Cover with wax paper and a tea towel. Set in a warm place, free from drafts, until double in bulk, about 1 hour or longer. Punch down.

Divide the dough into thirds and shape into loaves. Place in well-oiled pans and let rise in a warm place until nearly double in bulk. Bake 15 minutes at 400°. Remove immediately from pans and set on racks to cool. Freeze loaves. Finish baking when needed.

To Freeze:
Place pan with shaped loaf in a freezer bag and seal. This dough is excellent for freezing. It will keep in the freezer up to 4 weeks, but it is best if baked within 2 weeks.

To Bake Frozen Dough:
Remove from freezer and unwrap.
Place in a 250° oven for 45 minutes or until dough is double in bulk.
Raise temperature to 400° and bake for 35 minutes. Remove from pan and set on rack to cool.

RUTH'S BROWN AND SERVE ROLLS

YIELD: 4–5 DOZEN ROLLS
  3 *cups warm water*
  2 *tablespoons dry yeast*
  ¼ *cup unsulfured molasses*
  ¼ *cup unrefined corn germ oil*
  1 *egg, beaten*
  1 *tablespoon sea salt*

  7 *to 8 cups whole wheat flour*

☞ Have all ingredients at room temperature.
Stir the water, yeast, molasses, oil, egg, and salt until well blended. Gradually add the flour and knead until smooth.
Place the dough in an oiled bowl. Turn to coat the dough. Cover and let rise in a warm place until double in bulk. Punch down. Shape the dough into desired rolls and place in oiled muffin tins. Allow rolls to rise until double in size.
Bake for 40 minutes in a preheated oven at 275°. Remove from the oven. Let rolls cool in the tins for 20 minutes. Remove from tins and cool to room temperature. Wrap in freezer plastic and place in freezer.

These rolls will keep 1 week unrefrigerated, 2 weeks in the refrigerator, and 3 months in the freezer.

Refrigerator Rolls: When ready to serve, unwrap and place on an unoiled cookie sheet. Bake 8 to 10 minutes at 400° or until brown.

Freezer Rolls: Unwrap frozen rolls and place on cookie sheet. Put directly into the oven to brown without thawing first.

BASIC SWEET DOUGH

YIELD: ABOUT 3 COFFEE RINGS, OR ABOUT 2 LBS. OF ROLLS

2 cups warm milk
2 tablespoons dry yeast

½ cup unrefined safflower oil
⅔ cup raw honey
2 teaspoons sea salt
3 beaten eggs
grated rind and juice of 1 lemon

8 cups whole wheat flour
½ teaspoon of ground nutmeg,
   mace, or cardamom
1½ cups chopped nuts, raisins, citron,
   dates, etc., if desired

☞ Sprinkle yeast into milk. Stir until yeast is dissolved.
Add oil, honey, salt, eggs, and grated rind and lemon juice. Stir well.
Stir in flour and spice. Dough should be softer than for loaf bread.
Place the dough on a lightly floured board and knead. Put in an oiled bowl. Turn to oil the surface. Cover and let rise in a warm place until double in bulk. Punch down.
Shape into coffee cakes, cinnamon rolls, tea rings, twists, braids, etc. Brush with butter. Let rise until almost doubled.
Bake in 350° oven.

Bake some now, freeze some for company.
Wrap shaped breads, cakes, or rolls in freezer wrap and freeze. They will keep up to 4 weeks but are best when baked within 2 weeks.

HONEY TWIST COFFEE CAKE

YIELD: 1   8 x 8 INCH CAKE
   ¼ *Basic Sweet Dough*
   ¼ *cup butter*
   ½ *cup raw honey*
   1 *egg white*

   Garnish: chopped nuts

☞ Roll dough into a long rope about 1 inch in diameter. Coil in an oiled 9 inch layer cake tin, beginning at the outer edge and covering the bottom.
Cover and let rise until double in bulk. Bake at 350° for 20 minutes or until brown.
Cream the butter with the honey and stir in the egg white. Spread the mixture over the hot twist.
Sprinkle with chopped nuts.

To freeze: After shaping twist, wrap in freezer plastic and seal. Bake within 10 days. Unwrap and thaw 20 minutes at 200°. Raise temperature to 350° and bake 20 minutes more. Spread with honey and nut topping.

APRICOT TEA RING

YIELD: 1 TEA RING
   ¼ *Basic Sweet Dough*
   butter, melted

   1½ *cups cooked, honey-dipped,*
      dried apricots
   cinnamon

   butter, melted
   chopped pecans

☞ Roll dough into rectangle about ½ inch thick and 8 inches wide, any length.

Brush with butter and spread with the cooked apricots. Sprinkle with cinnamon.

Roll up like a jelly roll, sealing edge securely. Form into a ring on an oiled baking sheet. With scissors, cut through almost to center in slices about 1 inch thick. Turn each slice on its side, slightly overlapping the next slice. Brush lightly with butter. Let rise until double in bulk.

Bake 25 to 30 minutes at 350°. Brush with butter and sprinkle with chopped pecans. .

To freeze, seal ring in freezer wrap and place in freezer. Bake within 10 days for best results. Unwrap and thaw 20 minutes at 200°. Raise temperature to 350° and bake 20 minutes more. Brush with butter and sprinkle with nuts.

CINNAMON APPLE LOAF

YIELD: 2   9 X 5 INCH LOAVES
¼ *Basic Sweet Dough*

2 *tablespoons soft butter*
2 *teaspoons cinnamon*

2 *apples, finely chopped*
½ *cup chopped walnuts*
grated rind of 1 orange
1 *tablespoon orange juice*
⅔ *cup raw honey*
1 *tablespoon whole wheat flour*

Garnish: butter
      toasted sesame seeds

☞ Roll out dough on a floured board to a 11 x 15 inch rectangle, spread with soft butter, and sprinkle with cinnamon.

Combine apples, walnuts, grated orange rind and juice, honey, and flour. Spread on dough.
Starting with the 15 inch side, roll like a jelly roll and seal edges. Cut roll in half to form 2 shorter rolls.
Place each half in a well-oiled 9 x 5 inch loaf pan. Cut with scissors into 10 slices each.
Cover; let rise in a warm place until double in bulk, about one hour or more.
Bake at 350° for 40 minutes or until browned. Remove from pan. Brush with butter and sprinkle with toasted sesame seeds.

To freeze and bake: Place pan of shaped and sliced dough in freezer plastic and seal. For best results, bake within 10 days. Unwrap and thaw at 250° for 45 minutes or until double in bulk. Raise temperature to 400° and bake 35 minutes. Remove from pan. Cool on rack.

RAISIN NUT ROLLS

YIELD: 1 DOZEN SMALL ROLLS
¼ *Basic Sweet Dough*

¼ *cup raw honey*
¼ *cup butter*

½ *cup chopped nuts and raisins*
cinnamon

☞ Roll gently into a rectangle ¼ inch thick, 15 inches wide, and any length.
Brush with the mixture of honey and butter.
Sprinkle with chopped nuts and raisins. Dust lightly with cinnamon.
Roll up like a jelly roll, sealing long edge firmly.
Cut crosswise into 1 inch slices. Place close together, cut side up, in shallow, oiled pan. Brush top with more butter and dust with cinnamon.

Let rise until double in size. Bake about 25 minutes at 350°, depending on the size of the rolls.

These rolls freeze well. Bake within 10 days for best results. Unwrap frozen rolls and thaw 20 minutes at 200°. Raise temperature to 375° and bake 20 minutes or until brown.

SOURDOUGH BREADS

Sourdough bread is really the easiest and most dependable bread you can make. The total time needed to make sourdough bread is fairly long, but during most of that time the dough is taking care of itself.

The taste of the bread depends to a great extent on the starter. Make your own starter or get some from a friend. Passing sourdough starter around is a neighborly thing to do.

Sourdough also makes great rolls and pancakes. Take some starter along on your next camping trip.

MAKING YOUR OWN SOURDOUGH STARTER

½ package dry yeast or
½ cake fresh yeast
1 cup lukewarm water

1 cup whole wheat pastry flour
(any whole grain flour can be used,
but the pastry flour works quickest)

Dissolve yeast in water and let sit for 10 to 15 minutes.
Slowly add the flour and mix well. Place in scalded jar or crock. Let sit at room temperature for several days, until fermented and bubbly.
Stir well and refrigerate. Starter is now ready to feed for making bread.
Starters sometimes separate, especially after being refrigerated 2

or 3 weeks. The starter is still alive. Just stir it well when feeding it. Occasionally the liquid that separates will turn dark. This does not harm the starter, but you may pour off the darkened liquid if you wish.

The longer a starter ferments the stronger it tastes. The longer a starter is stored without being used, the stronger it tastes. It is best to keep your starter in shape by using it every week or 10 days.

FEEDING YOUR SOURDOUGH STARTER

1 cup starter from last time
(or from a friend)
2 cups warm water
2 cups whole wheat pastry flour

☞ Always use a ceramic or earthenware bowl to let the starter rise in. Never use metal.

Beat all the ingredients together with a fork. Do not leave the fork in the starter.

Let sit overnight.

Return at least 1 cup of the starter to the refrigerator in an airtight jar. Be sure to leave extra space in the jar for expansion.

Add more than 2 cups each of water and flour to the starter, especially if you're planning to make pancakes in the morning.

The ready-to-use starter should be the consistency of thick pancake batter.

SOURDOUGH BREAD

YIELD: 2 9 x 5 INCH LOAVES
1 cup sourdough starter
2 cups warm water
1 to 4 tablespoons raw honey
1 tablespoon sea salt
½ cup unrefined oil (or less)

6 cups whole wheat flour

Feed your starter the night before. Let it sit overnight.
Use a large ceramic or crock bowl.
Beat all the ingredients except the flour together. Add the flour.
Mix well by hand if necessary.
Cover the dough and let it rise 3 to 4 hours or until doubled. In
summer it may take less time.
Shape the dough into 2 loaves, kneading a little as you shape them.
Place in oiled loaf pans. Let rise 1 to 2 hours until doubled. The
bread will rise a little more while cooking.
Bake 30 to 40 minutes at 350°. Turn out on a rack to cool.

Use this recipe to make biscuits, rolls, or buns.
When the recipe is doubled, it does *not* make twice as much
dough, and therefore will not be quite sufficient for 4 loaves.

SOURDOUGH BAGELS

YIELD: 15
    2 cups sourdough starter
    4½ cups whole wheat flour
    1 teaspoon sea salt
    3 tablespoons unrefined oil
    ½ cup warm water

    Optional: 1 egg

    Glaze: oil, or egg mixed with water

 Add flour, salt, oil, and water (and egg if desired) to the starter.
Knead well. Cover and let rise for 3 hours in a warm place in an
oiled bowl.
Knead again and shape into rings by rolling dough like bread
sticks and pinching ends together, or roll out ½ inch thick with
a rolling pin and cut with a doughnut cutter. Let rise for 1½
hours.
Drop bagels into a large pot of boiling water (2 or 3 at a time).
When they rise to the surface, turn them over and boil 1 minute
longer.

Put boiled bagels on an oiled baking sheet. Brush with oil or beaten egg mixed with water.
Bake at 350° for about 50 minutes or until golden brown.

UNLEAVENED BREADS

Unleavened bread is the most basic bread of all. It is easy to make because it contains only the simplest ingredients. It is a tight textured bread, chewy and delicious. A loaf goes a long way when sliced thin with a very sharp knife. Make this bread when you're feeling earthy.

HINTS FOR UNLEAVENED BREAD

1. Always use warm liquid.
2. Adding fresh sprouts to the dough shortens rising time. It is best to grind the sprouts before adding, but it is not absolutely necessary.

UNLEAVENED BREAD

YIELD: 1 LOAF
1⅔ cups water
4 cups whole wheat flour (approximately)

☞ Put water in a large bowl. Add 3 cups of flour. Stir. Add the last cup of flour gradually, stirring until the batter is too stiff to stir. Knead in remaining amount of flour. Knead about 20 times, until the water and flour are well mixed. Shape into loaf as you knead. Oil a small loaf pan. Place the loaf in the pan. Cover with a damp towel and let rise in a warm place for 24 hours. In the summer rising time is less, depending on the temperature. (This does not apply to air-conditioned homes, of course.) The towel should be kept damp throughout the rising time.
Bake 1 hour at 350°. The crust will be chewy and hard. If the bread did not rise to the top of the loaf pan, bake 30 minutes at 250° and then at 350° until crust is hard. Cool on rack.
Different flours absorb water differently. You may need more or

less than 4 cups of flour. Artesian or other well water helps the bread rise.

When making variations of this recipe, always add supplementary ingredients *before* the flour.

VARIATIONS:

1. Add raisins, sunflower seeds, pumpkin seeds, sesame seeds, or nuts to the bread before adding flour for variety and nutrition.
2. Add wheat, mung bean, soybean, or pinto bean sprouts before adding the flour. The addition of sprouts will make the bread rise beautifully in 8 to 10 hours.
3. Substitute one cup of soy flour or other flour for one cup of wheat flour.
4. Add 1 or 2 cups of leftover cooked grains (rice, buckwheat groats, millet) to the water *before* adding the flour. Reduce the water to approximately 1¼ cups.

This tightly textured bread is very simple to make. Slice it thin with a sharp knife. It is delicious with old-fashioned peanut butter or sesame butter. Great toasted, too.

CHAPATI

SERVES 10

dough for unleavened bread
whole wheat flour for rolling out

☞ Pinch off a golf-ball-sized piece of the bread dough. Roll it out very thin on a well-floured surface.

Cook over low heat in skillet (try cast iron with no oil) until browned. Turn and cook the other side.

Refrigerate the dough so you can make just as many chapatis as you need for each meal.

VARIATION:

Roll the dough ⅛ inch thick or thinner and cut into small pieces with biscuit cutter or knife. Drop into hot oil. Turn. Cooks quickly.

PURI

(Indian Bread)

YIELD: ABOUT 2 DOZEN SMALL PUFFS

　　1¼ *cups whole wheat flour*
　　½ *teaspoon sea salt*
　　¼ *cup butter*
　　¾ *cup thick homemade yogurt*

　　unrefined safflower oil
　　　for deep frying

☞ Mix all ingredients together well, except the oil.

Have the oil 1 inch deep in a small but fairly deep saucepan. Heat on medium heat until a small piece of dough dropped in sizzles quickly.

Roll the dough out ⅛ inch thick or even a little thinner. Cut with biscuit cutter.

Drop in oil 2 at a time. Try to hold them under oil. They rise as soon as they begin to puff. They should puff and turn golden in just a few seconds. Drain.

Serve warm with honey or maple syrup (a few drops in each puff).

CRACKERS

Homemade crackers are so much more interesting than "store bought," and they're easy to make.

Newly baked crackers must be thoroughly cooled on racks. They should be stored in a dry place in tightly closed containers or plastic bags. Crackers will keep a week or two.

CORNMEAL PUFFS

YIELD: 2 DOZEN PUFFS

　　½ *cup stone-ground corn meal*
　　½ *teaspoon sea salt*
　　½ *cup boiling water*

2 egg whites, beaten until stiff

☞ Mix the corn meal and salt. Pour the boiling water into the meal and mix well.
Fold in the beaten egg whites.
Drop by the teaspoonful on an oiled cookie sheet.
Bake 20 to 25 minutes at 350°.

A crisp, puffy cracker.

SESAME CRACKERS

YIELD: ABOUT 6 DOZEN CRACKERS
3 cups whole wheat flour
1 cup stone-ground corn meal
1 teaspoon sea salt

¾ cup unrefined corn germ oil

water

sesame seeds

☞ Mix flours and salt together.
Stir in the oil.
Add water gradually until the dough holds together but is soft enough to roll. Do not knead too much.
Roll out thin, sprinkle with seeds, and lightly roll seeds into the dough. Cut into squares.
Bake at 375° for about 20 to 30 minutes, or until lightly browned.

To make bread sticks, use ⅓ cup of oil. Roll into long, thin sticks, and then roll in seeds. Bake until crisp.

WHOLE WHEAT CRACKERS

YIELD: 2 DOZEN CRACKERS
   1½ *cups whole wheat pastry flour, or*
      1 *cup pastry flour and* ½ *cup rice flour*
   ¼ *teaspoon sea salt*
   2 *tablespoons unrefined oil*
   4 *tablespoons water (approximately)*

☞ Mix the flour and the salt. Add the oil and rub in well by hand.
Add enough water to make a kneadable dough. Knead 5 minutes.
Roll out the dough to desired thickness and cut into shapes.
Place on an oiled cookie sheet. Bake 10 to 12 minutes at 325°.
Crackers can also be deep fried in oil.
For added crispness, try the rice flour.

CROUTONS

   whole wheat bread
   tamari soy sauce

☞ Cube the bread. Spread out the cubes on a cookie sheet and
sprinkle with tamari.
Bake until crisp at 350° or under a broiler until they are brown.
Watch closely so they don't burn.

SEASONED BREAD CRUMBS

YIELD: 4 CUPS
   4 *cups whole wheat bread crumbs*
   3 *tablespoons unrefined oil*

   1 *tablespoon sea salt*
   1 *tablespoon paprika*
   1 *tablespoon seasoned sea salt*
   1 *to 2 teaspoons seasoned pepper*
   dash of cayenne
   ¼ *cup chopped parsley*

Mix the bread crumbs and oil evenly.
Combine the seasonings and mix with the bread crumbs.
This mixture can be frozen for later use.

SIMPLE HERBED BREAD CRUMBS

YIELD: 1½ CUPS

1 cup whole wheat bread crumbs
⅓ cup grated Parmesan cheese
¼ cup chopped fresh parsley
¼ to ½ teaspoon sea salt
⅛ teaspoon pepper

Optional: ½ clove garlic, finely minced

 Combine ingredients thoroughly. Store in airtight jar.

Love 'Em or Leave 'Em
DESSERTS

Fresh fruits make the prettiest and most nutritious desserts. Serve them simply with yogurt or natural cheeses. (Ripe fresh fruits retain more food value and discolor more slowly if they are chilled before serving.) Or go elegant with a crystal bowl of fresh apricots and fresh cherries in ice water. Float sprigs of fresh mint and some flower blossoms on top for a beautiful dessert.

A bowl of luscious, cold grapes is a pretty centerpiece as well as a dessert. Tuck a few fresh ivy or mint leaves in the arrangement, and invest in some grape shears. After dinner, let guests snip off small bunches to eat with their cheese.

Watermelon baskets or scooped-out fresh pineapples make interesting containers for fresh fruit desserts. Or individual compotes piled high with pieces of fresh ripe fruit and topped with a complementary sauce and sprigs of mint make a most pleasant ending to a meal.

For other occasions, try a fruit pie or a carob cake. Birthdays certainly call for cake and ice cream. Occasionally you may want to fix a special treat for the children, though it is better to encourage them to eat fresh fruit rather than sweets.

SWEETENERS

Nature provides abundant natural sugars, particularly in fruits and some vegetables. Nature also provides vitamins and minerals, along with the sugars, to metabolize them without robbing the body of valuable nutrients as refined carbohydrates do. No concentrated sweetener, even a natural one, should be used in large amounts. But if your sweet tooth insists on being fed, delicious desserts can be made naturally. It is interesting that for years authorities in gourmet cooking have bypassed very sweet desserts in their menus, suggesting natural cheeses and fresh fruits instead.

As you begin to appreciate the many varied tastes of natural foods, the natural sweetness of whole foods will become more and more apparent. The usual desserts will come to taste cloying. While making the transition, there are several natural concentrated sweets available— such as honey and maple syrup. (But be sure the honey is unheated and unfiltered and the maple sap extracted without formaldehyde.)

Honey comes in many flavors, depending on the crop whose nectar the bees collected. Use honey in smaller amounts than the usual sweeteners. Start by cutting the amount in half. Cut down further as time goes by.

Other sweeteners have delicious but very distinctive flavors. Experiment with them and introduce them gradually—fruit purées, fruit juices, sprouted wheat, blackstrap molasses (very strong), unsulphured molasses (mild), date sugar, barley malt, carob syrup, and even well-sautéed onions.

HONEY TRICKS AND USES

1. Granulation of honey does not harm it. If you wish to return it to a liquid state, set the jar of honey in very warm water until the crystals melt.
2. Use honey to sweeten almost any drink—lemonade, tea, milk shakes.
3. Use on cereals or pancakes.
4. Mix with butter for a special hot roll spread.
5. One tablespoon of honey per egg white makes a delicious meringue.
6. Make your own jam by simmering honey and water with chopped dried fruits.

Try these simple changes and make your favorite desserts more flavorful and nutritious.

Replace refined sweeteners with natural ones. Use homemade safflower butter or unrefined oils in place of shortenings. Replace refined flours with whole grain flours and eliminate baking soda and powders or replace them with yeast and low-sodium baking powder. Stiffly beaten egg whites may replace the leavening agent in some sweets. Add non-instant milk powder. It does not change the flavor except to add natural sweetness, thus reducing the need for other sweeteners. Being highly concentrated, a little milk powder gives a big boost in protein and the other valuable milk nutrients. Mix it with the dry ingredients so it will not lump. Finally, try carob powder in place of chocolate or cocoa.

FRUIT DESSERTS

APPLESAUCE

FOR 1 QUART APPLESAUCE USE 8–10 LARGE APPLES

SAUCEPAN COOKING
apples, cut up
sea salt
cinnamon
Optional: lemon slice
vanilla

☞ Wash and cut the apples into quarters. Place them in a saucepan and add water to partially cover. Add a pinch of salt and the lemon if desired. Cook until tender. Purée.

Return the applesauce to the stove. Add a pinch of cinnamon and vanilla if desired. Cook until thick.

PRESSURE COOKING
whole apples
sea salt
Optional: cinnamon
vanilla

Wash apples and place whole in the pressure cooker with ½ cup water and a pinch of salt. (Do not cut apples or the skins will come loose and clog up the pressure cooker vent.) Pressure cook at 15 pounds for 20 minutes.

Bring pressure down. (If there is excess liquid after the pressure is brought down, drain it and use in cooking desserts or chill and drink.)

Purée through a food mill to remove the seeds.

Return to the stove and add spices if desired. Cook down if too watery.

VARIATION:
Applesauce can be made with dried apples too.

APPLE BUTTER

 Pour cooked applesauce into a heavy cast iron pot and continue cooking over low heat for several hours until the sauce turns brown. Stir often so that it doesn't stick to the bottom of the pot.

VARIATION:
Cook with the apples
    2 cups apple juice
    ½ cup raw honey
    2 teaspoons cinnamon
    1 teaspoon cloves
    ½ teaspoon allspice
    dash of sea salt
    juice and grated rind of 1 lemon

UNCOOKED APPLESAUCE

YIELD: ABOUT 3 CUPS
    2 tablespoons fruit juice
      (lemon, orange, lime, apple)
    3 apples, washed, cored, and unpeeled
    2 tablespoons raw honey

Optional: cinnamon

Cut the apples into chunks.
Blend the juice and one apple in a blender. Add the remaining apples and seasonings and blend again.

AMBROSIA

SERVES 6–8

6 to 8 fresh oranges, peeled, seeded,
  and cut up
3 cups fresh, unsweetened coconut
6 bananas, sliced in rounds

Optional: 1 to 4 tablespoons raw honey

 Toss all ingredients together lightly. Sweetening really isn't needed, but if you have to, add a little raw honey to taste.

BAKED APPLES

SERVES 6

6 red apples

1 tablespoon butter
½ cup raw honey
  (amount depends on tartness of apples)
2 tablespoons lemon juice

1 teaspoon cinnamon

½ cup chopped dates or
  raisins or dried apricots

Optional: ½ cup chopped nuts

1 to 2 tablespoons raw honey
¾ cup water

Wash and core apples, leaving a bit of the core in bottom to act as a plug. Place in glass baking dish.

Blend the butter, honey, and lemon juice. Partially fill each cavity with the honey mixture and sprinkle with cinnamon.

Finish filling each apple with raisins, dates, or chopped apricots and nuts, if used.

Add 1 or 2 tablespoons of honey to the water and pour in baking dish. Cover loosely with foil and bake 30 to 40 minutes at 350° or until apples are fork tender. Do not overcook. Approximately 10 minutes before apples are done, remove foil and baste with juice in pan. Return uncovered to oven and finish baking.

Serve with the juice or honey custard, whipped cream, or plain heavy cream.

BANANA DREAMS

SERVES 4

⅛ *teaspoon nutmeg*
⅛ *teaspoon cinnamon, or to taste*
3 tablespoons raw honey, or to taste
½ *cup homemade yogurt*
4 medium bananas, sliced in rounds

 Mix the spices, honey, and yogurt. Fold in the bananas. Chill.

Serve as a dessert or salad.

DRIED FRUITS

PRESSURE COOKED

	Pressure (lbs.)	Time (min.)	Prior Preparation
Apples	15	5	soak overnight
Apricots	15	1	no soaking
Peaches	15	5	soak overnight
Pears	15	5	soak overnight
Prunes	15	10	no soaking

☞ Place dried fruit in a pressure cooker. Add twice as much water and a pinch of salt.
Use leftover liquid in cakes, cookies, and breads.

SAUCEPAN COOKING
☞ All dried fruits may be simmered with liquid in a saucepan. Cover with water and/or fruit juices. Simmer 15 to 30 minutes or until desired consistency.

Cooked fruit should be refrigerated.

FRUIT QUARTET

dried peaches, pears, apricots, prunes
fresh orange slices
water and orange juice

☞ Combine fruits to your taste. Add several slices of fresh orange. Add water and orange juice to cover the fruit well. Simmer until the fruit is very tender and the sauce is thick.

BROILED GRAPEFRUIT

☞ Brush the top of a pink grapefruit with pure maple syrup or raw honey and a little butter.
Broil until warm and bubbly.

HONEY BAKED PEARS WITH LEMON SAUCE

SERVES 6
6 fresh, ripe, but firm pears

¼ cup raw honey
½ cup water
4 or 5 whole cloves

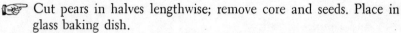 Cut pears in halves lengthwise; remove core and seeds. Place in glass baking dish.

Bring honey, water, and cloves to boiling point, but do not boil. Remove from fire, pour over pears.

Bake at 350° until pears are fork tender. Do not overcook. Serve while warm with a cold lemon sauce.

CREAMY LEMON SAUCE

YIELD: 2 CUPS

1 tablespoon arrowroot powder
1½ cups milk
1 stick cinnamon

grated rind of 2 lemons
¼ cup fresh lemon juice
¼ cup raw honey

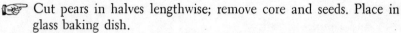 Dissolve the arrowroot in a little of the milk and place in a saucepan with the remaining milk and cinnamon. Stir and cook over low heat until slightly thickened.

Add lemon rind, juice, and honey. Remove from heat, cover, and chill.

Remove the cinnamon and pour the sauce over the pears just before serving time.

PRUNE-NUT WHIP

SERVES 4

1 cup of puréed prunes
(cook pitted prunes and blend to
make purée)
1 teaspoon lemon juice
1 tablespoon raw honey

½ cup heavy cream, whipped until stiff
1 tablespoon raw honey
dash of sea salt

¼ cup pecans or walnuts, chopped fine

Combine prune purée, lemon juice, and honey.
Combine whipped cream, and 1 tablespoon of honey, and salt.
Fold the prune mixture into the whipped cream. Chill.
Serve in sherbet glasses. Top with a spoonful of whipped cream
and chopped nuts.

CAKES

APPLESAUCE LOAF CAKE

YIELD: 1   9 X 5 INCH LOAF
   ¼ cup raw honey or pure maple syrup
   ⅓ cup unrefined corn germ oil
   1 egg

   1½ cups whole wheat flour
   ½ teaspoon sea salt
   1 teaspoon cinnamon
   ½ teaspoon ground cloves
   2 teaspoons low sodium baking powder

   1 cup raisins
   1 cup chopped nuts
   1 cup thick applesauce

 Beat the honey, oil, and egg together.
Sift together and add the flour and spices.
Lightly stir in raisins, nuts, and applesauce.
Spoon the batter into an oiled 9 x 5 inch loaf pan. Bake 40 min-
utes at 350°.

CARROT CAKE

YIELD: 1 SHEET CAKE (9 X 13 INCHES)
   7 carrots, grated fine
   2 cups whole wheat pastry flour
   1 cup chopped walnuts
   1 cup currants or chopped raisins
   4 eggs, beaten
   ⅓ cup pure maple syrup
   ⅓ cup unrefined corn germ oil
   1 teaspoon cinnamon
   1 teaspoon sea salt
   1 teaspoon vanilla
   ½ teaspoon nutmeg
   2 teaspoons low sodium baking powder

☞ Mix all the ingredients together well.
Pour into an oiled and floured 9 x 13 inch cake pan.
Bake one hour at 350°.

CHRISTMAS FRUIT CAKE

YIELD: 1 9 X 5 INCH LOAF
   2 cups (½ pound) dried pears
   4 cups water

   1 cup dried apricots
   2 cups water

   3 cups whole wheat pastry flour
   ½ teaspoon sea salt

   ¼ cup unrefined corn germ oil

   1 cup walnuts, roasted and chopped
   1 teaspoon vanilla
   rind of one orange

   orange juice

☞ Place pears and water in a saucepan. Cover and simmer for ½ hour. Purée.

Place apricots and water in a saucepan. Cover and simmer ½ hour. Chop.

Combine flour and salt.

Rub the oil into the flour by hand.

Add the pear purée, chopped apricots, walnuts, vanilla, and orange rind to the flour mixture. Add enough orange juice to make a moist batter.

Pour into an oiled 9 x 5 inch pan. Bake 1½ hours, or until done, at 300°.

Will keep well in refrigerator. Freezes well. Wrap in foil or plastic wrap.

QUICK CAKE

YIELD: 1 SHEET CAKE (9 x 13 INCHES)
    2¼ cups whole wheat pastry flour
    3 teaspoons low-sodium baking powder
    1 teaspoon sea salt

    1 cup raw honey
    ½ cup unrefined corn germ oil
    ½ cup milk

    ½ cup milk
    2 eggs
    2 teaspoons vanilla

☞ Mix the flour, baking powder, and salt.

Add the honey, oil, and ½ cup milk and beat 1 or 2 minutes.

Add the rest of the milk, eggs, and vanilla. Beat again.

Pour into an oiled and floured 9 x 13 inch cake pan.

Bake 30 to 35 minutes at 350°.

VARIATION:
Sauté 2 tablespoons sesame seeds in 1 tablespoon butter. Add them to the cake batter.

This is a simple cake for a birthday party.

SUSAN'S BIRTHDAY CAKE
(Carob Cake)

YIELD: 1 RING CAKE OR 2 LOAF CAKES
1½ cups butter, softened
1½ cups raw honey

6 eggs

3 cups whole wheat pastry flour or
  sifted whole wheat flour
½ cup carob powder
2 teaspoons low-sodium baking powder
¼ teaspoon sea salt

1 cup milk
1 teaspoon vanilla

☞ Cream butter and honey until light.
Add eggs, one at a time, beating well after each addition.
Stir flour, carob powder, baking powder, and salt together. Add,
alternating with milk, to the egg mixture.
Add the vanilla.
Pour the batter into a well-greased and floured angel food cake
pan or into 2 loaf pans. Bake 1¼ to 1½ hours at 325°. Do not
overcook. Turn out on rack to cool.

Ice with Maple Icing. This is a good "chocolate" birthday cake.

BUTTERMILK POUND CAKE

YIELD: 1   9 X 5 INCH LOAF CAKE
⅓ cup butter, softened
½ cup raw honey or pure maple syrup
⅓ cup buttermilk
2 cups whole wheat pastry flour
3 teaspoons low-sodium baking powder
8 eggs
⅛ teaspoon sea salt
1 teaspoon grated lemon rind or vanilla

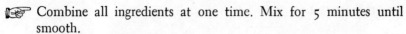 Combine all ingredients at one time. Mix for 5 minutes until smooth.
Pour into a greased and floured 9 x 5 inch loaf pan. Bake 30 to 40 minutes at 350°.

This recipe may be made into cupcakes or doubled and made into a layer cake.
Granola cake may be made by sprinkling granola on the bottom of the pan. Add the batter. Sprinkle granola on top of the batter.

PRISCILLA'S POUND CAKE

YIELD: 1   9 X 5 INCH LOAF CAKE
1 cup butter, softened slightly
¾ cup raw honey

juice and grated rind of one lemon

4 eggs

¼ teaspoon low-sodium baking powder
2 cups plus 4 tablespoons whole wheat
    flour

Cream the butter and honey five minutes.
Add the lemon juice.
Add the eggs, one at a time, beating well between each addition.
Mix the baking powder and flour. Stir into the egg mixture just until well mixed.
Pour into oiled loaf pan. Bake 75 minutes at 300°.

VARIATION:
Omit baking powder. Separate the eggs. Beat the yolks in as described. Fold the stiffly beaten whites in last.

CAROB BROWNIES

YIELD: 16 SQUARES
 1 *cup whole wheat pastry flour*
 1 *cup brown rice flour*
 ½ *cup carob powder*
 1 *teaspoon sea salt*

 2 *eggs, separated*
 ½ *cup unsulphured molasses or*
  pure maple syrup
 ¼ *cup unrefined corn germ oil*
 1 *cup water*
 1 *teaspoon vanilla*

 1 *cup chopped nuts*

☞ Mix flours, carob powder, and salt together in a large bowl.
In a small bowl combine the egg yolks, molasses or syrup, oil,
water, and vanilla. Add to the flours and mix well.
Add the nuts and stir.
Beat the egg whites until stiff and fold in.
Spread in an oiled 8 inch square pan. Bake 25 to 35 minutes at
325°.

MAYBERRY FRUIT SQUARES

SERVES 4–6
 2 *cups dried mixed fruit (or ½ pound)*
 juice and grated rind of ½ lemon
 ¼ *teaspoon sea salt*
 1 *cup boiling water*

 1½ *cups oat flakes*
 1 *cup whole wheat pastry flour*
 ¼ *teaspoon sea salt*

 ½ *cup unrefined oil*
 3 *tablespoons water*

Combine the fruit with the lemon juice, grated rind, salt, and boiling water in saucepan. Simmer 5 minutes. Cool.
Meanwhile, mix the oat flakes, pastry flour, and salt. Rub the oil in by hand until well mixed. Sprinkle with water and mix lightly. Press half the oat mixture into an 8 inch square pan.
Chop the fruit and spread over the crust. Then sprinkle the rest of the oat mixture over the fruit and press lightly.
Bake 25 minutes at 350°.
Cool. Cut into squares.

A single dried fruit such as apricots, or apples, may be used instead of mixed fruit.

WALNUT GINGERBREAD

SERVES 12
> ¼ cup raw honey
> ½ cup butter or unrefined safflower oil
>
> 2 or 3 eggs
>
> 1 cup unsulphured molasses
>
> 3 cups whole wheat flour
> 2½ teaspoons cinnamon
> 1½ teaspoons ginger
> 2 teaspoons low sodium baking powder
>
> 1 cup buttermilk or 1 cup fresh milk
>   mixed with the juice of one lemon
>
> 1 cup walnuts, coarsely chopped, or
>   1 cup toasted sunflower seeds

 Beat honey and butter well.
Add the eggs and beat well.
Add the molasses and continue beating.
Sift the dry ingredients together and add them alternately with the milk.
Add nuts.

Pour in an oiled and floured 9 x 13 inch pan. Bake 35 to 40 minutes at 325°.
Cool in pan for 10 minutes. Turn out on a flat tray. Cut in 3 x 3 inch squares.

Serve with lemon sauce or top with whipped cream and bananas or applesauce.

RAISIN SQUARES

YIELD: 1 SMALL CAKE (8 x 8 INCHES)
    2 cups raisins
    1½ cups water
    2 tablespoons butter
    ¼ teaspoon sea salt

    ½ cup raw honey or unsulphured molasses

    1 teaspoon each of allspice and cinnamon
    2 cups chopped nuts
    2 cups whole wheat pastry flour

☞ Boil the raisins, water, butter, and salt.
Add the honey while this mixture is still hot. Cool.
Mix the spices, nuts, and flour and add to the raisin mixture. Stir well.
Pour into an oiled and floured 8 x 8 inch cake pan. Bake 45 minutes to 1 hour at 350°.
Cool. Cut into chewy squares. These squares are best the second or third day.

SAUCES

APRICOT SAUCE

YIELD: 2 CUPS
   ½ pound dried apricots
   1 cup water
   pinch of sea salt

   Optional: 2 tablespoons raw honey

☞ Pressure cook the apricots, water, and salt together for 15 minutes after the pressure has come up. If you haven't a pressure cooker, stew the fruit with 1½ cups water for about 25 minutes. Put the mixture through a Foley food mill or blender until it is smooth.

Heat or chill. Serve over plain cake.
This sauce is tart 'n tasty. If you desire a sweeter sauce, add the honey while blending.

CAROB SAUCE

YIELD: 2 CUPS
   2 tablespoons butter
   2 tablespoons whole wheat flour
   2 tablespoons carob powder

   2 cups milk

   ¼ cup raw honey
   ½ teaspoon vanilla

☞ Melt the butter on low heat. Mix the flour and carob. Stir the flours into the butter. This will be quite thick.
Very slowly add milk, stirring constantly, making a smooth sauce. Continue cooking, stirring constantly until thick, about 10 minutes. Add honey to taste. Cool and add vanilla. Chill.

Use like chocolate syrup in milk or as a sauce over plain cake or ice cream.

CHERRY OR BERRY SYRUP

YIELD: 2½ CUPS
   ½ cup raw honey
   ½ cup water

   2 cups pitted cherries or other pitted
      berries

   1 tablespoon arrowroot powder mixed
      with 1 tablespoon hot water
   1 tablespoon lemon juice

☞ Simmer the honey and water.
Add the cherries or berries. Simmer 10 minutes.
Add the arrowroot mixture and lemon juice. Simmer 2 or 3 minutes until thick.

VARIATION:
For a quick, delicious syrup, blend the berries and honey in a blender. Omit the remaining ingredients.

LEMON DESSERT SAUCE

YIELD: 1 CUP
   1 cup boiling water
   ½ cup raw honey
   1 tablespoon arrowroot powder
      dissolved in 1 tablespoon water

   2 tablespoons butter
   2 tablespoons lemon juice
   ½ teaspoon nutmeg
   ¼ teaspoon sea salt

☞ Simmer the boiling water, honey, and arrowroot 2 minutes.
Add the butter, lemon juice, and spices. Simmer a few more minutes until thick, stirring constantly.

ORANGE SAUCE

YIELD: 2 CUPS

2 cups fresh orange juice
1 tablespoon lemon juice
¼ cup raw honey

Optional: 1 tablespoon butter
¼ cup chopped raisins

1 tablespoon arrowroot powder
dissolved in 1 tablespoon water

☞ Simmer orange juice, lemon juice, and honey.
Add butter and raisins if desired.
Add the arrowroot mixture and simmer until thick, stirring constantly, about 3 minutes.

ICINGS

These icings will seem a little too soft at first. However, they thicken as they sit.

YOGURT ICING OR DESSERT FONDUE SAUCE

YIELD: 1 CUP

½ cup homemade yogurt
¼ cup raw honey
⅓ cup non-instant milk powder
1 tablespoon lime juice
1 tablespoon butter

☞ Beat all ingredients until smooth. Add more milk powder to thicken (about ¼ cup).

ORANGE GLAZE OR HARD SAUCE

YIELD: 1 CUP
   2 tablespoons butter
   2 tablespoons raw honey
   4 tablespoons fresh orange juice
   ½ to ¾ cup non-instant milk powder

☞ Beat all ingredients until smooth and thick.

FRUIT JUICE ICING
   (Low fat)

YIELD: 1½ CUPS
   ¼ cup fruit juice
   2 tablespoons lemon juice
   ¼ cup raw honey
   1 cup non-instant milk powder

☞ Beat all ingredients until smooth. Add more milk powder (⅓ to ½ cup) to thicken.

CAROB FROSTING

YIELD: COVERS A 2 OR 3 LAYER CAKE
   2 tablespoons butter
   ¾ cup non-instant milk powder

   ¼ cup carob powder

   ¼ cup raw honey
   4 tablespoons milk
   1 teaspoon vanilla

☞ Cream the butter and milk powder. Add the carob powder and beat well.
Add the honey, milk, and vanilla. Beat with a rotary beater until smooth, 5 to 10 minutes.

Spread frosting on cool cake.
Spread apple butter between the layers for a surprising taste treat.

MAPLE ICING

YIELD: COVERS CAROB POUND CAKE
1½ *cups pure maple syrup*

4 *egg whites*
¼ *teaspoon sea salt*

☞ Bring the maple syrup to a boil in a heavy saucepan. Continue to cook at a low boil until the syrup spins a fine thread when dripped from spoon or to soft ball stage.
Have the egg whites and salt in bowl of electric mixer. Turn the mixer on high speed. Pour the hot maple syrup in a fine stream into the egg whites. Beat until the mixture is thick and stiff but still soft.
Spread on cooled Susan's Birthday Cake.

Although this delicious cake and icing are made entirely of natural, wholesome, unrefined ingredients, they are still sinfully rich. But everybody has to go sometime.

COOKIES

The cookie jar, an American institution, has a very special place in the natural food diet. When children reach into the cookie jar, it's nice to know that they will be enjoying delicious and nutritious treats—not "spoiling their supper."

If allowed to help make cookies, little children learn to enjoy making them of healthful ingredients. When offered cookies at a Christmas party, one 4-year-old asked his mother, "Do they have protein in them?"

APPLESAUCE COOKIES

YIELD: 4 DOZEN COOKIES
   2½ cups whole wheat pastry flour
   ½ teaspoon sea salt
   ¼ teaspoon cinnamon
   ¾ cup oat flakes

   ¼ cup unrefined safflower oil
   2 eggs, beaten
   ¼ cup pure maple syrup

   1⅓ cups applesauce
   1 cup raisins

☞ Mix the flour, salt, cinnamon, and oats.
Mix the oil, eggs, and maple syrup.
Mix the liquids with the dry mixture.
Add the applesauce and the raisins.
Drop the batter by the teaspoon onto oiled cookie sheets. Cookies
spread very little.
Bake 20 minutes at 400°.

ALMOND GEMS

YIELD: 3 DOZEN COOKIES
   1 cup unrefined oil
   4 tablespoons raw honey

   2 cups whole wheat pastry flour
   1 cup toasted almonds, ground
   1 teaspoon pure almond extract
   grated rind of 1 lemon
   ¼ teaspoon sea salt

☞ Mix the oil and honey well.
Add the flour, almonds, almond extract, lemon rind, and salt.
Shape the dough into small walnut-sized balls. Place on lightly
oiled cookie sheet. Bake 12 to 15 minutes at 400°.

CRUNCHY COOKIES

YIELD: 2–3 DOZEN COOKIES
   ½ cup unrefined safflower oil
   ¼ cup raw honey
   1 cup whole wheat flour
   ½ cup chopped nuts
   grated fruit rind (1 lemon or orange)

   2 cups (8 ounces) chopped dates

   4 ounces grated coconut

☞ Preheat oven to 400°. Mix the oil, honey, flour, nuts, and rind by hand. Spread loosely on ungreased pan and bake for 15 minutes. Take pan out of the oven and stir the mixture.
Cook the chopped dates in a small amount of water until really soft (approximately 5 minutes).
Stir dates into baked mixture and add the grated coconut.
Shape into a long roll; wrap in waxed paper. Refrigerate or freeze. Slice and eat like cookies.

GINGERSNAPS

YIELD: 2½ DOZEN COOKIES
   ¼ cup unrefined corn germ oil
   ¼ cup raw honey
   2 eggs
   ½ cup unsulphured molasses

   2½ cups whole wheat pastry flour
   ¼ teaspoon sea salt
   1 teaspoon cinnamon
   3 teaspoons ginger

☞ Beat the oil and the honey. Add the eggs and molasses. Beat again. Mix the flour, salt, cinnamon, and ginger together and slowly add to the liquid mixture, stirring constantly.
Drop by the teaspoonful onto an oiled cookie sheet. Bake 10 to 15 minutes at 350°, until lightly browned.

GRANOLA COOKIES

YIELD: 3–4 DOZEN COOKIES
    1 cup unrefined safflower oil
    1 cup raw honey

    2 eggs
    1 cup chopped pecans or
       sunflower seeds
    1 teaspoon vanilla

    2 cups whole wheat flour
    ½ teaspoon sea salt

    2½ cups granola

☞ Mix oil and honey.
Add the eggs, pecans, and vanilla.
Sift in the flour and salt.
Stir in the granola. Mix well.
Drop by the teaspoonful onto an oiled cookie sheet. Bake 15 to 20
minutes at 300° depending on whether you like moist, chewy, or
crunchy cookies.

HONEY-ORANGE COOKIES

YIELD: 3 DOZEN COOKIES
    1¼ cups whole wheat pastry flour
    1 teaspoon low-sodium baking powder
    ¼ teaspoon sea salt
    ½ teaspoon cinnamon

    ½ cup butter
    ½ cup raw honey
    2 eggs
    2 tablespoons orange juice
    grated rind of 1 orange

1 *cup oat flakes*
½ *cup chopped pecans*

☞ Mix the flour, baking powder, salt, and cinnamon.
Beat the butter, honey, and eggs well. Add the juice and rind.
Stir in the flour mixture.
Stir in the oat flakes and pecans.
Drop the dough by the teaspoonful onto an oiled baking sheet.
Bake 10 to 12 minutes at 350°.

PEANUT BUTTER COOKIES

YIELD: 2 DOZEN COOKIES
½ *cup old-fashioned peanut butter*
¼ *cup pure maple syrup or raw honey*

1¼ *cups whole wheat pastry flour*
2 *eggs, beaten*
¼ *cup unrefined safflower oil*
¼ *cup milk*
½ *teaspoon vanilla*
¼ *teaspoon sea salt*

☞ Cream the peanut butter and the maple syrup or honey together.
Add the pastry flour and the remaining ingredients. Stir well.
Drop the batter by the teaspoonful onto an oiled cookie sheet.
Flatten with a fork, dipping the fork in cold water between each cookie.
Bake 15 to 20 minutes at 375°.

RONNY'S BEST COOKIES

YIELD: 3 DOZEN COOKIES
> 1½ *cups oat flakes*
> 1 *cup sweet rice flour or brown rice flour*
> ½ *cup whole wheat pastry flour*
>
> ½ *cup unrefined corn germ oil*
>
> 1 *teaspoon sea salt*
> 4 *tablespoons pure maple syrup*
> *water*
> ½ *to* ¾ *cup raisins*
>
> *Optional:* 1 *cup chopped nuts*

☞ Mix the flours and oat flakes.
Rub the oil into the combined flours.
Add the salt, maple syrup, and enough water to make a wet but not runny batter. Stir in the raisins and nuts, if desired.
Drop by the teaspoonful onto an oiled cookie sheet. Press with the back of a spoon. Bake 20 minutes at 350°.

These cookies are more moist and chewy if the dough is refrigerated overnight. The next day, add more water, to make a wet but not runny dough. Bake.

SESAME-BANANA COOKIES

YIELD: 2–3 DOZEN COOKIES
> 1 *cup sesame seeds, lightly toasted*
>
> 2 *cups whole wheat flour*
> 1 *teaspoon sea salt*
> 1 *teaspoon low-sodium baking powder*
> ½ *teaspoon nutmeg*
>
> ¾ *cup sweet cream butter*
>   (*at room temperature*)
> 1 *cup raw honey*

1 *large egg*
1 *cup mashed banana*

1 *teaspoon pure vanilla*

☞ Preheat oven to 350°.
Spread the sesame seeds on a cookie sheet and toast lightly for 5 to 7 minutes while mixing other ingredients. Cool.
Measure and sift together all dry ingredients in the order listed. Cream the butter and honey together until fluffy.
Add the egg to the butter and honey. Beat well. Add bananas. Mix well.
Add dry ingredients to the honey mixture, ⅓ at a time. Mix well after each addition.
Add vanilla and sesame seeds last. Mix well.
Drop by the teaspoonful onto a lightly buttered cookie sheet. Bake 8 to 10 minutes at 350°.

These cookies are more chewy and moist if they're a bit under-cooked.

SORGHUM NUT COOKIES

YIELD: 2 DOZEN SMALL COOKIES

2 *cups whole wheat pastry flour or*
  sifted whole wheat flour
2 *tablespoons instant grain "coffee"*
½ *teaspoon sea salt*
¾ *cup chopped walnuts*
¼ *cup unrefined soybean oil*
¼ *cup unsulphured sorghum molasses*
2 *tablespoons water*

☞ Combine all ingredients in the order given, stirring after each addition. Mix well to make a stiff dough.
Drop by the teaspoonful onto an oiled cookie sheet. Bake 25 minutes at 325°.

Sorghum molasses is a high-quality sweetener derived from the stalk of the grain sorghum plant. It has its own distinct flavor, so if you use a substitute, such as honey or regular molasses, the cookies will have a distinctly different taste.

The special flavor of these cookies depends upon the use of pure, unrefined soybean oil. It is a strong tasting oil, suitable only with certain dishes, but it is especially high in lecithin content.

PIES

WHOLE WHEAT CRUST

YIELD: 1   10 INCH CRUST
    ¼ *teaspoon salt*
    1½ *cups whole wheat flour or*
       whole wheat pastry flour

    2 *tablespoons unrefined sesame oil*
    2 *tablespoons sesame tahini*
    4 *to 6 tablespoons cold water*

☞ Mix the salt and flour.
Rub the oil and tahini into the flour by hand until thoroughly distributed.
Add a little water. Knead until the dough is ear lobe consistency.
Roll out on a floured board. Place in pie plate. Trim excess.
If the crust is to be precooked, bake 15 minutes at 350°.

FLAKY PIE CRUST

YIELD: 2   9 INCH CRUSTS
    3 *cups whole wheat pastry flour*
    ½ *teaspoon sea salt*

    ½ *cup unrefined corn germ oil*
    1 *egg*
    1 *tablespoon cider vinegar*
    5 *tablespoons water*

Mix the flour and salt.

Mix the remaining ingredients together.

Make an indentation in the center of the flour and pour in the wet mixture. Mix with a fork, then knead lightly. Roll between waxed paper. Place in oiled 9 inch pie tin.

For baked shell, prick with fork to avoid puffing and then bake 10 minutes at 425°.

For other pies, partially bake the shell, then add filling and complete the baking.

For frozen crusts, place dough in pie tins, in freezer paper, and place in freezer. Use within 4 to 6 weeks.

WHEAT GERM PIE CRUST

YIELD: 1   8 INCH CRUST

1 cup wheat germ

¼ cup unrefined oil or butter

¼ teaspoon sea salt

Optional: 1 to 2 tablespoons raw honey

¼ cup wheat germ, toasted

 Blend 1 cup wheat germ, oil or butter, salt, and honey, if desired. Turn into oiled 8 inch pie tin, pressing on bottom and sides. Bake 8 minutes at 350°. Cool before filling.

Garnish with remaining wheat germ after filling.

PIE TOPPINGS

SUNFLOWER SEED TOPPING

raisins

grain flakes

any desired combination of nuts and seeds

small amount of unrefined safflower oil

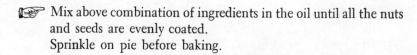 Mix above combination of ingredients in the oil until all the nuts
and seeds are evenly coated.
Sprinkle on pie before baking.

BLANCHED ALMOND TOPPING (Uncooked)
almonds, blanched
vanilla
water

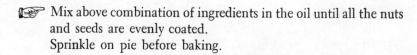 Blend in a blender almonds, vanilla, and enough water to make a
topping the consistency of whipped cream.
Serve like whipped cream, spooned on slices of pie.

GRANOLA TOPPING
granola
small amount of unrefined safflower oil
sea salt to taste

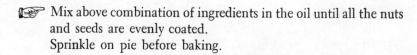 Mix granola with oil and salt.
Sprinkle over pie before baking.

VARIATION:
Substitute oat flakes and whole wheat pastry flour for granola.

APPLE BROWN BETTY

SERVES 6
    1½ cups whole wheat bread crumbs or
       oat flakes
    3 tablespoons unrefined corn germ oil

    5 apples, thinly sliced

    1½ cups applesauce
    ¼ teaspoon cinnamon
    ¼ teaspoon nutmeg
    1 teaspoon grated lemon rind
    ½ teaspoon vanilla
    pinch sea salt

    ½ cup raisins

Mix the bread crumbs or oat flakes and the oil.

Line the bottom of a deep, oiled 2 quart baking dish with ⅓ of the crumb mixture.

Arrange half the apples in the dish.

Mix the applesauce, cinnamon, nutmeg, lemon rind, vanilla, and sea salt.

Cover the apples with ½ of this mixture.

Add another ⅓ of the crumb mixture and ¼ cup of the raisins.

Add the remaining apples and cover with the remaining apple-sauce mixture and raisins.

Place the last third of the crumb mixture on the top.

Cover and bake 40 minutes at 350° until the apples are nearly tender. Remove the cover. Bake 15 minutes at 400° until browned. Serve with hard sauce or cream.

APPLE PIE

YIELD: 1 9 INCH PIE

unbaked whole wheat pie shell and
   dough for the top

4 cups juicy apples, washed and cored
   but not peeled, sliced ¼ inch thick
½ cup raw honey
2 tablespoons butter
1 tablespoon lemon juice
1 teaspoon cinnamon or mace or
   cardamom

 Fill shell with apple slices. Dribble honey over them. Dot with butter. Sprinkle with spice and lemon juice.

Add top crust. Pinch the edges together and prick the top with a fork.

Bake 35 to 40 minutes at 350°.

APPLE RAISIN PIE SUPREME

YIELD: 1   9 INCH PIE WITH DOUBLE CRUST
> *8 ounce package of sun-dried apples*
> *½ cup raisins*
> *1 cup fresh orange juice*
>   *(enough to cover apples and raisins)*
>
> *juice of one lemon*
> *¾ cup raw honey*
> *dash of sea salt*
> *¼ teaspoon nutmeg*
> *¼ teaspoon cinnamon*
>
> *unbaked whole wheat pastry shell and*
>   *dough for top crust*
>
> *2 tablespoons whole wheat flour*
> *2 tablespoons butter*
>
> *1 egg white, slightly beaten with*
>   *1 teaspoon honey*

☞ Soak apples and raisins overnight in orange juice. Drain and save any excess juice.

Add lemon juice, honey, salt, nutmeg, and cinnamon to the fruit. Put apples and raisins in bottom of uncooked crust. Dribble any remaining orange juice over fruit.

Sprinkle fruit with flour. Dot with butter. Make criss-cross top with strips of remaining pie dough. Brush dough with sweetened egg white.

Bake 10 minutes at 450°. Lower temperature to 300° and bake for 1 hour more.

VARIATION:
Add ½ cup chopped nuts or sunflower seeds to the fruit mixture.

BLUEBERRY OR CHERRY PIE

YIELD: 1   9 INCH PIE
1 unbaked 9 inch whole wheat pie crust

4 cups fresh blueberries or cherries,
  pitted
4 tablespoons whole wheat pastry flour
½ cup pure maple syrup or raw honey
1½ tablespoons lemon juice
2 tablespoons arrowroot powder
pinch of sea salt

☞ Mix the berries or cherries with the other ingredients and pour
into the crust. Let stand 15 minutes.
Add simple topping if desired.
Bake 45 minutes at 375°.

CAROB SILK PIE

YIELD: 1   8 INCH PIE
½ cup butter
½ cup raw honey

3 tablespoons carob powder
  dissolved in 2 tablespoons water
1 teaspoon vanilla

2 eggs

8 inch cooked pie crust (crumb type)

whipped cream

☞ Cream butter and honey together.
Add the dissolved carob and the vanilla.
Add 1 egg and beat in. Add the other egg and beat until the
filling turns from dark brown to a lighter color—about 2 to 3
minutes. If you beat too long at this stage, the filling will start to

separate. If this begins to happen, stop beating immediately. It does not affect the taste.

Turn filling into pie crust. Chill 3 to 4 hours. At serving time, cover with whipped cream.

This pie is very rich. Serve small pieces.

DRIED FRUIT PIE

YIELD: 1   9 INCH PIE

  4 cups water
  3 cups assorted dried fruits (1 cup
    raisins, 1 cup dates, 1 cup apples or
    apricots)

  2 tablespoons butter
  ¼ cup whole wheat flour

  1 cup chopped nuts

  1 partially baked 9 inch whole wheat
    pie crust

☞ Bring the water and fruit to a boil. Reduce the heat. Simmer until very thick.
Stir in the butter and flour. Remove from the heat.
Blend half of mixture at a time in a blender.
Stir in the chopped nuts.
Fill the crust.
Bake 20 minutes at 350°.

This pie looks like dark molasses pie. It is delicious and slightly tart. Add almond topping if desired.

OLD-FASHIONED PECAN MOLASSES PIE

YIELD: 1   9 OR 10 INCH PIE
  1½ cups unsulphured molasses
  4 eggs, beaten
  2 tablespoons whole wheat flour
  ¼ teaspoon sea salt
  ½ teaspoon nutmeg
  1 tablespoon butter

  1 cup pecans

  9 or 10 inch unbaked whole wheat
    pie crust

☞ Beat all ingredients well, except the pecans. Stir in the pecans.
Pour into the crust.
Bake 35 to 45 minutes at 350°.

VARIATION:
Substitute carob powder for the flour, for an extra rich pie.

For many years the lady who invented this recipe baked her pies
in an old wood stove stoked with oak wood on Hog Creek down
in central Texas.

PUDDINGS

APPLE MOUSSE

SERVES 8
> 2 tablespoons gelatin
> ½ cup pure apple juice
>
> 4 eggs, separated
>
> 1 cup pure apple juice
> ½ cup raw honey
> ¼ teaspoon sea salt
>
> Garnish: whipped cream,
>   rounds of red apple peel,
>   mint leaves
> freshly ground nutmeg

☞ Sprinkle gelatin over ½ cup apple juice.
Beat egg yolks until creamy. Add 1 cup apple juice, honey, and salt. Cook and stir in double boiler until thick.
Add gelatin mixture and stir until it dissolves.
Chill until mixture begins to set. Beat egg whites until stiff and fold into the gelatin mixture.
Pour into a 2 quart bowl and chill for several hours before serving. Spoon into individual serving bowls. Garnish with dollops of whipped cream, rounds of red apple peel, and mint leaves. Sprinkle with nutmeg.

This freezes well.

APRICOT ALMOND SOUFFLÉ

SERVES 4–6
> 1 cup dried apricots
> 2 tablespoons lemon juice

¼ cup pure maple syrup, or to taste

4 eggs, separated and beaten

½ cup toasted slivered almonds

☞ Cover apricots with water and simmer until soft. Add lemon juice. Purée in a blender or food mill.
Add the syrup. Let cool.
Add the beaten egg yolks. Beat the egg whites until stiff and fold into the apricot mixture.
Turn into buttered baking dish. Bake 30 minutes at 350°.

Place the soufflé in the oven just before you sit down for dinner. It will be light and perfect by dessert time. Top it with the almonds and serve warm.

APRICOT CUSTARD

YIELD: 6   ½ CUP SERVINGS
2 cups fresh milk
½ cup dried apricots, soaked and
    drained
⅓ cup raw honey
3 eggs

☞ Blend all ingredients until smooth.
Pour into oiled custard cups. Place cups in a pan of hot water.
Bake 45 minutes at 350°.

Very mild and delicious.

BAKED CUSTARD

YIELD: 6   ½-CUP SERVINGS
2 *cups milk*
2 *tablespoons raw honey or*
  3 *tablespoons pure maple syrup*
3 *eggs, beaten*
¼ *teaspoon sea salt*
½ *teaspoon vanilla*

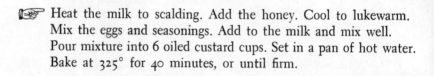 Heat the milk to scalding. Add the honey. Cool to lukewarm.
Mix the eggs and seasonings. Add to the milk and mix well.
Pour mixture into 6 oiled custard cups. Set in a pan of hot water.
Bake at 325° for 40 minutes, or until firm.

BREAD PUDDING

SERVES 4–6
2 *eggs, beaten*

½ *cup milk or soy milk*
1½ *cups apple juice*
¼ *teaspoon cinnamon*
¼ *cup raisins*

3 *cups whole wheat bread cubes*
  (*about 3 slices whole wheat bread*)

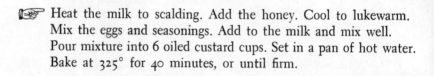 Add the milk, juice, cinnamon, and raisins to the beaten eggs.
Gently stir in bread cubes.
Pour into an oiled 8 inch square pan.
Bake 30 minutes at 350°.
Serve hot or cold with orange sauce.

DATE PUDDING

SERVES 6

3 tablespoons whole wheat flour
8 ounces (2 cups) pitted dates, chopped

2 eggs, beaten
1½ cups milk
¼ cup raw honey

½ cup chopped nuts

granola

☞ Mix the flour and dates in a saucepan.
Add the eggs, milk, and honey.
Cook over medium heat, stirring, until thick. Stir in the nuts.
Pour half of the mixture into an oiled, 1½ quart, deep baking dish.
Cover with a layer of granola, about ¼ inch thick. Pour in the
remaining mixture.
Bake 30 minutes at 350°.

Serve hot or cold with whipped cream, ice cream, or hard sauce
if desired.

BAKED INDIAN PUDDING

SERVES 6–8
    5 cups milk

    1 cup cold milk
    2 cups stone-ground corn meal
    ¼ cup whole wheat pastry flour

    3 eggs, well beaten
    2 tablespoons unrefined corn germ oil
    ¼ cup pure maple syrup
    1 teaspoon sea salt
    1½ teaspoons cinnamon
    ½ teaspoon nutmeg

    Optional: ½ cup raisins

☞ Boil the 5 cups of milk.
Mix 1 cup cold milk with the corn meal and pastry flour and add
to the boiled milk.
When cool, add the rest of the ingredients.
Cover and bake 2½ hours at 250°.

RICE PUDDING

SERVES 4–6
    2 eggs, well beaten
    ¼ teaspoon sea salt
    2 cups milk
    ½ cup unsulphured molasses

    1 cup cooked brown rice
    grated rind of 1 lemon
    1 tablespoon lemon juice
    ½ teaspoon nutmeg

    1 tablespoon unrefined corn germ oil

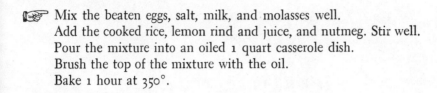 Mix the beaten eggs, salt, milk, and molasses well.
Add the cooked rice, lemon rind and juice, and nutmeg. Stir well.
Pour the mixture into an oiled 1 quart casserole dish.
Brush the top of the mixture with the oil.
Bake 1 hour at 350°.

ICE CREAMS

FRUIT YOGURT SHERBET

YIELD: 4 CUPS
1 cup homemade yogurt
juice of one orange
2 cups fresh or fresh frozen strawberries
1 tablespoon raw honey
1 pound can crushed pineapple
   (packed in its own juice), including juice
½ cup non-instant dry milk powder

Optional: 1 banana
          1 tablespoon lemon juice

☞ Blend all the ingredients until smooth. Freeze in ice cube trays
or other container. If possible, beat once before freezing is complete.

VARIATIONS:
Use other berries in place of or in combination with strawberries.

QUICK YOGURT SHERBET

homemade yogurt
fresh or fresh frozen fruit

Optional: raw honey to taste

Blend 1 part yogurt with 2 or 3 parts fruit.
Sweeten to taste. Freeze.

FROZEN FRUIT BOUQUET

YIELD: 2 QUARTS
   1½ *cups fresh orange juice*
   ¾ *cup fresh lemon juice*
   1½ *cups mashed ripe bananas*
   ½ *cup raw honey*
   1 *quart milk*

 Mix all ingredients; pour into refrigerator trays and place in freezer.
When partially frozen, remove from freezer, turn into bowl, and beat with electric beater. Return to tray and freeze—or double the recipe and freeze in a crank freezer.

PEACH ICE CREAM

YIELD: 1 GALLON
   6 *to 8 eggs, well beaten*
   1 *cup raw honey*
   3 *cups milk, partly cream*
   ⅛ *teaspoon sea salt*
   2 *cups cold milk*

   2 *tablespoons vanilla*
   1½ *cups homemade yogurt*
   6 *to 8 fresh peaches, peeled and cut*
      (*add ½ cup more honey if the fruit*
      is very tart)
   fresh milk to fill a gallon container
      ¾ *full*

 Mix the eggs, honey, milk, and salt. Cook over medium heat until the mixture begins to steam. Do not simmer or boil. Remove from the heat. Cool a few minutes, while preparing the peaches. Add 2 cups cold milk to cool more.

Stir in the vanilla, yogurt, peaches, and more honey if desired. Mix well.

Add enough fresh milk to fill the container ¾ full. Freeze.

STRAWBERRY ICE CREAM

YIELD: 1 GALLON

6 cups whole strawberries
   (fresh or fresh frozen—not in syrup)
1½ cups raw honey
1 tablespoon vanilla
pinch of sea salt
1 cup non-instant milk powder
fresh milk

Optional: 2 teaspoons finely ground
            kelp powder (no more than
            1 tablespoon)

☞ Blend all ingredients with enough milk to work the blender. Pour into a gallon freezer container. Add more milk until can is ¾ full. Freeze.

Kelp helps stabilize the mixture as well as adding nutrients. This amount does not harm the flavor. Kelp powder is available at natural food stores.

CONFECTIONS

APRICOT-NUT BALLS

YIELD: 3 DOZEN BALLS
    1 *pound dried apricots*
    6 *tablespoons raw honey*
    grated rind of one orange
    juice of 2 oranges

    1 *cup nuts, chopped fine*

☞ Put apricots through grinder. Combine with honey, rind, and juice. Mix thoroughly. Cook 10 minutes, stirring constantly. Add nuts. Cool. Shape in small balls. Roll in more ground nuts. Store in refrigerator.

DATE-DELIGHTS

YIELD: 2 DOZEN SMALL BALLS
    4 *tablespoons butter*
    4 *tablespoons raw honey*
    1 *cup finely chopped dates*

    1 *cup granola*
    1 *cup finely ground nuts or coconut*

☞ Melt the butter and honey in a saucepan on low heat. Add the chopped dates. Cook, stirring constantly, until the dates almost dissolve. Remove the date mix from heat.
Stir in the granola. When cool enough to handle, roll the mixture into small balls. Roll in finely ground nuts or coconut.

DATE TREATS

YIELD: ABOUT 4 DOZEN
 1 pound pitted stuffed dates
 ¼ cup old-fashioned peanut butter
 ½ cup chopped pecans or walnuts

☞ Mix peanut butter with chopped nuts and fill cavity of dates.

HALVAH

YIELD: 12 SMALL BALLS
 1 cup sesame seeds, lightly roasted
 and ground
 ¼ cup raw honey
 pinch of sea salt

 Optional: ⅛ teaspoon almond extract

☞ Mix all the ingredients together. Form into small balls. Store in the refrigerator.

The Thirst Quenchers
BEVERAGES

Tart and tangy, smooth and sweet, hot or cold! Great drinks are quick and easy to prepare! Make shakes, fresh fruit drinks, "hot chocolate" (without any chocolate), your own herb teas, and nut milk. Drink them all fresh.

Many extra nutrients may be slipped into your beverages while actually enriching the flavor. Non-instant milk powder adds natural sweetness as well as protein, minerals, and vitamins. Fresh lime or lemon juice gives a delightful spark to many fruit drinks and herb teas. Someone who hates yogurt will drink it without even knowing it. Homemade beverages are easy and good, and a real nutritional plus when you avoid commercially bottled drinks, many of which contain preservatives, artificial coloring, and a wide variety of chemical additives.

Use these recipes to spur your imagination. Trying out new beverage combinations can be the most enjoyable kind of "cooking." A blender helps too.

ALMOND MILK

YIELD: 2 CUPS
6 tablespoons ground almonds
(grind in hand mill or blender)
2 cups apple juice
pinch of sea salt

☞ Blend all ingredients together until creamy. Chill and serve as you would dairy milk. Do not keep more than 24 hours.

For variety, substitute one cup of water and one tablespoon of maple syrup for the apple juice.
Try it over granola.

APPLE-GRAPE JUICE

YIELD: 1 QUART
2 cups apple juice, chilled
2 cups grape juice, chilled
juice of one lime

Optional: 2 cups naturally carbonated
water, chilled.

☞ Mix all the juices together, adding the carbonated water if desired.

APPLE-MINT TEA

YIELD: 1 GALLON; SERVES 16 OR MORE
1 cup chopped fresh mint leaves
4 cups water

3 quarts apple juice
½ cup lemon juice
½ cup raw honey

Place mint in a tea pot. Heat water. Just before it boils, pour it over the mint leaves and steep for 5 minutes. Strain. Mix the mint tea with the remaining ingredients.

Serve hot with gingerbread in the winter time. Chill and serve anytime in the summer.

SPARKLING APPLE JUICE

2 parts apple juice, chilled
1 part naturally carbonated water,
chilled

 Mix and serve immediately.

Children love this.

BANANA SHAKE

YIELD: 2 CUPS
1 cup milk
⅓ cup non-instant milk powder
2 bananas
½ teaspoon vanilla
1 tablespoon raw honey
1 cup cracked ice

 Blend all together until smooth.

VARIATIONS:
1. Omit honey and vanilla. Add juice of ½ lime.
2. Omit the honey. Add ½ cup pitted dates.

CAROB MILK
(Hot or Cold)

YIELD: 2 CUPS
> 2 tablespoons carob powder dissolved
> in 2 tablespoons hot water
> 1 cup fresh milk
> ⅓ cup non-instant milk powder
> 1 teaspoon vanilla
> tiny pinch of sea salt
> 1 cup cracked ice or 1 cup hot milk or
> hot water

> Optional: 1 banana

☞ Combine carob, milk, milk powder, vanilla, salt, ice or hot liquid, and banana if desired.
Blend all until smooth.
Use cracked ice for a cold shake.
Use hot liquid for hot "chocolate" and heat all after blending.
No extra sweetening is necessary since carob powder and milk powder are both naturally sweet.

CARROT JUICE

YIELD: 2½ CUPS
> 2 cups orange juice
> 1 cup diced carrots
> honey to taste
> pinch of sea salt

☞ Blend until very smooth.

VARIATIONS:
Try your own combinations. Blend your favorite fresh vegetable with a compatible fruit juice.

HOT CIDER

YIELD: 1 SERVING

1 *cup apple juice or cider*
1 *teaspoon pure maple syrup, honey, or*
   molasses
3 *drops lemon juice or lime juice*
sprinkle of cinnamon or 1 cinnamon
   stick for stirring

Optional: ¼ teaspoon butter

Garnish: lemon slice

☞ Mix all ingredients together. Heat and serve.
Multiply recipe to serve desired number.

CHERRY FIZZ

YIELD: 2½ QUARTS

1 *cup pitted fresh cherries*
1 *pint apple juice, chilled*
2 *quarts naturally carbonated water,*
   chilled

☞ Mash ½ cup of the cherries and soak them in the juice for 15
minutes.
Add the water to the cherry mixture.
Pour into cups and put a whole cherry into each cup. Serve immediately.

Try this pretty drink at a child's birthday party. Children love it.

CRANBERRY JUICE

YIELD: 3 QUARTS
  2 *quarts boiling water*
  1 *quart fresh cranberries*
  2 *sticks cinnamon*

  juice of 2 lemons
  juice of 2 oranges
  raw honey, to taste

☞ Pour the cranberries and cinnamon into the boiling water. Bring
to a boil again.
Simmer 20 to 30 minutes until the berries are very mushy. Mash
the berries.
Cool the juice to lukewarm.
Strain the juice, pressing the berry pulp to get out all the juice.
Add the other fruit juices and honey to taste.
Chill.

SHAKE-A-DATE

YIELD: 3 CUPS
  ⅓ to ½ *cup chopped pitted dates*
  2 *cups milk*

  ⅓ *cup non-instant milk powder*
  1 *cup cracked ice*

☞ Blend the dates with a small amount of the milk until smooth.
Add the rest of the ingredients. Blend.

Dates are so sweet. Please do not add other sweeteners.

FOUR OF MARY'S FROZEN "DAIQUIRIS"

EACH RECIPE SERVES 6–8

I. 2 oranges, peeled
    1 banana, peeled
    2 cups apple juice
    1 tablespoon raw honey
    ½ teaspoon cinnamon
    crushed ice, about 2 cups

II. 3 cups fresh orange juice
    1 cup non-instant dry milk powder
    1 tablespoon raw honey
    1 teaspoon pure vanilla extract
    crushed ice, about 2 cups

III. 1 small ripe cantaloupe, peeled,
       seeded, and cubed
     1 orange, peeled
     juice of 1 lime
     1 tablespoon raw honey
     crushed ice, about 2 cups

IV. 1 cup coconut milk
    ½ cup orange juice
    1 cup pineapple juice
    juice of 1 lime
    ½ cup almonds, blanched
    crushed ice, about 2 cups

☞ Make these drinks in a blender and serve them in long-stemmed glasses. They are festive, delectable, and naturally nutritious. The combination of fruits to use in fresh fruit daiquiris is endless, depending on the fruits in season. Any time you can find fresh papayas or fresh mangoes, use them in your daiquiris. Fresh lime juice complements both of these fruits.

Garnish if desired with fresh mint or fresh citrus fruit slices.

PARTY GRAPEFRUIT JUICE

SERVES 50
      10 pink grapefruit

      40 to 50 grapefruit

      fresh mint
      water to cover

☞ Squeeze 10 pink grapefruit. Fill a star-shaped mold with the juice and place in the freezer.
Squeeze the remaining grapefruit.
Pick a handful of fresh mint, place in a small pan, cover with water, and simmer a few minutes. Strain and add to grapefruit juice. Serve very cold, over ice mold.

Grapefruit juice is a real thirst-quencher any time.

LEMONADE OR LIMEADE

YIELD: 2 CUPS
      juice of one lemon or lime
      2 tablespoons raw honey
      enough water to bring total liquid
         measure to one pint (2 cups)

☞ Stir all ingredients until the honey is dissolved. Serve cold with ice.

A mixture of lemon and lime juice is a delicious treat.

MINT TEA

YIELD: 1 QUART
   1 quart water
   7 or more sprigs of fresh mint, crushed
   1 slice of lemon

☞ Bring the water to a boil. Turn off heat. Add the mint and the lemon and steep 5 to 10 minutes. Serve this tea hot or cold. If served cold, you may want to use additional mint.

Serve this delightful tea with dessert.

MOCK SANGRIA

YIELD: 2½ QUARTS
   1 quart grape juice
   juice of two oranges
   juice of one lemon
   ½ orange, sliced thin
   1 lemon, sliced thin
   1 quart naturally carbonated water

☞ Mix all liquids well. Add the sliced fruits. Chill thoroughly.

VARIATION:
Try apple juice in place of the grape juice.

Serve in tall glasses garnished with orange slices.

MOLASSES MILK DRINK

YIELD: 2½ CUPS
   2 cups cold fresh milk
   ⅛ teaspoon sea salt
   4 teaspoons unsulphured molasses
   pinch of nutmeg
   ⅓ cup non-instant milk powder

☞ Blend. Serve ice cold.

SUPER GRACE MALT

YIELD: 4 CUPS
   ½ cup homemade yogurt
   2 cups milk
   ½ cup non-instant milk powder
   1 teaspoon vanilla
   juice of 2 oranges

   Optional: honey to taste
              1 banana

   1 cup cracked ice

☞ Blend all until smooth.

PINEAPPLE-MINT DRINK

YIELD: 4 CUPS
   2 cups water
   ½ to 1 cup fresh pineapple
   ⅓ cup lemon juice
       (or juice of 1 lemon and 1 lime)
   ½ cup raw honey
   2 or 3 sprigs fresh mint
   1 cup cracked ice

☞ Blend until smooth in a blender.

VARIATION:
Substitute ½ cup fresh alfalfa sprouts for the mint.

RUSSIAN PARTY TEA

YIELD: 2 QUARTS
   5 teaspoons of blended teas
      (orange, mint, herb, or your choice)
   4 cups boiling water

   raw honey to taste

   peel and juice of 1 lemon
   juice of 2 oranges and peel of one
   juice of 1 grapefruit
   about ¼ peel of grapefruit

   Optional: 1 cup pure grape juice

☞ Pour water over the tea leaves and steep; strain.
Sweeten to taste with honey.
Add juices and peelings. Cover and refrigerate overnight.
Use some of the tea to make an ice ring in a ring mold; garnish
it with thin slices of oranges and lemons. At party time, place
ring in bowl; remove peelings from tea and pour tea over ice.

The Russians probably never heard of this tea, but it can be served
—Russian-style—in glasses. Or serve hot.

SOY MILK

YIELD: ABOUT 4 CUPS
    1 cup dry soybeans, soaked 24 hours
     and drained
    1 quart water

    Optional: Add 1 tablespoon raw honey,
              1 tablespoon unrefined oil,
              and a pinch of sea salt.

☞ Blend the soaked beans (about 2 cups after soaking) with 1 quart water.
Strain through cheesecloth into a saucepan.
Bring the liquid to a boil. Remove from heat immediately. Cool and strain again.

MARGIE'S STRAWBERRY MILK SHAKE
(or Ice Cream)

YIELD: 4 CUPS
    2 cups fresh milk
    2 cups fresh or fresh frozen strawberries
    1 teaspoon vanilla
    2 tablespoons raw honey
    ½ cup non-instant dry milk powder

☞ Blend all ingredients. Add a few ice cubes and blend until very cold.
For ice cream: Omit the ice. Freeze the liquid in ice cube trays, stirring once before freezing is complete.

SUMMER TEA

YIELD: 4 CUPS
    2 cups bancha twig tea
    2 cups apple juice

1 lemon
2 or 3 sprigs fresh mint

☞ Mix the tea and the apple juice together in a 2 quart jar or pitcher. Cut the lemon in half, squeeze the juice into the jar, and put the whole rest of the lemon in the jar.
Crush the mint against the inside of the jar and leave the sprigs in the liquid.
Chill. Serve cold.

This is the perfect drink for a picnic.

Hey Diddle Diddle
CHILDREN'S FOOD

Children, little ones especially, love to help cook. They are eager to learn and quickly soak up knowledge of foods and nutrition if you will take time to explain simple principles. They also seem to eat better after they have helped prepare the food, if you can keep them from tasting too often in the kitchen.

Included in this section are foods children particularly like to eat and cook. Girls are usually introduced to cooking early in life. Encourage the boys, too. They make very adept cooks if given the opportunity.

To complete the cycle, start a garden if you don't already have one. Give the children a section of their own. They may pull the plants up by the roots to see if they're growing, but they also develop a love for growing things. If you have no garden spot, put the children in charge of growing the sprouts for salads. The rapid transition from seeds to edible sprouts is fascinating for children and adults too.

Also included in this section is a discussion on preparing baby foods at home.

BABIES AND TODDLERS

The best food for a baby is mother's milk, provided the mother is eating well. If her diet is poor, the baby will not be properly nourished, or will get by only at the expense of the mother. The nursing mother needs a wide variety of wholesome, natural foods. Some need an extra nutritional boost and/or increase in liquids to increase milk production. Fresh alfalfa sprouts, in salads and fruit drinks, are a good choice. Alfalfa seeds are easy to sprout, taste good, and are an excellent source of the vitamins, minerals, and enzymes common to fresh greens, which are often not available, or are anything but fresh during much of the year. Sea vegetables (certain types of seaweed) are much like dried garden greens, but are much higher in mineral content. They make delicious, brothy soups. Drinks and soups are excellent ways of getting the extra fluids that may be necessary in nursing. Natural malt and nutritional yeast mixed in juices also add valuable nutrients. Seeds and nuts, especially fresh sunflower seeds, are nutritious snacks.

ALFALFA SPROUT DRINK:

Blend fresh sprouts with fruit juice, a sprig of fresh mint, and ice, if desired. Add raw honey to taste.

If nursing is not possible, make the formula at home. Unrefined carbohydrates may be used instead of the refined ones found in many prepared formulas, and natural nutrients may be added, such as nutritional yeast, non-instant milk powder or soy powder, and natural vitamins. *Let's Have Healthy Children*, by nutritionist Adele Davis, offers much good advice.

A baby's digestive system is not ready for solids until he begins to produce some of the enzymes (Ptyalin, for instance) necessary to digest them. The baby does not produce adequate starch-digesting enzymes until he is at least a year old, and sometimes not until the age of two. The production of these enzymes is thought by some physicians to correspond to the eruption of the first baby teeth and the later eruption of the molar teeth. Other physicians believe there is good reason for giving some solids before those times, however. At any rate, from time immemorial, mothers have chewed whole grain foods, in order to start the digestive process, and then fed them to their small babies. A healthy mother today could still do the same. By the time his molar teeth erupt, a baby should be able to handle almost any type of food.

When your baby is able to utilize solid foods properly, make them fresh at home. Commercial baby foods are prepared with preservatives, salt, and sugar, to please the mother's eye and taste. These have no place in baby foods. Salt in baby foods is suspected of contributing to heart disease later in life. Sweeteners lead to a "sweet tooth," dental problems, and lowered resistance to disease. Commercial baby cereals and grain products are also highly refined. A growing child needs complete nutrition, not the partial nutrition of refined foods.

Preparing whole foods for your baby at home is simple with the help of a blender or "Happy Baby Food Grinder."[1] There is no need to cook special foods. Just take the baby's portion out of the natural foods you cook for the rest of your family before you add any seasonings. Grind or blend to the proper consistency for your baby. Protein and B vitamin content of almost any food may be increased by blending in non-instant dry milk powder, soy powder, or nutritional yeast.

Prepare extra baby foods and freeze them for those days when there isn't time to prepare a balanced meal. Blend any unseasoned, cooked foods and freeze them in cubes in ice cube trays. When the food is frozen, dump the cubes into plastic bags or airtight containers to prevent freezer burn. Return them to the freezer. The small cubes are a very handy size and thaw quickly in the top of a double boiler.

CEREALS

When your baby is ready for his first solids, cook rice or another grain until very soft (6 parts water to 1 part rice). Skim the "milk" off the top of the grain and feed this to the baby or mix this milk with the grain and blend or grind in a baby food grinder. Rice is a good first grain for your baby since it is easier to digest than some other grains.

Make baby cereals from rice, barley, millet, oat, or wheat flour. To insure freshness roast the whole grain first and then grind it in a hand grinder or a blender. Cook cereal about an hour in a double boiler for the young baby (6 months).

☞ Place 2 tablespoons flour in the top of a double boiler.
Add ½ to 1 cup water or milk to the flour.
Place directly over low heat and simmer until thickened, 5 to 10 minutes.

---

[1] "Happy Baby Food Grinders" can be purchased at natural food stores or ordered from: Bowland-Jacobs Mfg. Co., Spring Valley, Illinois.

Now place the cereal over boiling water and cook 45 minutes to
1 hour.

SOUPS

Purée a portion of the family's soup before adding any seasoning.
Thicken, if desired, with a little flour.
Purée vegetables and/or cooked grain with a little water or milk.
Add liquid to desired consistency and warm

VEGETABLES

Steam, pressure cook, or sauté vegetables until they are very tender.
Remember to omit all seasonings.

☞ ½ cup cooked fresh vegetable—no seasoning
2 tablespoons milk, water or unseasoned vegetable stock
Blend until smooth. Serve immediately or refrigerate in a tightly
closed container.

When your baby is older (12–18 months), blend cooked vegetables with whole cooked grains or cooked grain flakes. The older baby
may also eat cooked dry beans in small amounts if they are first soaked
and then well cooked before puréeing.

FRUITS

Babies love fresh fruits. Try uncooked applesauce or a scraped raw
apple. Bananas are a favorite of children of all ages. Cooked fresh or
dried fruits are excellent, too.

Fresh fruits:
Blend a ripe banana with ½ cup fresh fruit such as avocado, apple,
apricots, or with soaked dried fruits.

Cooked fruits:
¾ cup cooked fresh or dried fruits, no seasonings
1 tablespoon fruit juice, vegetable stock, or milk
Blend until smooth. Serve immediately or refrigerate in a tightly
closed container.

BEVERAGES

If your baby continues to drink milk after being weaned from mother's milk, he may find goat's milk easier to digest than cow's milk because the fats in goat's milk are slightly more digestible. If (and this is a big if in many parts of the country) safe, tested, and approved raw milk is available, it is an excellent milk that has additional nutrients that are destroyed in processed milk by the heat of pasteurization. Homemade yogurt is excellent for all ages.

Your baby will enjoy other liquids, too. Try apple juice, carrot juice, mild herb teas (but not strong teas, such as Mu Tea, or those containing tannic acid), blended fruits and juices, and of course water.

Carrot juice:
Finely grate or blend a carrot. Squeeze the juice through cheese-cloth.

MIXED FRUIT DRINKS.

½ cup milk or juice
¼ cup soaked dried apricots or 1 small banana
⅓ cup other fresh fruit
Optional: 1 teaspoon or more nutritional yeast
Blend all ingredients until smooth.

PROTEINS

When your baby can handle concentrated proteins, simply grind or blend a portion of the family's protein dish. Remember to take the baby's portion out before adding seasonings.

Older babies and toddlers particularly like foods they can feed themselves and which are easy to chew—such as firmly cooked eggs and cheese.

A *word of warning:* Add only one new food at a time—no more than one a week—to your baby's diet. In this way it will be easier to isolate the offending food should the baby develop a food allergy.

As your baby gets older and is able to chew well, increase the variety and texture of the foods in his diet—cereals made from more coarsely ground grains, diced vegetables, dried fruits, whole grain breads spread with nut butters, and all kinds of "finger foods."

All children have likes and dislikes about foods as about anything else. They are very changeable, too. Next week they may love whatever they hated this week. Offer your child a variety of well prepared wholesome natural foods. He may eat a lot of one food and none of another, but it will all balance out over a period of time. If your child is not introduced to sweets at an early age, he will develop a taste for fruits and vegetables instead. It's amazing to watch a 3 year old beg for more squash or broccoli.

SCHOOL LUNCHES

Let the kids help prepare their own lunches. You may get tired of peanut butter and honey sandwiches, but they never seem to. If the peanut butter is the old-fashioned variety containing only ground, roasted peanuts and is spread on stone-ground whole wheat or whole grain bread, the sandwiches will provide excellent protein even if they are gooey. Include thin slices of crisp apple in the sandwich for a special treat.

For sandwich variety use other nut butter and cheeses on the kids' favorite homemade bread. Alfalfa sprouts are an interesting change from the usual limp lettuce in sandwiches, too.

Small wide-mouth thermoses are excellent for individual servings of soup or hot "chocolate" (carob) on a cold day.

Include pickles, carrot sticks, celery sticks filled with peanut butter, and fresh fruit for dessert.

Encourage your children to eat fresh fruit for after-school snacks— or cheese toast, granola, high-protein milk shakes, or fruit drinks.

CUSTARD EGGS

SERVES 4–6
   2 tablespoons butter
   1 to 2 tablespoons raw honey

10 *eggs*
½ *cup milk*
½ *teaspoon sea salt*
½ *teaspoon cinnamon*
¼ *teaspoon nutmeg*
½ *teaspoon vanilla*

☞ Melt the butter in a large skillet on low heat. Add the honey and just melt.
Meanwhile, beat the eggs, milk, and spices. Pour into the skillet and stir.
Cook like scrambled eggs on low heat, stirring frequently, until soft and custardy.

SKILLET MACARONI AND CHEESE

SERVES 4
1 *tablespoon unrefined oil*

Optional: 1 *onion, sliced thinly*

1 *package pasta (8 ounces whole wheat*
spaghetti or 2 cups whole wheat
macaroni or noodles), cooked

2 *to* 3 *tablespoons tamari soy sauce*
1 *cup grated cheddar cheese*

☞ Heat a large skillet. Add the oil, and onion if desired, and sauté 5 minutes.
Add macaroni and stir until it is heated thoroughly.
Add the tamari and grated cheese. Cover and steam a few minutes on low heat until the cheese melts.

This is great for lunch. It's really quick and easy.

PIZZA

Use any of the following for the crust:

CRUSTS
1. Make whole wheat pie crust dough. Roll out ⅛ inch thick. Place on ungreased cookie sheet with raised edges.
2. Make whole wheat bread dough and allow to rise partially. Roll out. Place on an oiled cookie sheet.
3. Use lightly toasted whole wheat bread slices.

SAUCE
Make Simple Tomato Sauce with chopped mushrooms and oregano as in Pizza variation.
Add ½ to 1 cup cooked soybean flakes, or other cooked beans if desired.

Spread the sauce thickly on one of the crusts. Sprinkle with grated cheese, cheddar, jack, mozarella, or swiss.
Bake 5 to 10 minutes at 450° for sliced bread crust, 15 minutes for the other crusts. Add more grated cheese and serve.

VARIATION:
Spread old-fashioned peanut butter on the crust before adding the sauce and cheese. Amazing, but it's really good!

Pizza is a favorite with the whole family—teenagers especially. Use whole wheat toast for the crust if you're in a hurry; it's delicious and gives each person his own individual pizza. Serve with a green salad and Paul's salad dressing.

FRESH FRUIT SALAD

cantaloupe chunks
apricot halves
pineapple chunks
apple pieces (with peel)

berries, whole
bananas, sliced
grapes, seeded

lemon juice or homemade yogurt

☞ Mix the fruits gently.
Add lemon juice and/or yogurt to coat the fruit.

HONEY-ORANGE SAUCE FOR FRUIT SALAD

YIELD: 1¼ CUPS
  ½ cup raw honey
  ¾ cup fresh orange juice
  1 teaspoon grated orange rind
  pinch of sea salt

☞ Beat all ingredients together. Chill.

Serve with a mixed fruit salad or spooned over pear halves. A little goes a long way!

MOON DISKS

brown rice cakes (crackers)—or
  any whole wheat cracker
swiss cheese, sliced ⅛ inch thick

☞ Place swiss cheese on top of crackers. Bake 10 minutes at 400°

Brown rice cakes are available at natural food stores.

PEANUT BUTTER MUFFINS

YIELD: 1½ DOZEN
2 cups whole wheat flour
3 teaspoons low-sodium baking powder
½ teaspoon sea salt

¼ cup old-fashioned peanut butter
⅓ cup unrefined oil

1½ cups milk
4 tablespoons raw honey

☞ Sift the flour, baking powder, and salt together.
Cut in peanut butter and oil with fork or pastry blender until the mixture is like small grains. This may be done at low speed in an electric mixer.
Add the milk and honey and stir just until well mixed, but do not beat.
Fill oiled muffin tins or muffin cups ⅔ full.
Bake 12 to 15 minutes at 350°.

PEANUT BUTTER SANDWICH SPREAD

YIELD: 1½ CUPS
½ cup old-fashioned peanut butter
½ cup wheat germ
½ cup raw honey, or less to taste
3 tablespoons soft butter

☞ Stir all ingredients until well blended.

Children love to eat this spread on homemade bread.

CARAMEL APPLES

YIELD: 10–12 APPLES

3 cups pure maple syrup
1 cup light sweet cream

4 tablespoons real butter

1 to 1½ cups non-instant milk powder
10 to 12 apples with sticks

☞ Mix the maple syrup and milk in a large saucepan. *Slowly* bring the mixture to simmering, stirring constantly. If the mixture begins to curdle, it is heating too rapidly. Immediately reduce the heat and continue cooking. The mixture will not be harmed.
When it simmers, continue cooking the mixture to the soft ball stage, stirring often.
Pour the hot sauce into a large mixing bowl. Add the butter. Cool slightly.
Beat in the milk powder until the still-warm mixture will pour very slowly.
Have a pot of boiling water ready. If the caramel mixture hardens or cools too much, set the mixing bowl over boiling water for a minute or two until it softens again.
Coat each apple by turning it in the warm caramel sauce. Let the excess drip off. Place the coated apples on a buttered cookie sheet in the refrigerator until the caramel hardens.

CRACKER JACKS

unrefined safflower oil, small amount

peanuts
pumpkin seeds
sunflower seeds
sesame seeds
chia seeds

nut meats (any kind)
coconut

raw honey or pure maple syrup

☞ Heat a heavy skillet on medium heat. Add oil, just enough to barely coat the bottom of the pan.
Add the peanuts and seeds. Roast lightly.
Add the nut meats and coconut. Continue roasting until the coconut begins to turn golden.
Remove from heat and stir in honey or maple syrup to taste—just enough to coat the nuts and seeds lightly.
Eat while warm.

Children enjoy this snack as a change from popcorn.

GINGERBREAD PEOPLE

YIELD: 18–24 GINGERBREAD PEOPLE
   3 *cups whole wheat flour or*
      1½ *cups whole wheat and*
      1½ *cups brown rice flour*
   ¾ *teaspoon sea salt*
   1 *teaspoon powdered ginger*
   ½ *teaspoon cinnamon*
   ¼ *teaspoon nutmeg*

½ *cup unrefined corn germ oil*
½ *cup unsulphured molasses*

Garnish: raisins or currants

☞ Combine the dry ingredients.
Stir in the oil and molasses.
Add enough water to make a wet but rollable dough. Work as little as possible. Roll out ⅜″ thick. Cut into desired shapes with a cookie cutter or knife. Place on oiled cookie sheets. Decorate with raisins.
Bake 20 to 30 minutes at 350° or until browned.

ICE CREAM CONES

YIELD: 1 DOZEN CONES
2 *cups whole wheat pastry flour*
¼ *teaspoon sea salt*
¼ *cup unrefined corn germ oil*
water

unrefined safflower oil for deep frying

small metal cornucopia molds*

☞ Combine the flour and the salt. Add the oil and mix thoroughly. Add enough water to make the dough ear lobe consistency. Form the dough into small balls and roll thin.
Shape the dough around the cornucopia molds, wetting edges to seal. Trim any excess at the top of the mold.
Heat the oil to 350° and set the dough and mold in the oil. Fry until golden. Cone and mold will separate while cooking in the oil. Remove from the oil. Drain.

* These molds are available in restaurant supply stores, gourmet cooking ware stores, and some department stores.

STRAWBERRY MONKEY JUICE

YIELD: 2 CUPS
   1 cup fresh or fresh frozen strawberries
   juice of one lime
   1 banana
   juice of 2 oranges

   Optional: 1 cup cracked ice

☞ Blend the strawberries, lime juice, banana, and a little orange juice in a blender until smooth. Add the remaining orange juice and cracked ice if desired. Blend again.

YOGURT AND ORANGE JUICE POPSICLES

   thick homemade yogurt
   fresh orange juice

   Optional: raw honey to taste

   popsicle sticks

☞ Mix all to taste. Pour into popsicle molds or ice cube trays. When frozen to a mush, put in sticks. Freeze.

PLAY DOUGH
   (Not to Be Eaten)

   2 cups water
   1 cup salt

   2 tablespoons oil
   food coloring

   4 teaspoons cream of tartar
   2 cups flour

Heat the water on low heat in a large 6 to 8 quart pan. Teflon
works best.

Add the salt and simmer until it is completely dissolved.

Add the oil and food coloring for desired color.

Mix the flour and tartar. Add to the water, stirring constantly
with a wooden spoon.

Don't worry about lumps. Work them out when the dough cools.

Trail Foods

Natural foods were made for camping and cooking out. The whole grains—especially wheat, rice, buckwheat, and millet—lend themselves well to "one pot" cooking. Pinto beans, split peas, lentils, soybeans, mung beans, chickpeas, and other beans can be cooked easily and quickly with your favorite seasonings, and are easily carried in your pack on the outgoing trail.

Sunflower seeds, sesame seeds, almonds, and other seeds and nuts pack a lot of food value in small packages. Dried apples, peaches, apricots, prunes, raisins, and other dried fruits are convenient, delicious, and great for quick energy. Even sourdough can make the trip. All these items will keep without refrigeration and require only the simplest cooking equipment.

You can usually supplement these staple foods with wild greens and vegetables picked near your campsite. You might take along a good wild food plant encyclopedia, such as *Edible Wild Plants* by Oliver Medsger, published in 1972 by the Macmillan Co. in paperback. Mung beans and alfalfa seeds may be sprouted on longer camps, and the sprouts can be used both as salads and as ingredients for delicious soups and other dishes.

There is no need to carry a lot of expensive equipment and perish-

311

able food when you head for the great out-of-doors. You can camp the natural foods way and really get away from it all while enjoying the freedom of traveling light. Here are just a few recipe ideas; if you are a camper, you will probably have many more.

CAMPER'S BREAKFAST

brown rice, cracked wheat, or other grains
pinch of sea salt
boiling water
thermos

☞ Fill a thermos ⅓ full of rice, wheat, or other whole grain. Add a pinch of salt.

Fill the remainder of the thermos with boiling water. Seal immediately and let sit overnight.

The grain will be ready for breakfast. You can't ask for an easier breakfast than that.

Serve with sunflower seeds and/or raisins.

PANCAKE MIX

YIELD: ENOUGH FOR 3 BREAKFASTS FOR 4 PEOPLE
6 cups whole wheat flour
1 cup non-instant milk powder
2 tablespoons low-sodium baking powder
1 tablespoon sea salt

☞ Mix all ingredients together. Carry in a tightly closed half-gallon container.

When ready to use, add 2 cups water, 2 eggs, and 2 tablespoons unrefined oil to each 2⅓ cups of the dry mix. If you don't carry eggs, increase the amount of oil to 3 or 4 tablespoons.

PAUL BUNYAN'S BUCKWHEAT CREAM

SERVES 4
  1½ *cups buckwheat flour*
  3 *cups boiling water*
  ½ *teaspoon sea salt*

  Garnish: tamari soy sauce
      chopped scallions

☞ Heat a skillet and roast the buckwheat flour well—at least 5 minutes.
Remove from heat and pour boiling water over the buckwheat flour. Add salt.
Mix well and serve with chopped scallions and tamari.

This is a very hardy tasting cereal for cold mornings.

BAKED APPLES

  1 *large apple per person*

  raw honey
  raisins
  butter
  cinnamon

  A *dutch oven with lid and a pan that*
      will fit inside the oven.

☞ Wash and core the apples but do not cut completely through the bottom.
Fill the cavity with a mixture of the remaining ingredients.
Place the apples in the greased pan. Pour water in the pan to a depth of ¼ to ½ inch.
Place pebbles in the bottom of the dutch oven. Set the pan of apples on the pebbles. Cover and set the dutch oven in hot coals.
Bake about 20 minutes.

HIKER'S SNACK

whole grain flakes
sesame seeds
sunflower seeds

nut meats
raisins
dried fruits, chopped

☞ Toast the grain flakes and seeds in a dry skillet.
Pour into a bowl and mix with nut meats, raisins, and any desired chopped dried fruits.
Cool the mixture completely. Carry in tightly closed plastic bags or other containers.

DUTCH OVEN POTATOES

1 potato per person

A dutch oven with lid. A pan that
    fits inside the oven.

Optional: foil for wrapping potatoes,
            butter, sea salt, yogurt

☞ Scrub the potatoes. Puncture the skins. Oil lightly, wrap in foil if desired. Place the potatoes in the pan. If the potatoes are not wrapped, oil the pan and add a little water.
Place pebbles in the bottom of the dutch oven. Place the pan of potatoes on the pebbles.
Cover and set the dutch oven into hot coals. Place hot coals on the lid too. Bake about an hour.
Serve with butter, salt, and yogurt if desired.

HOE CAKES

SERVES 4
> 2 cups stone-ground corn meal
> 1 teaspoon sea salt
> boiling milk or water

☞ Combine corn meal and salt. Add enough liquid to make a thick batter.
Drop by the tablespoonful and flatten on a hot, oiled griddle. Bake until brown, turning once.

TAKE SOURDOUGH TO CAMP

> 1 cup sourdough starter
> whole wheat flour—take plenty

☞ Knead enough flour into the starter to make a soft dough. Sprinkle the dough with more flour.
Carry the dough in a plastic bag containing a cup of dry flour. Keep the bag tightly closed. Sourdough starter must be mixed with flour because it can only be stored in liquid form in glass or ceramic containers, which are too heavy and inconvenient for camping.
The starter will keep a week or more. Keep the starter fresh by feeding and using it once a week or more.

To use the starter:
Place the soft dough starter in a bowl. Add 2 to 4 cups of warm water and 2 to 4 cups of flour.
Set the bowl in a warm place 3 to 4 hours or overnight (near a warm fire in winter).
Now the starter is ready to use in any sourdough recipe.

SOURDOUGH PANCAKES

☞ Refer to sourdough pancake recipe in the Breakfast section.

SOURDOUGH ON A STICK

> *sourdough bread dough—or thick*
> *sourdough pancake batter with*
> *enough flour added to make a soft*
> *dough. Or use dough made from*
> *plain pancake batter using less liquid*
> *than called for.*

> *green sticks, peeled*
> *hot coals from camp fire*

> *Optional: honey, cinnamon, butter*

☞ Prepare the dough. Roll pieces of dough into long skinny sausages about ¼ inch thick.
Wet the green stick and heat it over the coals. Wrap the dough around the warmed stick. Hold the dough over the hot coals until baked, turning to prevent burning.
Dip the dough in a mixture of melted honey, butter, and cinnamon before baking if desired.

Of course somebody always drops the dough in the ashes. But that's all right. Out-of-doors even ashes taste pretty good.

PRIMITIVE BREAD

> *sourdough bread dough*
> *plenty of green leaves (maple, aspen,*
> * bay, magnolia, birch, etc.)*
> *hot coals*

☞ Allow the bread dough to rise once.
Pat the dough into a ½-inch-thick cake.
Place the dough on several thicknesses of leaves.
Scrape coals and ashes to one side. Place the leaves and dough on the hot fire base.

Cover the dough well with more green leaves. Then cover with ashes, followed by a layer of hot coals.
Let the bread bake under the ashes and coals about 10 to 15 minutes. Test after 10 minutes by poking the bread with a long, thin twig. If it comes out clean, the bread is done.

THROW-IT-IN-THE-POT STEW

2 cups whole grain—
   wheat, millet, or rice
6 cups water
carrots, cut in ½ inch pieces
onions, quartered
potatoes, cut in chunks
1 teaspoon sea salt

Optional: chopped wild greens

tamari soy sauce to taste

☞ Place all ingredients, except greens and tamari, in large pot and cook until grain is tender. Add chopped wild greens, if available, for the last 5 to 10 minutes of cooking. Add tamari to taste.
Any vegetables may be added to this stew.

VARIATION:
Roast millet until golden brown before adding other ingredients.

Some menu ideas for a group of eight adventurers on a two-day outing in the lake country, woods, or mountains—and the amounts to put in the packs—might go like this:

Breakfast: Stewed prunes, boiled cracked wheat cereal with a little maple syrup on it, and a few almonds for a snack as you pack up and move out.

Lunch: Dried apples, sliced cheese, whole rye crackers, cold fruit juice—and you are on your way again to the high country.

Supper: Now you are ready to do some basic cooking—and eating! Camper's Stew—wheat flakes, rice with onions, carrots and potatoes cut into small chunks and boiled for about an hour. Add a little corn oil, tamari, and seasoning. Serve with corn chips. Oatmeal cookies from home with some cinnamon-spiced hot apple juice or a good herb tea make a good dessert as you sit around the campfire.

Breakfast: Whole wheat pancakes (see recipe, this section) topped with poached eggs and maple syrup. Grain coffee.

Lunch: A quick soybean chili made with soybean flakes, wheat flakes, onions, salt, and a little chili powder. Dried pears or peaches.

A *late afternoon snack* of Maple-Nut Granola on the down-hill trail.

In the packs: 4 potatoes, 4 carrots, 3 onions. Small containers of corn oil, tamari, maple syrup. Packets of grain coffee, herb tea, salt, and seasonings. 2 lb. pkgs. cracked wheat cereal and rice. 1 lb. pkgs. soybean flakes, wheat flakes, granola, and almonds. 2 lbs. whole wheat flour, oatmeal cookies, 1 dozen eggs. 2 pkgs. corn chips, 1 lb. cheese, 1 lb. rye crackers, 4 pkgs. dried fruits, 2 qts. apple juice.

Total weight: Less than 25 lbs., if you drink the apple juice before you start.

Natural Foods from Deaf Smith County

The whole, natural foods shipped from Deaf Smith County, bearing "Olde Mill," "Arrowhead Mills," "Deaf Smith," and other labels respected in the natural foods movement, provided the ingredients for most of the dishes in these tested recipes. The foods were lab tested for pesticide residue as a part of a continuing program of quality control that actually begins with the soil.

Farmers growing produce for these companies, in Deaf Smith County and in several other areas of the country, use biodynamic compost, marine humus trace minerals, green manure crops, and other materials to increase the humus content and beneficial bacterial action in the soil.

Predatory insects like ladybugs, lacewing flies, and trichogramma wasps are introduced into the fields when needed to bolster the efforts of indigenous beneficial insects that aid in the control of aphids and other insect pests. In this way, the use of poisonous chemicals is avoided. It is interesting to note that healthy plants raised on healthy, balanced soil are less subject to insect attack.

When the grains, beans, or seeds are brought from the fields, they are stored in clean, dry grain bins without the use of fumigants. All

319

foods are cleaned thoroughly before being bagged for shipment. No preservatives or other "nonfood" additives are ever used in processing.

On each of the small packages shipped by Arrowhead Mills there are recipes, a statement of purpose, and as much information as possible about the methods used in growing and storing the food contained in the package, where it was grown, and, in some cases, by whom. In this way, a closer bond can develop between growers and consumers of natural foods.

NATURAL FOOD PRODUCTS

Following are brief descriptions of some of the staple foods available to the natural food cook. These descriptions apply only to those foods used by the authors. They may not apply to every similar product. These basic items are emphasized because they form a basis for natural food cooking. Such staple foods are generally the most economical to buy. They ship well, are widely available, and keep well with proper storage.

Many staple items are available in either bulk or small quantities. If you are able to use the products fairly rapidly and have storage space, it will pay you to buy in larger quantities. If not, buy only what you can use in a couple of weeks. It is best to refrigerate some items, such as flours, oils after being opened, and raw nuts. In Deaf Smith County's high, dry climate these foods can be kept unrefrigerated for months, but in hotter or more humid climates more care should be taken.

There is a great variety of other natural foods, not so generally available. Each region usually has its own specialties. A trip to your nearest natural food store will turn up many interesting items.

WHOLE GRAINS

The less that is done to a grain the greater the retention of natural nutrients. Therefore, it is an excellent practice to use whole grains that have not even been cracked or ground. There are several ways to do this: (1) sprouting, (2) soaking, or (3) cooking until tender. The grains are then ready to eat or to be included in breads, cereals, soups, salads, casseroles, patties, cookies, etc. They add taste, texture, and important nutrients to almost any recipe.

Unrefined whole grains all contribute a wide range of trace minerals. The refining of most commercial grain products does a tremendous amount of harm by drastically reducing the trace mineral content. Trace minerals, except iron, are not replaced even in synthetic form in so-called enriched foods.

Whole grains are important sources of nearly all the B vitamins as well as Vitamin E, unsaturated fatty acids, and quality protein. Refining removes the greater percentage of these vitamins, fatty acids, and proteins. Only 3 B vitamins and iron are partially replenished in enriched foods, and they are synthetic. The rest of the B complex (13 or more vitamins) as well as other vitamins, minerals, and proteins—all of which are necessary—are virtually ignored. All nutrients are interdependent, so that eliminating or weakening any one of them cripples the whole nutritional process.

Hulled Barley   The best barley in the world is grown in the Red River Valley of Minnesota and North Dakota, on rich "gumbo" soil. This barley is consistently highest in protein and minerals.

Almost all barley available in stores has been pearled in order to remove the tenacious hull. However, the important factor is the degree of pearling. The whiter the barley, the more it has been pearled, some of the nutrients having been removed along with the outer layers. The barley available in natural food stores should be browner than that available in supermarkets. This darker barley is often called just "hulled barley." It is practically impossible to cook unhulled barley. Barley is delicious in soups and casseroles.

Buckwheat   Grown in an area from Pennsylvania north into Canada, this grain crop is not fertilized because fertilization decreases the yield by encouraging excessive leaf growth. Nor is it sprayed, since spraying would kill the bees needed for pollination.

Buckwheat is very carefully hulled and graded. The best is whole groats, which are the whole buckwheat grains. It may be purchased unroasted (white) or roasted (brown). However, the unroasted is a more vital grain and is easily roasted at home. The flavor is much better when it is freshly roasted. Buckwheat is high in B vitamins. It cooks quickly, in 15 to 20 minutes, and may be used as a hot cereal (especially good in winter), in casseroles, and in stuffed cabbage leaves and knishes, the most familiar uses of buckwheat.

Yellow Corn   Yellow corn is organically grown in the Deaf Smith area. The protein content is higher than average—about 10 percent. This corn makes excellent meal, high in Vitamin A. Like other whole grains, whole yellow corn contributes many trace minerals and B vitamins.

White Corn   White corn meal is not refined from yellow meal, but comes from a white corn variety. White corn is grown under the same conditions as yellow corn. It too makes an excellent meal, though it is not as high in Vitamin A as yellow corn meal. Its flavor is more subtle than that of yellow corn.

Millet   Grown in the Red River Valley of North Dakota, this grain is sometimes known as "poor man's rice," although it is not as flavorful as rice or wheat. It is used heavily in China, Japan, and Africa. Millet provides well-balanced, low-gluten protein, calcium, and lecithin. It is good in soups and stews or as a hot cereal, and makes an excellent breakfast, cooked with onions, when camping out. For variety try millet in place of rice in almost any recipe.

Oat Groats   Like millet and barley, these oats are grown in the Red River Valley of Minnesota and North Dakota. Oats are carefully hulled to remove all "clingers," the last bits of hull that tend to cling to the crease in the grain.

Oats were originally a staple food of Scotland. Today they are generally used in the form of rolled oats. However, whole oats may be used in soups like barley, or may be made into a porridge.

Brown Rice   Brown rice is whole grain rice as opposed to white rice, which has been stripped of its bran and much of its nutrition. Long- and medium-grain brown rice is grown on the Brookshire-Huckley Prairie of southeast Texas and in Louisiana. This rice is carefully rotated with native grasses and soybeans and is watered with deep well water. The soil fertility is enhanced by adding marine humus, natural colloidal phosphates, and a mixture of mined minerals. This rice is higher in protein than ordinary rice, either brown or white. The rice is hulled by a special huller to protect the bran layers.

The long-grain rice cooks up light and fluffy, while the medium grain is tender and moist. Try alternating varieties for more interesting rice dishes.

Organically grown short-grain brown rice is also available from

California. Short-grain rice is more glutinous and sticks together when cooked. Its delicious flavor is preferred by many.

Rice is one crop that is more expensive to grow organically. You can be sure that cheap brown rice is not organically grown. Most commercial rice farming entails ecologically unsound practices and staggering amounts of poisons. Commercial rice is one of the most heavily chemicalized food crops. Be especially careful of your source of brown rice. The name of every organic rice supplier is well known, so ask.

Rye   Rye is grown in the high plains of eastern Colorado. The soil on which this rye is grown has been free of chemicals for well over 5 years. Rye grows through the winter and is harvested in the early summer. The weeds and stubble are returned to the soil to enrich it. Rye is delicious in casseroles and may be sprouted, flaked, or ground into grits or flour. Its taste is quite mild. The flavor of caraway seed, often used in rye bread, is mistakenly identified as rye by many people.

Triticale   This grain is grown in Texas, Oklahoma, and Kansas, but at present most organically grown triticale comes from dry land areas of Kansas. Triticale is a fairly new grain variety. Originally it was a cross between durham wheat, hard red winter wheat, and rye, but it is now a true breeding grain variety. Triticale is slightly higher in protein (around 17 percent) and has a better balance of the amino acids than some other grains. Therefore it is a very nutritious grain when cooked whole, sprouted, or flaked for use in cereals, casseroles, meat loaves, cookies, etc. Triticale flour also makes excellent breads, but it must be mixed with other, higher gluten flours, for its protein contains little gluten. It has a distinctive, slightly sweet taste. For these reasons triticale is a very interesting and nutritious addition to the selection of whole grains, flakes, and flours.

Whole Wheat Berries (*whole wheat grains*)   Hard red winter wheat is organically grown in Deaf Smith County, where the soil is famous for its high trace mineral content. This wheat contains about 15 percent protein. "Tascosa" and "Centurk" are the varieties used for flour and baking purposes because of the high gluten fraction in the protein. The same high-quality, high-test weight wheat is sold as whole berries, flaked, cracked for cereal, and ground for flour. Wheat has many uses aside from breads.

Soft Wheat   Soft wheat is organically grown in several areas of this country. This wheat variety is lower in protein and in gluten than hard winter wheat. Therefore it is most suitable for grinding into pastry flour to use in place of unbleached white flour.

WHOLE GRAIN FLAKES AND
WHOLE BEAN FLAKES

The whole grain flakes from Deaf Smith County, Texas, are made from exactly the same nutritious whole grains described previously. Some are made from whole dry beans. Except for oat flakes, however, these flakes are made by an entirely different process than commercial products. The whole grains or beans are quickly cooked (about 15 to 20 seconds) under dry radiant heat, each grain or bean acting, in effect, as its own little pressure cooker. Then the grains or beans drop into rollers and are flattened into completely whole grain or whole bean flakes. Thus, all refining or possible leaching of nutrients through wet methods is eliminated. The inventor of this procedure is Chardo Pierce of Lubbock, Texas. Although he originally developed the method to improve animal nutrition, it was obvious to Chardo that it could also improve human nutrition.

When the flakes were first produced, the question was where to use them, other than in the obvious cereals. The answer is "everywhere"! They add taste, texture, protein, and other nutrients to breads, cakes, cookies, cereals, casseroles of every kind, dips, soups, sauces, and stews. Use them instead of or in addition to cracker and bread crumbs. Flakes are dry, light in weight, and quickly cooked, so they also make excellent trail foods for campers.

Oat flakes, rice flakes, rye flakes, triticale flakes, wheat flakes, soybean flakes, and pinto bean flakes are available now. It is possible to flake almost any grain, bean, or seed, so other varieties may be available at a future time. See charts giving directions for cooking grain and bean flakes.

CEREALS

Almost any whole grain may be cracked, flaked, or ground for use as a cereal. The following are readily available and are the most frequently used. Refer to the breakfast section for directions and further discussion. See the chart that outlines cooking procedures for various kinds of cereals.

Bulgur Bulgur is whole grain wheat that has been parboiled, then dried, and then cracked. It is a staple food in the Middle East where many delicious dishes are made from it. Bulgur and cracked wheat (which has not been cooked) are usually interchangeable in recipes.

Flakes as Cereals See the preceding description of flakes. All the flaked grains make delicious cooked cereals and granola. The grain flakes cook quickly and are more tender than the whole or cracked grains. The variety of grain flakes greatly increases the number of cereal possibilities. Try mixing several grains.

Rice Cream This delicious cereal is made from whole, long-grain brown rice. The rice is roasted by the dry radiant method and then stone ground a little coarser than rice flour. Children love it for breakfast.

Whole Grains Whole grain berries, cooked as is, make excellent cereals as well as bases for main dishes. These are perhaps the simplest and most healthful of all cereals.

Granola Basically a mixture of flaked grains, seeds, nuts, and/or fruits, this cereal can easily be made in endless varieties at home. There are also several good varieties on the market. Maple-Nut Granola is one of the tastiest and most nutritious. It contains wheat, rye, and oat flakes; seedless raisins; natural sesame seeds, sunflower seeds; slivered almonds and hazel nuts; pure maple syrup; unrefined soy oil; sea salt; and pure vanilla extract. Granola is a hearty cold breakfast cereal, not the over-refined, artificially sweetened type now common in this country. Really good granola requires some chewing and is even recommended by some dentists to their patients. Granola is an excellent dry snack food and a great trail food. Try granola in toppings for ice cream, cakes, and pies; in cookies; and in crumb crusts.

DRY BEANS (LEGUMES)

Beans are among the most versatile foods available. There are so many varieties, and all are important sources of protein, minerals, and

B vitamins. Beans may be sprouted, flaked, ground into flours, or cooked whole in everything from "meat" patties to party pies. See the chart for information about cooking beans.

Black Beans   These beans are really black and are a variety of soybeans. They have been a major food and source of protein in Mexico and the Southwest for many, many years. Black beans are good in any bean recipe, but they are particularly delicious in soup.

Chick Peas   Also known as garbanzo beans, these legumes come from California. They are very light brown in color and irregularly shaped. Chick peas are high in protein and are a source of calcium, iron, potassium, and B vitamins. They may be served as a vegetable, dip, sauce, or in soups and salads. Chick peas are a traditional food in the Middle East and are becoming popular in this country.

Lentils   Lentils are grown in Washington and in western Idaho, the most famous lentil-growing area in the United States. The soils are enriched by the mineral deposits of ancient volcanoes and are free of sprays and residues. Lentils are good sources of protein, iron, and B vitamins. They are excellent in soups and casseroles and they sprout well.

Mung Beans   These small green dried beans are grown in Oklahoma and Texas. They are a soil-building crop, are very clean, and have a high germination rate. They are most commonly used as sprouts because they sprout so easily. The sprouts are excellent as a quickly cooked vegetable or a fresh and tangy addition to salads.

Split Peas   Dry split green peas also come from eastern Washington and western Idaho. They are good sources of protein and minerals, and are most popular in delicious soups.

Pinto Beans   Brown-speckled pintos are a favorite in the South and Southwest. The tenderest and most flavorful pintos are grown at high altitudes. They cook more quickly than pinto beans grown under other conditions, and blend well with any kind of seasoning—sweet or spicy. Like nearly all dry beans, pintos provide important protein and minerals.

Pinto Bean Flakes   Pintos are flaked just as grains are flaked. Flaking greatly shortens the cooking time—from several hours to one hour or less. However, flaking loosens the outer skins, which rise to the top in cooking. Just stir them back in.

Soybeans Soybeans have been the "meat" of the Orient for hundreds of years and are now being grown extensively in this country. Soybeans are grown in the mineral-rich soil of Deaf Smith County, Texas, and in Arkansas and Louisiana.

Soybeans are rich in minerals, B vitamins, and the unsaturated fats that help the body break cholesterol down into harmless particles. (Soybeans are high in lecithin.) They are also high in both amount and quality of protein.

Because of their high concentration of nutrients and very mild flavor after cooking, soybeans may be made into or used in an amazing array of foods. Refer to other sections for descriptions of such soy products such as tamari soy sauce, miso (soy paste), tofu (soy cheese), and soy milk.

Always sprout or cook soybeans before eating in order to destroy the urease and antitrypsin enzymes that interfere with digestion.

Soybean Flakes These flakes are among the most useful of all the flaked products because raw soybeans require much soaking and cooking. The flakes require no soaking and only 1½ to 2 hours cooking. Here too the skins separate during cooking and should be stirred back into the beans.

FLOURS

If one staple food can be said to be more important than any other, it must be whole grain flour. Some kind of flour may be included in almost any conceivable recipe. Stone-ground flours from Deaf Smith County, Texas, are stone ground by large granite stones hand-quarried in North Carolina. Stone grinding evenly distributes the germ and other nutrients in the grains without breaking them down and without cooking the flour.

Buckwheat Flour (*dark*) This dark flour is ground whole grain buckwheat. (It is important to note that light buckwheat flour is made from sifted flour, not unroasted buckwheat groats as is generally believed.) Buckwheat flour is used to make spaghetti and Japanese "soba" noodles. It is excellent in bread, muffins, and cereal, although it is most often used in buckwheat pancakes and waffles.

White Corn Meal This meal is coarsely ground whole white corn grown in the Deaf Smith area. It is traditionally used in southern spoon bread, cereal, and johnny cakes. It is sweeter and lighter than yellow corn meal, but it contains less Vitamin A.

Yellow Corn Meal This meal is stone-ground organically grown whole yellow corn. It makes great corn bread. Try using a little in breads, cookies, pancakes, and waffles for a subtle and delicious change in taste and texture.

Brown Rice Flour This flour is stone-ground long-grain brown rice. It may be combined with whole wheat flour in breads and in batters, or used alone in cookies for crispness. Rice flour is slightly sweet, although not as sweet as that made from a special sweet rice variety.

Rye Flour Rye flour is stone-ground whole grain rye. It is generally mixed with whole wheat flour because rye by itself tends to be heavy, although some people prefer a heavier bread. Caraway seeds in rye bread add a delightful flavor that most people identify as rye. Rye bread is a traditional bread of northern Europe. It is a delicious sandwich and party bread.

Soybean Flour Since soybeans must be sprouted or cooked before being eaten, the beans are first flaked and then ground into flour. Precooking tames the strong taste of the raw flour and also increases the uses of soy flour.

Soy flour, like the beans, is an excellent source of high quality protein and B vitamins. It is lower in starch than other flours. Try substituting soy flour for part of the wheat flour in breads, muffins, and pancake recipes.

Triticale Flour A new taste in breads is possible using the flour of this new grain variety. Though high in protein, this flour is low in gluten and must be combined with higher gluten flours in order to bake well. You will enjoy the naturally sweet taste of breads made with triticale flour.

Whole Wheat Pastry Flour Pastry flour is ground whole grain soft wheat. Use pastry flour in place of unbleached white flour. While it acts much like unbleached white flour, soft wheat flour is actually a whole grain, unrefined flour and nutritionally superior to the white flour. Flaky pie crusts and light cakes and cookies are more easily made with this variety of whole grain wheat flour. (Sifted whole wheat flour may be used in place of pastry flour.)

Whole Wheat Flour Whole wheat flour is hard red winter wheat stone ground into a beautiful light brown flour. Tascosa and Centurk wheat varieties do well in this part of the country, are high in protein and have enough gluten to be good for baking. Stone-ground whole wheat flour is the favorite of many people and is possibly the most versatile flour of all. Use it in any kind of baked goods. But a loaf of brown, crusty homemade bread right out of the oven is still the best of all.

PASTA

Macaroni, spaghetti, and noodles made of whole grain flours are so delicious and easy to cook you will never settle for anything less again.

Buckwheat Spaghetti This spaghetti is a blend of whole buckwheat flour and soft wheat flour. Use it in any spaghetti recipe for a slightly different flavor.

Whole Wheat Spaghetti and Macaroni Two varieties of wheat combine to make this delicious spaghetti—unrefined durham wheat from North Dakota and Montana and soft white wheat grown in the volcanic soils of eastern Washington. The whole grains are carefully ground into a fine textured flour made fresh for each batch of spaghetti. Use spaghetti in soups, casseroles, and salads, or serve with a vegetable sauce or fried like Chinese noodles with vegetables. Spaghetti is wonderful for a quick meal.

Whole Wheat Flat Noodles Made of the same ingredients as whole wheat spaghetti, these noodles are excellent in vegetable casseroles. Try making your own whole wheat noodles at home. They're great!

NUTS AND SEEDS

Like beans, nuts and seeds are very versatile. Besides being everyone's favorite snack foods, nuts and seeds add flavor, nutrition, and interesting texture to every kind of dish. They contribute valuable protein, unsaturated fatty acids, some B vitamins, and minerals. Nuts and seeds are often recommended as sources for magnesium, which has recently been found to be deficient in many American diets.

Every kind of nut has different amounts of unsaturated fatty acids as well as different combinations of nutrients, so it is a good practice to eat a variety of seeds and nuts for optimum nutrition. Try using them in unusual ways, in vegetable and grain dishes or blended in soups. The following are among the most nutritious varieties.

Alfalfa Seeds   Alfalfa seeds are grown in the North Texas area on dry land farms. The seeds are carefully and gently cleaned twice by a cleaner with felt rollers. These tiny seeds become big nutrition when sprouted. The sprouts are crisp and tangy and add sparkle to green salads. Try using them in sandwiches instead of lettuce.

Almonds   Almonds are grown in California. Many call them the "king of nuts" because of their high mineral content. Delicious milk may be made from them. Almonds may be eaten raw or roasted with tamari for a delicious snack. For a real treat blanch them, roast them, and grind them into almond butter.

Peanuts   Peanuts are actually not a nut but rather a legume with good nutrition as well as great taste. These peanuts are grown in New Mexico and Texas and are field dried in bright sunshine. (Many commercial peanuts are gas dried.) The famous Valencia peanut, an especially good eating variety, makes a great peanut butter too.

Pecans and Walnuts   Pecans from Texas and New Mexico; walnuts from California. These well-known and delicious nuts each contribute valuable nutrients. Walnuts are higher in protein and iron. Pecans are higher in potassium and B vitamins.

Sesame Seeds   Sesame seeds are grown in southern Mexico. The farming is still done by hand labor and no sprays are used. After entry into this country, they are cleaned, washed, and bagged.

Sesame seeds are an excellent source of protein, calcium, magnesium, and unsaturated fatty acids. Unhulled sesame seeds are superior to the hulled because much of the mineral content is in the hulls. Sesame seeds are a great addition to breads, cookies, grains, and vegetables. Sesame butter, made of ground roasted sesame seeds, is an unusual and delicious spread.

Sunflower Seeds   These delicious and nutritious seeds are grown in the northern states. They are subjected to some of the most exacting grading in the food industry. After extensive culling the seeds pass an electric eye to remove all broken seeds and hulls. Finally they are hand-sorted. Sunflower seeds are one of the few vegetable sources of Vitamin D. They are rich in protein, minerals, and several of the B vitamins. Eat sunflower seeds raw or toasted for a great energy snack, or include them in breads, cookies, and granola.

Tamari Roasted Nuts   Whole nuts are soaked in tamari soy sauce and then dry roasted for the richest-tasting snacks you will ever treat yourself to. Try tamari roasted almonds, cashews, sunflower and pumpkin seeds, and soybeans.

SEED AND NUT BUTTERS

While eating peanut butter is practically a national pastime, comparatively few people are familiar with other interesting nut and seed butters or with their different uses.

The old-fashioned butters shipped from Deaf Smith County, Texas, are good sources of proteins, trace minerals, and vitamins as well as unrefined, unsaturated oils. There is no question of content in these butters. Peanut butter is 100 percent peanuts; sesame butter is 100 percent sesame seeds, etc.

Besides being good spreads for breads and crackers, they are excellent breads and other baked goods, salad dressings, and sauces. They can replace thickeners, binders, shortenings, and other fats.

Peanut Butter   "Deaf Smith" old-fashioned peanut butter is the real thing. Made only from delicious Valencia peanuts, it needs no salt. Single grinding keeps all but a tiny amount of the peanut oil spread throughout the butter. If you are a peanut butter fan, you may take to eating this one with a spoon.

Sesame Butter   Sesame butter is made by grinding toasted, unhulled sesame seeds. The hull contributes a stronger taste and a high trace-mineral content. Sesame butter and sesame tahini are extensively used in the Middle East. Use them as spreads or include them in a variety of recipes.

Sesame tahini is made from hulled sesame seed, so it is not as high in minerals as sesame butter. Tahini is very mild and sweet. It makes delicious salad dressing and is a good binder and thickener. If tahini is runny, adding water will actually thicken it! Its mild flavor allows it to be used anywhere.

Home Grinding All seed and nut butters may be made at home with the help of a small home grinder. Roast the nuts and seeds first and then grind.

UNREFINED OILS

There is much confusion about the processing of oils. Almost all oils, including some labeled "cold pressed," are made by heating the grains, beans, or seeds before the oils are extracted. Commercial processors also use chemical solvents to extract the oils. After extraction, the oils are almost universally refined, bleached, and deodorized. This results in a light, clear, odorless product with no "impurities"—a term that unfortunately applies to the vanished nutrients.

In producing "unrefined" oils the grains, beans, or seeds are first heated and then expeller pressed without the use of any chemicals or solvents. No further processing takes place. Unrefined oils will have some sediments in the bottle, particles of the germ left in order not to remove nutrients by over-filtering.

Like other unrefined foods these oils contain all the nutrients naturally present in the oils of the grains, beans, or seeds. Unrefined oils are excellent sources of the important unsaturated fatty acids. To be properly utilized, these must be accompanied by Vitamin E, mostly destroyed in refined products, but which is also available in unrefined oils. Every oil differs from every other oil in the amounts and percentages of the essential fatty acids it possesses. For this reason it is a good practice to use a variety of these oils. You may even mix several oils.

Unrefined oils also have their own natural odors and mild, nutty flavors. Those used to highly refined foods may find this very noticeable at first. The mildest oil for most uses is unrefined safflower oil. Unrefined corn germ oil gives a rich buttery taste to baked goods. Unrefined sesame, sunflower, and olive oils are also mild. Any of these work well in salad dressings and other recipes. Unrefined peanut and soy oils are rather strong and are best used in sautéing, where they lose their strong flavor during cooking.

Most unrefined oils should not be heated over 350 degrees. At higher temperatures the germ will scorch and many nutrients will be lost. It is damaging to cook any fat at extremely high temperatures, though high-temperature cooking is often advertised as an "advantage" of refined, preserved oils. High heat changes the chemical make-up of oils, making them detrimental to health. If the oil is allowed to overheat and begins to smoke, throw it out. For deep frying (400 degrees) use unrefined safflower oil, for it can withstand higher heats than most other oils. It is not necessary to go above 400 degrees for deep frying.

Some oils, particularly peanut and olive oils, may partially solidify if they get too cold in the refrigerator. Simply run them under hot tap water or set them out at room temperature and they will become liquid again.

Make your own unsaturated soft spread by blending unrefined safflower oil and real, fresh butter. This combination gives excellent flavor and eliminates the artificial hydrogenation and preservatives present in the commercial products.

Substitute unrefined oils for solid fats in recipes. It may be necessary to reduce the other liquids slightly or to increase the dry ingredients.

Unrefined corn germ oil, unrefined safflower oil, unrefined sesame oil, unrefined soy oil, unrefined olive oil, and unrefined peanut oil are presently available. Other unrefined oils will probably be available in the future.

DRIED FRUITS

Untreated dried fruits are excellent for satisfying that sweet tooth naturally. Although they may appear drier than the usual commercial varieties, dried fruits are especially flavorful. They are free from chemical preservatives, although some are "honey dipped" for natural preservation.

Dried fruits combine well in almost any kind of dish—casseroles, salads, breads, and desserts. Dried fruits, like all fruits, are great snack foods. Eat them as is or soften them by soaking in a little water or juice. For quick energy as well as convenience take dried fruits along when hiking or camping out.

Dried apples, apricots, dates, peaches, pears, prunes, and raisins are available either in small packages or in bulk. Small sizes come plain or "honey dipped." Mixed bags of fruit are also available.

SEASONINGS

Sea Salt   Unrefined sea salt is solar evaporated and briefly kiln dried. Longer kiln drying makes salt less soluble and harder for the body to assimilate. The best reason for using unrefined sea salt is that it is high in natural essential trace minerals and is not just sodium chloride with perhaps some synthetic iodine added. No extraneous chemicals are added to make this sea salt "pour."

Tamari Soy Sauce   Real soy sauce is made of soybeans, wheat, sea salt, and water by a process of natural fermentation, without the use of any chemicals. It is aged about 2 years in wooden kegs. Use tamari in place of salt in cooking (2 or 3 parts tamari in place of 1 part salt). It is excellent with soups, rice, and other grains. Keep a small bottle on the table along with the salt and pepper.

Miso Soybean Paste   Made from soybeans, barley, water, sea salt, and koji rice (a fermented rice), miso is most commonly made into soup and is eaten every day for breakfast in the Orient. It is also used to make pickles and sauces. It is an energy giver and helps in the digestion and assimilation of other foods.

Vinegar   Try to use only apple-cider vinegar, preferably made from unsprayed apples.

OTHER FOODS YOU'LL NEED

Agar-Agar (*Kanten*)   A gelatinous sea vegetable used like gelatin to make molded salads and desserts, agar-agar comes in flakes, powder, or stick form.

Arrowroot Powder   Is made from the root of the arrowroot plant. It is preferable to cornstarch as a thickener and is especially good for sauces. It should be dissolved in cold water before being added to hot foods to prevent lumping. Simmer the sauce 5 minutes after thickening to blend the flavors.

Baking Powder, Low-Sodium   Because it is free from both sodium compounds and aluminum compounds, low-sodium baking powder is much preferable to the usual baking powders. You may even make your own.

Carob Powder (*St. John's Bread*) Use carob in place of chocolate and cocoa (3 tablespoons of carob plus 2 tablespoons of water or milk equals one square of chocolate). It is ground from the pods of the carob tree and is available toasted or untoasted. You may toast it at home just prior to use for a fresher flavor. Carob is rich in minerals and natural sugars and is low in fat. The addition of carob reduces the need for other sweeteners. Mix the carob powder thoroughly with the dry ingredients or dissolve it in a little water or milk before adding it to liquids.

Milk Powder Non-instant dry milk powder is one of the most useful and nutritionally important foods around. It is very concentrated, so a small amount gives a big nutritional boost to any recipe. (Stir it with the dry ingredients for easiest mixing.) The price per pound is the same as the lowest priced instant milk powder. Non-instant milk powder is also a great natural sweetener. Its inclusion reduces the amounts of concentrated sweets needed in dessert recipes.

Sea Vegetables These plants are worthy of mention because they are superior sources of minerals and vitamins. Powdered kelp may be used as a salt substitute. Other sea vegetables may be roasted and crumbled into soups and vegetable dishes. Still others must be cooked, much like ordinary greens, before eating. Americans tend to turn up their noses at "sea weeds," so just remember that they are merely vegetables, dried for easy keeping, with an extra dose of the minerals the sea is so rich in. There are many varieties. Wakame, nori, and dulse are the best known. Be sure to ask for directions if you're unfamiliar with them.

Sweeteners Natural food stores offer a variety of natural sweeteners. Be sure to look for raw, unfiltered honey; unsulphured sorghum molasses; date sugar; and pure maple syrup. Try carob powder for delicious, healthful "chocolate" goodies. Refer to the chapter on desserts for more suggestions.

RECOMMENDED BOOKS

Refer to these books for nutritional information and more recipes.

DAVIS, ADELE, *Let's Cook It Right*. New York: Harcourt, Brace, & World, 1970. Available in paperback.

HUNTER, BEATRICE TRUM, *Natural Foods Primer*. New York: Simon & Schuster, 1972.

MEDSGER, OLIVER, *Edible Wild Plants*. New York: Macmillan Publishing Co., Inc., 1972. Available in paperback.

LAPPE, FRANCES MOORE, *Diet for a Small Planet*. New York: Ballantine Books, 1971. Available in paperback.

U.S. DEPT. OF AGRICULTURE, *Composition of Foods, Agricultural Handbook #8*. Available in large paperback.

Rodale Press Publications. Emmaus, Pennsylvania.

Natural Food and Farming Journal, Natural Food Associates, Atlanta, Texas.

336

Index